SACRED
Covenants

SACRED
Covenants

OUR AGREEMENT *with* GOD *to be* EXALTED

JEFFERY A HOGGE

CFI

AN IMPRINT OF CEDAR FORT, INC.
SPRINGVILLE, UTAH

This is not an official publication of The Church of Jesus Christ of Latter-day Saints. The opinions and views expressed herein belong solely to the author and do not necessarily represent the opinions or views of Cedar Fort, Inc. Permission for the use of sources, graphics, and photos is also solely the responsibility of the author.

ISBN 13: 978-1-4621-3767-1

Published by CFI, an imprint of Cedar Fort, Inc.
2373 W. 700 S., Springville, UT 84663
Distributed by Cedar Fort, Inc., www.cedarfort.com

   Library of Congress Control Number: 2020931793

Cover design by Shawnda T. Craig
Cover design © 2020 Cedar Fort, Inc.

Printed in the United States of America

10 9 8 7 6 5 4 3 2 1

Printed on acid-free paper

For my grandchildren,
beginning with Mari

Contents

CONTENTS

Acknowledgments

I owe a debt of gratitude to many people for their encouragement and inspiration for this book.

I am grateful to Hon. George W. Nicholson (ret.), who provided valuable input and insight. He has been a friend and mentor for thirty years, and he is a friend of The Church of Jesus Christ of Latter-day Saints.

My parents laid the foundation of my faith and testimony.

My children have been my audience, sometimes a willing audience. Mindy, Spencer, and Bradford provided encouragement. Sarah is a gifted editor. Joe excels at organization. And Hilary is my social media advisor.

I am also grateful to my dear wife, Kim, for her love and encouragement. I am a blessed man.

Preface

Covenants are exciting to me. I am drawn to the subject by my background in the law, having analyzed legal relationships for many years and having observed the order and predictability that legal relationships can bring to our lives and associations when those relationships are carefully defined and virtuously honored. And to think that I may have that kind of relationship, carefully defined and virtuously honored, with a loving Heavenly Father who wants me to return to Him is exhilarating—truly positive and faith-promoting. It is with this excitement that I approach the subject of sacred covenants.

I began this project years ago with two goals in mind: (1) to share with my grandchildren what I believe deep down in the depths of my heart and the marrow of my bones, and (2) to organize the universe in my mind so that I could better understand it. This book is the result. It is not a self-help book, but it certainly may be if the reader's increased understanding of doctrine leads to better behavior. In that way, this book is an invitation to make and keep covenants that will lead to eternal life.

I don't have authority to declare God's doctrine. That authority belongs to the prophets and apostles. The ideas in this book are my thoughts and my beliefs, and I am the only one responsible for them.

Nine principles are foundational for me. They are the most basic things that we need to know about Heavenly Father and His plan. They include the following:

1. God is our Father, and He loves us.
2. Jesus is the Christ, the Son of God and Redeemer of the World, and He loves us.

3. The family is essential to God's plan for the eternal destiny of His children.
4. Joseph Smith was and is a true prophet.
5. The Book of Mormon is true.
6. The Church of Jesus Christ was restored through Joseph Smith.
7. Russell M. Nelson, or whoever succeeds him as president of The Church of Jesus Christ of Latter-day Saints, is God's prophet on the earth today.
8. The authority and keys to provide the saving ordinances reside in The Church of Jesus Christ of Latter-day Saints.
9. Living the gospel of Jesus Christ brings peace in this world and eternal life in the world to come.

These truths bring me peace and joy. I know they can bring peace and joy to you too. And, if you believe and embrace these truths, this book will be easier to understand.

I have included many analogies in this book. Each one is imperfect, by definition. Taken to its extreme, every analogy breaks down. But analogies can be useful in thinking about the many abstract concepts discussed in this book. Just be careful.

Finally, a word of warning: my training and vocation are as a lawyer. I admittedly have come to think like a lawyer; it is simply who I am. Considering my training and vocation, you may not be surprised that I have come to conclude that God's plan for us is all about law and covenants—those binding agreements between God and man. While I cannot simply shed my learning and predilections, I firmly believe that this point of view—seeing God's plan for us as a series of covenants—can be helpful to anyone truly seeking to return to God and be like Him.

Introduction

THE COVENANT PATH

Keep on the covenant path.

—Russell M. Nelson

On January 16, 2018, the thirteen Apostles of the Lord Jesus Christ living on the earth met in the Salt Lake Temple to broadcast an announcement to the members of The Church of Jesus Christ of Latter-day Saints. Just four days earlier, the Apostles and members of the Church had laid to rest Thomas S. Monson, the sixteenth President of the Church. In this historic broadcast from the temple, the members were introduced to the new President of the Church, Russell M. Nelson, who had been ordained and set apart by the other Apostles in the orderly succession of the most senior Apostle to be President of the Church.

Directing his message to each member of the Church, President Nelson said: "Keep on the covenant path. Your commitment to follow the Savior by making covenants with Him and then keeping those covenants will open the door to every spiritual blessing and privilege available to men, women, and children everywhere."[1]

What is this covenant path, and why is it so important that a new President of the Church included this appeal in his first words to Church members? To understand the importance of President Nelson's appeal to keep on the covenant path, it is helpful to retrace history more than 180 years to the beginnings of The Church of Jesus Christ of Latter-day Saints.

In February 1832, Joseph Smith was busy in Hiram, Ohio, translating a more correct version of the Bible, in addition to fulfilling his other duties as the temporal leader and prophet of a fledgling church founded less than two years earlier. With Sidney Rigdon as scribe, Joseph was translating chapter 5 of the Gospel of John.

As recorded in John 5, Jesus healed a man on the Sabbath and directed the man to take up his bed and walk. The leaders of the Jews were incensed that Jesus would violate the law of Moses, or at least their interpretation of the law, by doing this "work" on the Sabbath. Responding to their criticism, Jesus compared himself to God: "My Father worketh hitherto, and I work" (John 5:17). He told them that, to honor the Father, they must honor the Son, clearly referring to Himself (see John 5:23).

The leaders of the Jews were so enraged that they sought to kill Jesus because "not only had [he] broken the sabbath, but said also that God was his Father, making himself equal with God" (John 5:18). Jesus responded to this indignation, not by condemnation but instead by a clearer explanation of His relationship with His Father, leaving no doubt in the minds of the leaders of the Jews that Jesus claimed to be the very Son of God. He told them that whoever believes in Him will have everlasting life (see John 5:24). Continuing the sermon, Jesus said the dead "shall come forth; they that have done good, unto the resurrection of life; and they that have done evil, unto the resurrection of damnation" (John 5:29).

This passage perplexed and intrigued Joseph, who had been wondering about the final state of those who die. Joseph said later, referring to this time, "'It appeared self-evident from what truths were left [in the Bible], that if God rewarded every one according to the deeds done in the body, the term 'Heaven,' as intended for the Saints' eternal home, must include more kingdoms than one" (D&C 76, introduction).

God resolved Joseph's confusion with a revelation. Joseph and Sidney received a vision of the kingdoms of glory where most of God's children will receive their rewards, as well as a state of darkness, known as outer darkness, for those who have known the light of God but yet "deny the truth and defy [God's] power" (D&C 76:31).

Joseph and Sidney saw and conversed with the Son of God (see D&C 76:14). In "the Vision," as it became known among the Latter-day Saints, God identified the inhabitants of this earth as "sons and daughters of God" (D&C 76:24), paralleling the statement of Jesus to the leaders of the Jews that He was the Son of God. If that were not enough to evoke images of a divine nature in us, the Vision continued with a clear explanation that not only are we sons and daughters of God, but we can also truly be like Him.

The righteous "shall come forth in the resurrection of the just" (D&C 76:50). "Wherefore, as it is written, they are gods, even the sons of God. Wherefore, all things are theirs, whether life or death, or things present, or things to come, all are theirs and they are Christ's, and Christ is God's" (D&C 76:58–59).

As Jesus proclaimed Himself the Son of God, so that same Son of God told Joseph and Sidney that we, being sons and daughters of God, may become all that God is. As expressed by the First Presidency in 1909, "Man is the child of God, formed in the divine image and endowed with divine attributes, and even as the infant son of an earthly father and mother is capable in due time of becoming a man, so the undeveloped offspring of celestial parentage is capable, by experience through ages and aeons, of evolving into a God."[2]

The Vision was remarkable and controversial.

In the early 1800s, the Second Great Awakening swept through Joseph Smith's area of New England. Christian denominations vied for new members, resulting in tumultuous competition (see Joseph Smith—History 1:5–6).

From this tumult emerged The Church of Jesus Christ of Latter-day Saints, organized by young Joseph in 1830. Within two years after the organization of the Church, Joseph received revelations, especially in the course of translating the Bible, that challenged the prevailing doctrines about whether, and in what way, we could become like God. The closest any of the other denominations came to embracing a tenet that we may become gods was that we could so perfect ourselves that we might have God within us or participate in His nature, certainly not that we, ourselves, could become gods.

One prominent doctrine of modern Christianity, predominating in New England of Joseph's day, naturally limits development of any principle allowing that we may become gods. That doctrine is creation out of nothing (*creatio ex nihilo*). It holds that God is self-existent. He has always existed and, therefore, was never created. On the other hand, He created everything else out of nothing. There was no pre-existing material for Him to use. The whole universe is composed of what God created out of nothing, so He is different in nature from everything else in the universe because He, alone, has no prior cause, having always existed.

In this doctrine of creation out of nothing, God is the creator, the self-existent One; we are the created or "creatures." Just like everything around us, God created us out of nothing. As a result, we can never become like God because, as the tenets of the surrounding religions taught in Joseph's day, we are not self-existent. We did not always exist. Unlike Him, we are created. That basic difference between God and humans is an insurmountable barrier to our ever becoming like Him. At best, we may participate in His nature (in some of His attributes) but never in His essence, what makes Him God. We can never become gods, just as the building can never become the builder, or the work of art can never become the artist.

Into this prevailing doctrinal tradition, Joseph was born in the early 1800s. When he received the Vision in 1832 that we may become gods and have eternal life, the life that God has, it ran counter to the religious traditions and culture of his day.

Certainly, this newly restored theology, emanating line-by-line and precept-by-precept from God through this new prophet, differed from other Christian theology in many other important ways. For example, God has a body as tangible as man's; the members of the Godhead are separate and distinct personages; and family relationships can be eternal. But the rejection of the doctrine of creation out of nothing allowed for the prospect that we could become like God—not just to participate in some way in His divine nature, but to be divine ourselves.

Directly contradicting the doctrine of creation out of nothing, Joseph wrote: "Man was also in the beginning with God" (D&C 93:29). Joseph completed the repudiation of Christian theology that limits our potential when he said, "The mind or the intelligence which man possesses is co-equal with God himself."[3] He continued: "The first principles of man are self-existent with God. God himself, finding he was in the midst of spirits and glory, because he was more intelligent, saw proper to institute laws whereby the rest could have a privilege to advance like himself."[4]

As self-existent beings, we have no temporal barrier to our becoming like God. We can have all his attributes, including the attribute of having no beginning, which attribute we already possess. But becoming like God is not inevitable; instead, it is a choice, or more accurately a combination of a multitude of choices that eventually allow us to ascend in character and attributes to the summit of our potential.

These are not concepts foreign to the Bible. The Psalmist lyricized: "I have said, Ye are gods; and all of you are children of the most High"

(Psalm 82:6). And Paul testified: "The Spirit itself beareth witness with our spirit, that we are the children of God: And if children, then heirs; heirs of God, and joint-heirs with Christ; if so be that we suffer with him, that we may be also glorified together" (Romans 8:16–17). The difference in the theology of The Church of Jesus Christ of Latter-day Saints from the theologies of the rest of Christendom is that we take these scriptures as literal declarations of our own divine potential.

Today, the Church plainly teaches, "All human beings—male and female—are created in the image of God. Each is a beloved spirit son or daughter of heavenly parents, and, as such, each has a divine nature and destiny."[5] And "spirit sons and daughters knew and worshipped God as their Eternal Father and accepted His plan by which His children could obtain a physical body and gain earthly experience to progress toward perfection and ultimately realize their divine destiny as heirs of eternal life."[6]

If we can become gods, as sons and daughters of God, how do we achieve that ultimate destiny? The answer lies in President Nelson's appeal to "keep on the covenant path." It is by obedience to the laws and ordinances of the gospel that we may have eternal life, not just living forever but living the life God lives.

In President Nelson's message to Church members from the temple, he said: "The end for which each of us strives is to be endowed with power in a house of the Lord, sealed as families, faithful to covenants made in a temple that qualify us for the greatest gift of God, that of eternal life. The ordinances of the temple and the covenants you make there are key to strengthening your life, your marriage and family, and your ability to resist the attacks of the adversary. Your worship in the temple and your service there for your ancestors will bless you with increased personal revelation and peace and will fortify your commitment to stay on the covenant path."[7]

Endnotes

1. Nelson, "As We Go Forward Together," 7.
2. First Presidency, "The Origin of Man," 81.
3. *Teachings of the Prophet Joseph Smith*, 353.
4. *Teachings of the Prophet Joseph Smith*, 354.
5. "The Family: A Proclamation to the World" (1995).
6. Ibid.
7. Nelson, "As We Go Forward Together," 7.

PART I

COVENANT
FOUNDATIONS

Chapter 1

AGENCY, ACCOUNTABILITY, AND ATONEMENT

Wherefore, men are free according to the flesh. . . . And they are free to choose liberty and eternal life, through the great Mediator of all men, or to choose captivity and death, according to the captivity and power of the devil.

—2 Nephi 2:27

President Russell M. Nelson's counsel to stay on the covenant path refers to God's plan for us. God provided a plan for our salvation, for our eternal happiness. It started with a promise: We promised to obey. And God promised to send His Son to bring us back to Him. It really is that simple. With that premortal covenant to obey God, we began our journey. As spirits, we accepted His plan. In this life we receive a physical body, and we have experiences to help us progress toward exaltation. Along the way, we must make additional covenants with God. Some of these covenants, such as the covenants we make when we are baptized, are milestones, both marking our progress in returning to God and allowing us to continue progressing.

Covenants

A covenant, in this divine context, is a mutual promise, an agreement, between God and His children. God determines the terms of the covenant, but we decide whether to make and keep the covenant. Once made, the covenant binds God if we keep the covenant (see D&C 82:10).

Divine covenants may be compared to a train ticket. The railroad agrees to transport us to the correct destination, but we must agree to pay for the ticket and board the right train.

I had an experience several years ago that emphasized in my mind the importance of not only paying for the ticket but boarding the right train. My wife, Kim, and I traveled to Italy. Our home base for the tour of Italy was Milan, where we stayed in a hotel close to Central Station. From that train station, we took many day trips to various parts of northern Italy.

One of those day trips was to Florence. We got up early and went to Central Station, where we bought round-trip tickets to Florence—our agreement with the state railroad to conduct us to and from Florence in relative comfort. Tickets in hand, we boarded the train and arrived in Florence later that morning without incident. All day, we toured Florence on foot. We walked to the museum that houses Michelangelo's *David*, to the city cathedral and adjacent baptistery with the famous Gates of Paradise, and down to Ponte Vecchio, the old bridge over the Arno River. As the time approached for our return train to depart, we made our way back to the station. Exhausted and ready to settle in to a comfortable train seat (I don't remember trains being that comfortable several decades ago when I served as a missionary in Italy), we found our train already in the station thirty minutes before departure.

Kim and I gratefully boarded the train and sank into our seats. Within about five minutes, the train began rolling out of the station. I was alarmed. Italian trains are generally on time but never early. I quickly took my book of train schedules out of my backpack and searched for a train that was to leave from Florence a few minutes before our train to Milan. To my dismay, I discovered we were on a train headed for Venice. I love Venice, but we had already visited there, and our hotel was in Milan. Besides, we did not have tickets for a trip to Venice. I had visions of being thrown off the train in the Tuscan countryside.

Recognizing my mistake, I quickly found a conductor and explained our predicament. He was amused at my error and my imperfect command of the Italian language in my panicked condition. But he explained to me that it was not a major problem. The train we were on was scheduled to stop in Bologna, and the train we were supposed to be on would also stop there. So we could catch the right train—the train for which we had tickets—by getting off in Bologna and boarding the Milan-bound train. We did that and finally arrived in Milan that evening. We were tired and a little addled (although I think Kim was also more than a bit amused at my bumbling), but we were in the right city.

Covenants will get us to the right destination, but it is our responsibility to buy the ticket and board the right train. We buy the ticket by entering into agreements with God—by making sacred covenants. We must also board the right train by keeping those covenants. But if we find ourselves on the wrong train from time to time, we can get on the right course by finding out from the conductor how to get back on the right train. We can repent. After all, God wants us to arrive safely at our eternal destination.

President Lorenzo Snow used a similar train analogy to illustrate the importance of staying the course. He was unjustly imprisoned because of an illegal interpretation of the polygamy laws until the United States Supreme Court finally ordered his release. Soon after his release, he delivered a sermon in Brigham City, Utah, putting the prison experience, as well as the mortal experience, in perspective. At that time a member of the Quorum of the Twelve Apostles, he said:

> I do not propose to curse the United States because they have taken away from us a good many of our rights. We will live to enjoy ourselves. It will not make any difference to the Gospel nor its principles. That pathway to celestial glory is still open for every one, just the same as it was before they took away our rights. I feel to look on the best side of the question. We have prospects before us of dwelling in the presence of God.
>
> While I was confined in the Penitentiary I could look forward and see that the cars were still traveling; I could see I was traveling nearer towards the presence of God every day. Now, for instance, if you are on a moving train of cars, as long as you sit still and occupy your seat that train will take you to the point you wish to go; but if you step off the cars it will be dangerous, and it may be a long time before another train will come along. It is the same with us—if we are living right, doing our work, we are going along, and if we are keeping our covenants, we are doing the work of God and accomplishing His purposes, and we will be prepared for the time when Jesus the Son of God will come in honor and glory, and will confer upon all those who prove faithful all the blessing that they anticipate, and a thousand times more.[1]

Elder David A. Bednar emphasized the importance of consistently keeping our covenants: "Steady and sustained progress along the covenant pathway is the course of life that is pleasing to Him."[2]

Everyone must make covenants with God to complete His plan for us and reach exaltation, to receive those blessings referred to by President Snow "and a thousand times more." These include covenants associated with baptism by immersion for the remission of sins and covenants we make in the temple. But why must we make covenants to return to God and live with Him? The answer lies in the concept of agency, the freedom to choose our destiny.

Joseph Smith taught that "all was voluntary."[3] "God would not exert any compulsory means, and the devil could not."[4] God cannot force us; we must agree to be exalted. Our covenants with Him serve the purpose of accepting His offer to return to live with Him. As Alma taught his son Corianton, "Whosoever will come may come and partake of the waters of life freely; and whosoever will not come the same is not compelled to come" (Alma 42:27).

The difference between living a good life with covenants and living a good life but failing to make covenants with God is like the difference between making monthly payments to rent a home and making monthly payments to buy a home. Consider the not-unheard-of scenario of paying as much each month to rent a home as to buy one. The monthly payments serve much the same function: they allow you to live in the home that month. The difference, however, is the long-term effect. If you have entered into a contract to buy the home by making monthly payments, those monthly payments give you the benefit of living in the home but also give you ownership of the home. But renting gives you nothing in the future, just a place to live now.

Similarly, living the commandments brings blessings whether or not you have made covenants with God. If I love my neighbor, practice honesty, and live a righteous life, I will be blessed, even if I never get baptized or receive temple ordinances. Over time I will become a better person, but I have not given my consent to be exalted. On the other hand, if I love my neighbor, practice honesty, and live a righteous life as part of the covenant path, I am doing more than just trying to be a good person and live a good life. I am accomplishing more than receiving the just consequences of my actions. I am pressing forward on the covenant path to eternal life.

No matter how good I am, no matter how closely I follow God's laws, I cannot save myself. I need the Savior. I must covenant with God and accept the Atonement of Jesus Christ to be exalted. Without the Savior, I am a permanent renter, unentitled to the incidents of ownership. With the Savior, I may become an owner, an inheritor of eternal life. Without sacred covenants with God, even a good person will be ever a renter and never an owner.

Joseph Smith taught that all would be resurrected; "nevertheless, they shall return again to their own place, to enjoy that which they are willing to receive, because they were not willing to enjoy that which they might have received" (D&C 88:32). "God will force no man to heav'n."[5]

This fundamental perspective helps answer questions about how God acts toward His children on earth. Why doesn't God save everyone? Why doesn't God save someone who tries to be good but isn't baptized? What covenants must we make with God to receive the greatest blessings that He offers us?

It also raises some questions about justice and fairness: Why is each person born into different circumstances on this earth—some born into circumstances of privilege and plenty and others born into circumstances of misfortune and poverty? What about someone who never has the opportunity to make essential covenants with God in this life?

These questions, and more, are the focus of this book. Understanding covenants, especially what we may call the covenants of exaltation or saving covenants, and recognizing our ability to make and keep these covenants clarify our mortal purpose and should deepen our commitment to God.

But first, we must be familiar with three foundational and eternal doctrines to grasp the significance of this book. These doctrines are agency, accountability, and Atonement. If you don't have a working knowledge of these doctrines, then, as Charles Dickens might say, "nothing wonderful can come of the story I am going to relate."[6]

Agency

We have agency, which is the capacity and opportunity to choose. This truth is essential to God's plan of salvation. Without agency, there is no opportunity to make covenants because covenants without agency are void. And the freedom to choose without the capacity to choose isn't freedom at all. Therefore, an understanding of agency is the first step in a study of covenants.

Agency and freedom can be explained with everyday contracts. I can enter into an agreement to buy a car by offering money to the dealer in return for a car. I am free to refuse to buy the car, but if I take the car I must pay for it. On the other hand, an animal—a dog, for example—has no agency, at least not in any way we recognize legally. If a person offers a meal to a dog, requiring only that the dog pay for the meal, no lawful contract is formed when the dog happily accepts the meal. The dog has no capacity to enter into an agreement.

When we think of agency, we normally think of authorizing someone else to do something on our behalf. For example, if we want to buy property, we may hire a real estate agent to act on our behalf in locating suitable property and negotiating with the owner to buy it. Agency in the sense intended with respect to the Lord's plan, however, is different. It is your own capacity and opportunity to choose and act for yourself.[7]

An example from professional baseball can help us understand agency as used with respect to God's plan for our salvation. Owners of baseball clubs make contracts with baseball players to play for the owners' clubs—a simple enough arrangement, at least ostensibly giving players freedom to play for the owner offering the most lucrative contract. Under the contract, the player agrees to play for the owner's club for a specified number of years, and the owner agrees to pay the player a specified salary. There are complexities involved in the system, but it is an agreement between a player and an owner for the player's services. However, before 1975, every contract between a player and an owner also included what was called a "reserve clause."

The reserve clause stated that for one year after the expiration of the contract between the player and the owner, the owner still retained the "rights" to the player. This meant that although the player's duty to play and the owner's duty to pay under the contract had expired, the owner could prevent the player from agreeing to play for any other team. It forced the player either to enter into another contract to play for the same owner or to seek the owner's generosity in releasing the player to make a contract with another owner. The owner holding the contract with the reserve clause could also trade to another owner the rights to the player. Thus, the reserve clause reduced the bargaining power of the player, resulting in lower player salaries.

In 1969, a baseball player challenged the reserve clause. Curt Flood was a talented outfielder for the St. Louis Cardinals. After Flood had played for the Cardinals for twelve years, the team owners exercised their rights under their reserve clause and traded him to the Philadelphia Phillies. Flood objected to the trade, challenging the reserve clause. He wrote to the commissioner of baseball, explaining that he did not feel he was a piece of property to be bought and sold irrespective of his wishes.

Flood sued Major League Baseball, arguing that the reserve clause was illegal, and took his case all the way to the United States Supreme Court, where he lost.[8] Despite Flood's loss, however, his case was the beginning of the end for the reserve clause. Soon after Flood's case was resolved against him, a concerted effort by the players brought about the end of the reserve clause. It was replaced in 1975 with the principle of free agency. Under free agency, the current system, a player who has completed the term of contract with his team can freely contract with another team for his services. Major League Baseball free agency is more complicated than I am making it sound, but this simple description suits our purpose here.

The "free agency" adopted by Major League Baseball is similar to the agency essential to the plan of salvation. It is not an arrangement with someone else to act on our behalf. Instead, it is the freedom to choose and act for ourselves. We are agents unto ourselves. Like a baseball player who can freely choose among offers from various owners and enter into a contract to play for the owner's club, we are free to choose between good and evil, right and wrong—between the Lord's offer and Satan's offer. The choice of teams is ours.

Agency is at the core of who we are, and it always has been. By exercising our agency, we progressed to where we are now, having successfully completed our premortal existence (the first estate) and moved on to our mortal existence (the second estate). How we exercise our agency will continue to determine our progress.

Elder John A. Widtsoe was a twentieth century Apostle of The Church of Jesus Christ of Latter-day Saints and an intellectual who excelled in his studies at Harvard and presided over two different universities, garnering worldwide renown as a scientist. He identified agency as a concept essential to understanding the universe and our place in it. He said:

> No one attribute so clearly distinguishes man as does the intelligent will or the will to act intelligently. It was by the exercise of their wills that the spirits in the beginning gathered information rapidly or slowly, acquired experiences freely or laboriously. Through the exercise of their wills they grew, or remained passive. . . . The reaction of the will upon the material universe within reach, enabled the intelligent beings, little by little, to acquire power. By the use of his will upon the contents of the universe, man must have become what he now is.[9]

Use of this free will to choose between right and wrong is *moral agency*. We make choices each day, many of which are simply choices that do not implicate morality. We can choose between having oatmeal or eggs for breakfast, and it is really no more than a matter of preference. The choices that matter most are moral choices, such as deciding whether to lie or tell the truth. We have the moral agency to make that choice between right and wrong.

The modern trend is to deny that any of our choices are moral choices. They are simply alternatives bearing no good or evil connotations. This drift from morality is a tool of the adversary to lead God's children astray. If, for example, cheating on an exam is neither right nor wrong but simply a choice, then one could reason that getting the better grade through cheating provided the greatest advantage. The result justifies the means because there is no right or wrong course.

President Thomas S. Monson identified this drift away from moral choices and warned that the drift is dangerous. President Monson's remarks were based on a study by a Notre Dame research group. The group asked research subjects questions to identify their understanding of moral choices. Tellingly, many of the people who were questioned could not identify a moral dilemma: "'When asked to describe a moral dilemma they had faced, two-thirds of the young people either couldn't answer the question or described problems that are not moral at all, like whether they could afford to rent a certain apartment or whether they had enough quarters to feed the meter at a parking spot.'"[10]

When the morality of a choice is removed from the equation, our selfish desires prevail. The Notre Dame study found support for this conclusion:

> The default position, which most of them came back to again and again, is that moral choices are just a matter of individual taste. "It's personal," the respondents typically said. "It's up to the individual. Who am I to say?"
>
> Rejecting blind deference to authority, many of the young people have gone off to the other extreme [saying]: "I would do what I thought made me happy or how I felt. I have no other way of knowing what to do but how I internally feel."[11]

Some modern neuroscientists believe there is no real personal responsibility for decisions because there is no such thing as free will. To them, we are nothing more than animals because our brains are wired to respond without any real choice. Much like the beating of our hearts, the apparent choices we make are no more than a reaction based on our brain's chemistry and architecture. If we could completely understand the brain's chemistry and architecture, we could predict every action.

There is certainly some truth to the theory that our brain's chemistry and architecture have a role in our thoughts and deeds, even to the extent that at times it leads us to think and do things out of our own control (think of the deeply depressed individual or the victim of brain damage). But the gospel of Jesus Christ teaches us that we are agents unto ourselves. We are "free to choose" (2 Nephi 2:27). The Lord would not tell us so if we were preprogrammed for predetermined responses simply by our brain's chemistry and architecture—creatures of nature having no real say in our thoughts and deeds or in our destiny.

The adversary leads us astray by suggesting that there is no right or wrong; there is no good or bad; indeed, there is no evil. He wants us to believe that there is no such thing as moral agency, only agency that allows us to do whatever we want or, as in the thinking of some neuroscientists, that our actions are determined solely by instinctive firing of neurons in the brain in reaction to outward stimuli. In many ways Satan has succeeded when society sees whether to water your front lawn as a moral decision while considering whether to have sexual relations before marriage simply a matter of personal preference.

While serving as the prophet, President Monson warned us about the failure to develop a moral intuition, a sense of what is right and what is wrong: "None within the sound of my voice should be in any doubt concerning what is moral and what is not. . . . We have been and continue to be taught God's laws. Despite what you may see or hear elsewhere, these laws are unchanging."[12]

Our Heavenly Father's willingness to allow one-third of the heavenly host in the premortal life to choose Satan's plan of eternal misery rather than our Father's own plan of happiness is proof of how jealously He guards our agency. And the Savior is similarly prohibited from violating our agency. He can save us *from* our sins but not *in* our sins: "The Lord surely [came] to redeem his people, but [he came not] to redeem them in their sins, but to redeem them from their sins. And he hath power given unto him from the Father to redeem them from their sins because of repentance" (Helaman 5:10–11). We must choose to accept His atoning sacrifice by repenting. Only then can the Lord intervene in our behalf—after we have accepted His offered intervention.

God *commands* everyone everywhere to repent (see D&C 18:9). But He *compels* no one to repent (see Alma 42:27).

Accountability

Choosing to repent, or not to repent, has consequences. Having made the choices, we are responsible for the consequences. We are accountable.

In a profound discourse, Lehi described both agency and accountability to his son Jacob: "Wherefore, men are free according to the flesh; and all things are given them which are expedient unto man. And they are free to choose liberty and eternal life, through the great Mediator of all men, or to choose captivity and death, according to the captivity and power of the devil; for he seeketh that all men might be miserable like unto himself" (2 Nephi 2:27).

Recalling the analogy of baseball and its system of free agency, we must choose whether to play on the Lord's team or Satan's team. If we choose to play on the Lord's team, we will receive the Lord's wages. If we select Satan's team, we will receive Satan's wages.

Given this option, the choice between the Lord's wages or Satan's, it is important to understand what Satan will give us (as opposed to what he offers). What the Lord promises and what the Lord provides are the same. When we obey, He will bless us as promised. He must. When we do not obey, He will not give us the blessing. He cannot (see D&C 82:10). On the other hand, Satan's promises are empty. And his eventual reward to us is always the same: abandonment. "He rewardeth you no good thing" (Alma 34:39). We do well to learn this lesson from Korihor's experience, as related in the Book of Mormon.

Korihor was an influential and aggressive orator when Alma the Younger was the high priest of the Nephites. Bowing to the influence of Satan, Korihor preached against the Church of God. Satan appeared to Korihor in the form of an angel and deceived Korihor, convincing him that he must reclaim the people from their belief in what he characterized as "an unknown God" (Alma 30:53). Korihor led many astray, teaching that there is no Christ, no Atonement, no spirit of prophecy, and no wrong.

Alarmed citizens eventually took Korihor to Alma. Korihor argued with Alma, asserting that there is no evidence that there is a God. Caught up in his own rhetorical talents, Korihor demanded from Alma a sign to prove God's existence. The demand was answered with a fitting sign from God: Korihor was struck dumb.

Korihor implored Alma to remove the curse, but the Lord revealed to Alma the intent of Korihor's heart—to return to his evil ways and again lead away the hearts of the people once the curse was removed. Unable to convince Alma to remove the curse, Korihor found himself without friends, unable to speak, and among strangers. Eventually, he was knocked down in a crowd and trampled, dying ignominiously. After recounting the story of Korihor, the narrator added this insight: "And thus we see the end of him who perverteth the ways of the Lord; and thus we see that the devil will not support his children at the last day, but doth speedily drag them down to hell" (Alma 30:60).

The story of Korihor teaches that although agency can be exercised contrary to the laws of God, we cannot avoid the consequences of that exercise. The adversary inevitably will abandon those who follow him. The promises of the adversary are empty. He is a liar and has been from the foundation of the world.

Moral agency and accountability are inextricably intertwined. If we have agency, we are accountable. President Russell M. Nelson described this interrelationship between personal responsibility and our eventual exaltation or eternal life in God's kingdom: "The final responsibility to prepare for salvation and exaltation rests upon each person, accountable for individual agency, acting in one's own family."[13]

Some, however, are not accountable, either because they do not have capacity to choose or because they have insufficient knowledge upon which to base a moral choice. This condition involving lack of agency deserves explanation.

Some do not have agency because they do not have capacity to choose between right and wrong. In an eternal sense, this condition of being unaccountable is temporary. Mortal infancy, for example, results in an absence of capacity to choose between right and wrong. The same may be true of some who are intellectually impaired, even in adulthood and throughout mortal life.[14]

The other class of people who are not accountable are those who do not know the law. That may sound wrong at first because we hold people accountable to know our societal laws. Ignorance is no excuse for breaking the law. To an extent, this societal approach may be unfair, but it is necessary to make society work.

Under God's plan, on the other hand, no one is responsible for violating laws they don't know about. Jacob explained this aspect of God's mercy: "Wherefore, he has given a law; and where there is no law given there is no punishment" (2 Nephi 9:25).

Because moral agency unavoidably produces accountability, we may not avoid accountability by declining to exercise our moral agency. There is no avoiding accountability. Pretending to make no choice is a choice all the same. There is no neutrality because life continually presents moral dilemmas that we must work through. Elder Tad R. Callister associated that continual exercise of agency with the temptations we necessarily face: "Neutrality is a nonexistent condition in this life. We are always choosing, always taking sides. That is part of the human experience—facing temptations on a daily, almost moment-by-moment basis—facing them not only on the good days but on the days we are down, the days we are tired, rejected, discouraged, or sick."[15]

A most unfortunate and serious consequence of some choices is that we lose our agency. While God will not take our agency away, we may make choices that limit or even eliminate our agency. President Marion G. Romney explained: "Every wrong decision one makes restricts the area in which he can thereafter exercise his agency. The further one goes in the making of wrong decisions in the exercise of free agency, the more difficult it is for him to recover the lost ground. One can, by persisting long enough, reach the point of no return. He then becomes an abject slave. By the exercise of his free agency, he has decreased the area in which he can act, almost to the vanishing point."[16]

The decision to smoke cigarettes simply illustrates this forfeiture of agency. I am free to choose to smoke cigarettes. However, if I smoke I can become addicted and lose the ability to abstain, limiting my later choice not to smoke because of the prospect of painful withdrawal.

The ultimate illustration of this forfeiture of agency is failing to repent during this probationary mortal life and, by that choice, forfeiting our freedom to choose to continue on to eternal life (see Helaman 13:32, 36–38).

Brigham Young preached accountability, explaining it in personal terms:

> If Brother Brigham shall take a wrong track, and be shut out of the Kingdom of heaven, no person will be to blame but Brother Brigham. I am the only being in heaven, earth, or hell, that can be blamed.
>
> This will equally apply to every Latter-day Saint. Salvation is an individual operation. I am the only person that can possibly save myself. When salvation is sent to me, I can reject or receive it. In receiving it, I yield implicit obedience and submission to its great Author throughout my life, and to those whom he shall appoint to instruct me; in rejecting it, I follow the dictates of my own will in preference to the will of my Creator.[17]

Implicit in Brigham Young's statement is that how we exercise our agency affects our chances for salvation. Blessedly, however, we are not left to earn our salvation on our own because we would inevitably fail.

Atonement

While we have agency and are accountable, we are imperfect and will eventually make choices that are wrong. "If we say that we have no sin, we deceive ourselves, and the truth is not in us" (1 John 1:8). When we consider this truth, along with the truth that we must be completely clean to return to God and live with Him (see 1 Nephi 10:21), our doom naturally follows. But God's plan for us provides a Savior from this doom. Through the Atonement of Jesus Christ, we can become clean if we meet the conditions of that gift.

Jesus Christ accomplished the Atonement as He suffered for the sins of the world in the Garden of Gethsemane and as He gave His life on the Cross of Calvary. It was the ultimate proxy act. He paid for our sins so that we can present ourselves clean, free of sins, at the judgment seat of God. This is the only way we can be saved in the celestial kingdom of our Heavenly Father.

"Had agency come to man without the Atonement," taught President Boyd K. Packer, "it would have been a fatal gift."[18] Through the Atonement of Jesus Christ, all mankind may be saved (see Articles of Faith 1:3). Without the Atonement of Jesus Christ, no one could be saved.

President Gordon B. Hinckley summed up agency, accountability, and Atonement in God's plan: "Man would have his agency, and with that agency would go accountability. Man would walk the ways of the world and sin and stumble. But the Son of God would take upon Himself flesh and offer Himself a sacrifice to atone for the sins of all men. Through unspeakable suffering He would become the great Redeemer, the Savior of all mankind."[19]

Agency, accountability, and the Atonement of Jesus Christ allow us to covenant with God to return to Him and live with Him—and not just to covenant but to have the possibility that, by the grace of God, those covenants may provide the way to exaltation. The covenants of exaltation are agreements that bridge the gap between (1) our desire to become like our Heavenly Father but our failure because of sin and (2) the Savior's ability to save if we accept His Atonement. Agency and Atonement combine to provide the means for us to be exalted, despite accountability for sin.

In summary, you are free to choose, but there will be consequences. Without the Atonement of Jesus Christ, the unfavorable consequences would be eternal.[20]

Endnotes

1. Snow, "Discourse Delivered by Apostle Lorenzo Snow in the Tabernacle at Brigham City, March 6, 1887," 244.
2. Bednar, "If Ye Had Known Me," 104.
3. *Teachings of Presidents of the Church: Joseph Smith*, 214.
4. Ibid.
5. Anon., "Know This, That Every Soul is Free," in *Hymns of The Church of Jesus Christ of Latter-day Saints*, no. 240.
6. Dickens, *A Christmas Carol*, 5.
7. *True to the Faith*, s.v. "Agency," 12.
8. *Flood v. Kuhn* (1972) 407 U.S. 258.
9. Widtsoe, *A Rational Theology as Taught by the Church of Jesus Christ of Latter-day Saints*, 17.
10. Monson, "Dare to Stand Alone," 60.
11. Ibid.
12. Ibid.
13. Nelson, "Salvation and Exaltation," 10.
14. See chapter 7 for additional discussion of agency.
15. Callister, *The Infinite Atonement*, 106.
16. Romney, in Conference Report, Oct. 1981, 63.
17. *Discourses of Brigham Young*, 390.
18. Packer, in Conference Report, Apr. 1988, 83.
19. Hinckley, "We Look to Christ," 90.
20. See chapter 11 for additional discussion of the Atonement of Jesus Christ.

Chapter 2

OPPOSITES AND COUNTERFEITS

---

*For it must needs be, that there is an
opposition in all things.*

—2 Nephi 2:11

gency is based on the fundamental principle of opposites. Understanding opposites activates our agency and allows us to make
covenants. The adversary, however, would distract us from our
sacred covenants by tempting us with counterfeits. We must choose
between making and keeping covenants, which exalt us, or settling for
counterfeits, which impede our progress.

Opposites

Opposition is closely associated with agency and covenants. Certainly
we must have trials and obstacles in this life to grow spiritually, but that
is not exactly the type of opposition I mean here. Opposition in the sense
used here is the principle of opposites: right and wrong, joy and pain, light
and darkness, and many other opposites including the most important
opposition for us to understand—good and evil.

Lehi's teachings to his son Jacob comprise the most-recognized explanation of opposites for those who are familiar with the Book of Mormon. Lehi
told Jacob that there must be "an opposition in all things" (2 Nephi 2:11).

And Lehi explained this concept by illustrating: "If not so, . . . righteousness could not be brought to pass, neither wickedness, neither holiness nor misery, neither good nor bad. Wherefore, all things must needs be a compound in one; wherefore, if it should be one body it must needs remain as dead, having no life neither death, nor corruption nor incorruption, happiness nor misery, neither sense nor insensibility" (2 Nephi 2:11).

Joseph Smith also received revelation on opposites and their relation to agency: "And it must needs be that the devil should tempt the children of men, or they could not be agents unto themselves; for if they never should have bitter they could not know the sweet" (D&C 29:39).

Comprehending opposites, as every rational and mature thinker does, we are tempted to limit this concept merely to how we *understand* things, our point of view—that opposites are just a matter of viewing our existence. For example, if you do not know misery, you cannot understand happiness. If you have not felt cold, you do not understand warmth. Understanding opposites is an important part of what Lehi was saying. But Lehi's teachings were much deeper than merely understanding opposites.

Brigham Young observed that "every fact that exists in this world is demonstrated by its opposite"[1] and "every effect can only be fully manifested by its opposite."[2] This is more than point of view; opposites give life.

Lehi knew that without opposites there is no existence. If there are no opposites, "all things [are] a compound in one" (2 Nephi 2:11–12), without life. From this idea follows the importance of opposites. If there is no right or wrong, there is no sin. If there is no sin, there is no righteousness. If there is no righteousness, there is no happiness. And if there is no happiness, there is no misery (see 2 Nephi 2:13). Lehi concluded that if there are no opposites, God does not exist: "And if these things are not there is no God. . . . Wherefore, all things must have vanished away" (2 Nephi 2:13).

Elder Bruce R. McConkie said that Lucifer's offer of exaltation without the possibility of eternal damnation was "a philosophical impossibility."[3] He explained: "Opposites must exist in every department of creation and in all phases of life. There could be no salvation unless there was also damnation."[4]

Thus, opposites, or, as Lehi said, "an opposition in all things," animate everything. It is a fundamental principle that allows all things to exist, even God. And understanding this principle is essential to understanding agency and covenants. Without opposites, there is no choice to be made. And without a choice to be made, there is no agency. There is no point to life or existence.

Opposites are all around us. For example, digital technology, one of the greatest innovations of the latter days, is based entirely on opposites— off or on. This binary system in which every number is expressed using only two symbols (0 and 1) is now used as the basis for the programming in almost every computer in the world, including the phones we carry. Within the computer, the logic of the programming starts with a simple on or off. A question is asked of the computer, and the answer is either yes or no. That simple concept is used over and over, hundreds of billions of times per second, making possible logical computations of almost unfathomable levels of complexity. Tremendous complexity can be produced based on a simple concept of opposites—on or off.

Like digital technology, the great plan of salvation is based entirely on opposites. As Lehi said, without opposites no aspect of the plan of salvation would have life.

That is not to say that every question we face has an easy yes or no answer. The decisions we must make involve complex systems of opposites—opposites upon opposites upon opposites. We must consider that complexity, both consciously and subconsciously.

If I am deciding whether to have oatmeal or eggs for breakfast, I must take numerous things into consideration. Do I like oatmeal? Do I like the texture? Do I like the taste? Is oatmeal good for me? Do I care if it is good for me? And if I conclude that I like oatmeal and want to eat it for breakfast, do I want it more than eggs? Do I like eggs? Are they good for me? Do I care if they are good for me? And must I really choose between oatmeal and eggs? Can't I have both? Or can I have something different all together? This is just the tip of the iceberg in the complexity of choices. Every choice involves levels upon levels of opposites.

A computer only works well if at each level the choices between opposites (the on-or-off decisions) lead to a useful result. Similarly, our progression within the plan of salvation is optimal only if the choices we make between opposites lead us in the best direction, back to our Heavenly Father.

Relating this concept of opposites to our progress toward exaltation, Brigham Young said: "We must know and understand the opposition that is in all things, in order to discern, choose, and receive that which we do know will exalt us to the presence of God. You cannot know the one without knowing the other."[5] He concluded: "You cannot give any persons their exaltation unless they know what evil is, what sin, sorrow, and misery are, for no person could comprehend, appreciate and enjoy an exaltation upon any other principle."[6]

When Jesus visited the American continent after His resurrection, He taught the people about the resurrection and judgment, using the eternal principle of opposites. He said that all people would be resurrected "if they be good, to the resurrection of everlasting life; and if they be evil, to the resurrection of damnation; *being on a parallel, the one, on the one hand and the other on the other hand*" (3 Nephi 26:5; italics added).

Gravity can teach us about opposites. Gravity is useful, but it can also cause pain. We necessarily learn about gravity and harness its power to live successfully as mortals here on earth. Likewise, we must understand opposites and choose good over evil to live successfully as spiritual beings.

We each have our stories, both trivial and tragic, about gaining an understanding of gravity. We were born mercifully small so that as we learned to move about we were always close to the ground. When we fell, we rarely sustained lasting injury. As we grew and increasingly risked injury from falling, we also increased our understanding of gravity and our ability to avoid falling. Yet we still suffer harmful effects of gravity whenever we fail to control our acceleration toward earth.

I have plenty of my own stories about gravity. One experience happened a few years ago when I had the opportunity to take my family to a session of general conference in the Conference Center in Salt Lake City. I was pleased as I shepherded kids, in-laws, and Kim into the expansive hall. As we moved down the steps toward our seats, I paid more attention to the beautiful surroundings and my family members than to the stairs, and I did not use the handrails. I think I was actually looking back when I stepped off a stair I had not seen.

Few things are more surprising and disconcerting than the momentary feeling of stepping into thin air rather than onto anticipated firm ground. I immediately clicked into "I'm-falling-and-I-must-save-myself" mode, desperately trying to avoid the effects of gravity. I staggered forward, unable to gain my balance and flailed my arms around as I tried to turn my body in the direction I was falling. In one revolution of what may have been many, I hit my hand against something, probably either a chair or, ironically, the handrail. Finally, I caught hold of the handrail just as my backside hit the floor.

My family and the nearest spectators collectively gasped as I scrambled to my feet. Ushers came running, and I was suddenly the unwilling object of way too much attention. As my hand throbbed, I told everyone I was fine, and I even forced a smile and a goofy laugh. I'm sure it took several minutes after I was seated and all ushers had returned to their posts before the red in my face faded and I was able to see that my hand was bruised but not broken.

I have been in the Conference Center several times since that day, and I am always careful to grasp the handrail and pay attention to every step. I learned my lesson.

The mortal lessons we learn about opposites can also be unanticipated, embarrassing, and painful. The most momentous of all such lessons resulted from Adam and Eve's decision to eat the forbidden fruit. Presented with the opposites of life and death, Adam and Eve chose death. But even that decision was more complex than simply choosing life or death.

Placed in the Garden of Eden, Adam and Eve were commanded not to eat from the tree of knowledge of good and evil. The Lord told them: "Remember that I forbid it, for in the day thou eatest thereof thou shalt surely die" (Moses 3:17). But they were also commanded to "be fruitful, and multiply, and replenish the earth" (Genesis 1:28). By eating the forbidden fruit, Adam and Eve chose to have posterity; they chose to obey the commandment to multiply and replenish the earth; they chose to know good from evil; and, of course, they chose death over life.

The immediate consequences of their transgression were grave. Instead of enjoying the spontaneous beauty of the Garden of Eden, they were cast out into the telestial world. This separation from God is a spiritual death, and for Adam and Eve it prefigured their eventual physical death. Instead of being nurtured in the presence of God, they were cast out of His presence—on their own. It was a crash-course in opposites. The essence of the Fall is Adam and Eve's exposure to opposites. Presented with opposites, they were allowed "to follow after their own will" (Alma 42:7).

President George Q. Cannon highlighted the most important opposites that Adam and Eve learned from the Fall: "[Adam and Eve] had a knowledge of good and evil just as the Gods have. They became as Gods; for that is one of the features, one of the peculiar attributes of those who attain unto that glory—they understand the difference between good and evil. . . . God has given unto us this probation for the express purpose of obtaining a knowledge of good and evil—of understanding evil and being able to overcome the evil—and by overcoming it receive the exaltation and glory that He has in store for us."[7]

Like the choice between opposites given to Adam and Eve, gravity is dangerous. It can cause injury or death. Our survival and health depend on our understanding of gravity and our vigilance in applying that understanding. And yet gravity is also critical to our physical growth and well-being. Astronauts have found that when they spend time in space in zero gravity, their muscles used to fight gravity rapidly atrophy because they are not needed. Too much time in space can cause such weakness that astronauts cannot walk until they strengthen those muscles again. They also lose bone density in zero gravity. Even an astronaut's heart is at risk because it normally must pump hard to fight gravity and maintain blood pressure throughout the body. When it doesn't need to pump as hard, the heart atrophies. It takes about one day on earth for each day in space for an astronaut's body to recover from the absence of gravity. Although gravity is dangerous, it is also necessary for our mortal bodies.

Opposites are also dangerous but necessary. Choices between opposites determine destiny. And wrong choices between opposites can result in spiritual injury and death. Yet without opposites we could not progress. Applying our agency wisely to choices between opposites builds our spiritual muscles.

If we cannot figuratively fall down the stairs of choices between opposites, we cannot gain the experience to avoid such a fall and become like our Heavenly Father. But we are not left without a handrail. That handrail consists of moral guides. Some of those guides are the honorable elements of our culture, gospel teaching, family values, inspired leaders, the Light of Christ, and the Holy Ghost. With these moral guides, we can choose wisely between opposites.

We must know and experience opposites—pain and darkness, good and evil—to become like God and comprehend joy and light, even the exalted goodness of God, who told Joseph Smith,: "And above all, if the very jaws of hell shall gape open the mouth wide after thee, know thou, my son, that all these things shall give thee experience, and shall be for thy good" (D&C 122:7).

Without opposites our spiritual muscles atrophy. If there are no opposites, there are no choices. If there are no choices, there is no agency and no possibility of making covenants with God. If there is no agency, there is no purpose to mortal life because it cannot be a probation. And if there is no mortal probation, we cannot progress to become like God.

Brigham Young summarized the role of opposites in the eternal plan:

> The reason of our being made subject to sin and misery, pain, woe, and death, is, that we may become acquainted with the opposites of

happiness and pleasure. The absence of light brings darkness, and darkness an appreciation of light; pain an appreciation of ease and comfort; and ignorance, falsehood, folly, and sin, in comparison with wisdom, knowledge, righteousness, and truth, make the latter the more desirable to mankind. Facts are made apparent to the human mind by their opposites. We find ourselves surrounded in this mortality by an almost endless combination of opposites, through which we must pass to gain experience and information to fit us for an eternal progression. Those who are enlightened by the spirit of truth, have no difficulty in seeing the propriety and the benefit to us of this state of things.[8]

Because opposites are essential to our agency and our covenants, there is value in understanding what opposites are. Lehi used examples, and effectively so. Good is the opposite of bad. Righteousness is the opposite of wickedness. Happiness is the opposite of misery. These examples help the reader of the Book of Mormon to get the point, as I am sure they helped Jacob. But it may be possible, and empowering, to delve deeper into the principle.

Counterfeits and Secret Combinations

Asked what opposites are, we might casually answer that they are two things or concepts that are most dissimilar. But that casual answer would be wrong. Instead, opposites are the two things that are most alike. Think about it. The opposite of boy is girl, not table. A boy is a young human male. A girl is a young human female. There is only one definitional difference, even if that difference is critical. The same applies to concepts such as good and evil. Good is a positive moral value, while evil is a negative moral value.

That opposites are the two things that are most alike is a useful tool to the adversary. He deals in counterfeits, and counterfeits are as close as possible to the real thing without actually being the real thing and having the benefits of the real thing. For example, a counterfeit hundred-dollar bill is like a real hundred-dollar bill in every way that the counterfeiter can make it. The essential difference is that it was made by a counterfeiter and therefore has no value, while the real hundred-dollar bill is made by the government and is legal tender. Applying this to the way the adversary uses counterfeits, we see, for example, that living together without marriage—"living in sin," which term the adversary has succeeded in rendering an archaic description—is the counterfeit of marriage. Baptism without authority is the counterfeit of baptism with authority. Communism is the counterfeit of the law of consecration. The adversary disguises his ambitions by making his plan look as similar as possible to the Lord's plan, tempting us to settle for the counterfeits.

Brigham Young identified counterfeits as one of the adversary's important tools: "If true principles are revealed from heaven to men, and if there are angels, and there is a possibility of their communicating to the human family, always look for an opposite power, and evil power, to give manifestations also; look out for the counterfeit."[9]

Understanding that opposites are alike except for one key characteristic is useful for us because it helps us to avoid counterfeits, as long as we understand the importance of that one definitional characteristic. One example is how we identify proper priesthood authority. If we know that the key definitional characteristics of priesthood authority require the conferring of that priesthood by one who is "called of God, by prophecy, and by the laying on of hands by those who are in authority, to preach the Gospel and administer in the ordinances thereof" (Articles of Faith 1:5), then we can determine for ourselves whether the person purporting to bear priesthood authority is real or counterfeit. If any one of the definitional characteristics is missing, the priesthood authority is counterfeit.

Abraham came face to face with counterfeits in his early years. Born in the time between Noah and Moses, Abraham was entitled by birth to administer in the patriarchal priesthood (see Abraham 1:2–4). He knew that Adam had so administered by making animal sacrifices to remind them of the future sacrifice of Jesus Christ for our sins, by "offer[ing] the firstlings of their flocks, for an offering unto the Lord" (Moses 5:5), in "similitude of the sacrifice of the Only Begotten of the Father" (Moses 5:7).

Abraham was raised in Ur, in the land of the Chaldeans, where idol worship had taken the place of the proper worship of God. Just like in the true religion, the priests of the false gods offered sacrifices. But those sacrifices were not of the proper kind or done with the proper authority. Instead of animal sacrifices, they sacrificed men, women, and children. Instead of authority from the true and living God, they derived authority from false and dead gods (see Abraham 1:5–8).

Abraham was a follower of righteousness and sought the blessings of administering in the true priesthood of God. As a result, he rejected the false worship in Ur and incurred the wrath of the false priests. Eventually, Abraham was captured, bound, and placed on a false altar to be sacrificed, ironically because of his goodness. Even Abraham's father approved of the barbarity. But an angel of the Lord appeared and rescued Abraham (see Abraham 1:12, 15, 30).

Counterfeits mimic but detest the real thing. And so, Abraham's brush with counterfeits was nearly fatal.

Applying this understanding of counterfeits to our study of covenants, we can see that secret combinations are counterfeit covenants. As there is opposition in all things, there are also evil covenants in opposition to righteous covenants. Cain covenanted with Satan: "And Satan said unto Cain: Swear unto me by thy throat, and if thou tell it thou shalt die; and swear thy brethren by their heads, and by the living God, that they tell it not; for if they tell it, they shall surely die" (Moses 5:29).

Notice that in this covenant between Cain and Satan—this secret combination—Satan promises Cain death if Cain and his brethren (his cohorts) reveal the secret, as if they could conceal their covenant and their wrongdoing from the Lord. "All these things were done in secret" (Moses 5:30). This promise of death for revealing the covenant contrasts with the covenant that the Lord makes with us that, if we keep our covenants we will live—that is, have eternal life. And Satan's promise of death was no idle threat. When one of Cain's descendants who had entered into this evil covenant revealed the secret combinations to someone not under the covenant, he was killed by another covenanter, "for the oath's sake" (Moses 5:50).

After generations of these secret combinations, the Lord told the prophet Enoch: "And for these many generations, even since the day that I created them, have they gone astray, and have denied me, and have sought their own counsels in the dark; and in their own abominations have they devised murder, and have not kept the commandments, which I gave unto their father, Adam. Wherefore, they have foresworn themselves, and, by their oaths, they have brought upon themselves death; and a hell I have prepared for them, if they repent not" (Moses 6:28–29).

Secret combinations were not limited to the first few generations of Adam's posterity. The Book of Mormon reveals that the same evil covenants were made among the Jaredites (see Ether 8:15–25) and, later, among the Nephites and Lamanites (see 3 Nephi 6:27–30; Ether 8:20), where the covenanters became known as the Gadianton robbers (see Helaman 6:18).

The object of these secret combinations was and is to lead men away from God. In that diabolical pursuit, the Gadianton robbers of old and of today seek power and money, and they stop at nothing to get them. Murder, plunder, dishonesty, and sexual immorality are in the arsenal of the adversary and his mortal minions. They agree to keep their plans secret so that they can more easily rob the people of their possessions, their liberty, their virtue, and their lives (see Ether 8:15–18).

Secret combinations are an exercise of agency that attempts to avoid accountability. But accountability is unavoidable. Although it may seem for a time that Gadianton robbers have gotten away with their wickedness, the Lord will always uncover it and require that the price of sin be paid, whether in this world or in the life to come. "For there is nothing covered, that shall not be revealed; neither hid, that shall not be known. Therefore whatsoever ye have spoken in darkness shall be heard in the light; and that which ye have spoken in the ear in closets shall be proclaimed upon the housetops" (Luke 12:2–3).

Getting his "reward" in this life for secret combinations was the subject of a story in the Book of Mormon about a man named Seantum. It happened not long before Jesus Christ's visit to the American continent—a time when the wicked became more wicked. Some of the judges were Gadianton robbers who wanted to punish Nephi, son of Helaman, for speaking out against government corruption. "Those judges were angry with him because he spake plainly unto them concerning their secret works of darkness" (Helaman 8:4). As is often the case with Gadianton robbers, these judges were cowards, however, and "durst not lay their own hands upon [Nephi], for they feared the people lest they should cry out against them" (Helaman 8:4). So, instead, they tried to stir up the people to anger against Nephi. But they were unsuccessful because there were still people who believed that Nephi was a prophet (see Helaman 8:7).

One of these corrupt judges was Seantum, whose brother was Seezoram, the chief judge. Under the law, the chief judge was the highest government official and held great power. Both Seantum and Seezoram were Gadianton robbers. Seantum coveted Seezoram's status as chief judge, so, to obtain the position for himself, he murdered his own brother.

Seantum may have believed he got away with it, especially when five others were accused of the murder. But the Lord knew better, and He revealed the truth to Nephi. When Nephi told the people that Seantum was the murderer, they went to Seantum, who had blood on his robes. At first Seantum denied the murder, but when the blood was discovered, the coward trembled and turned pale. By that, they knew he was the murderer, and he confessed.

The Lord always knows who the Gadianton robbers are. Justice is always served in the end. The eternal law of accountability always catches up to them, and they are left to pay the price. Unlike sacred covenants, counterfeit covenants have no power to save.

The Lord, on the other hand, never works by such diabolical means as secret combinations. He provides His children with the opportunity to exercise their agency by choosing between opposites and entering into covenants. If they accept His invitation, they reap the rewards—the rewards of the righteous. They receive life.

Endnotes

1. Young, in *Journal of Discourses*, 14:71.
2. *Discourses of Brigham Young*, 345.
3. McConkie, *A New Witness for the Articles of Faith*, 92.
4. Ibid.
5. *Discourses of Brigham Young*, 346.
6. Ibid., 55.
7. Cannon, in *Journal of Discourses*, 26:190–191.
8. Young, in *Journal of Discourses*, 11:42–43.
9. *Discourses of Brigham Young*, 68–69.

Chapter 3

EXALTATION

This is life eternal, that they might know thee the only true God, and Jesus Christ, whom thou hast sent.

—John 17:3

If we desire to covenant with God, we must know Him. Believing in God and understanding who He is are the first willful steps we take toward making those sacred covenants toward exaltation. Covenants can only be understood in this context. To someone without this context, covenants appear restricting. To someone with this context, covenants are liberating; they open up possibilities before unimaginable.

Context

As we learn and grow through childhood and into adulthood, we build context—a philosophy of life. This growing comprehension brings meaning to our lives. The child reared in the gospel-centered home may build a context of eternal life and covenants, rather than believing solely in the here and now. The convert to the Church often must change drastically the context built into life. In that sense, "convert" is an appropriate term for the process of coming unto Christ because the whole person, including the mind, must be converted, or changed, into something it was not before.

Elder John A. Widtsoe said that our context is our religion whether or not it includes a belief in God. It is our attempt to place ourselves in the system of existence. And he added: "Those who have no life-philosophy at all become the playthings of unknown forces. Every act of a man's life is influenced by the philosophy of his life."[1] Our religion, or philosophy of life, is "the most compelling power in life."[2]

Whether we believe in God is part of that context of life. What we believe God expects of us is also part of that context. These beliefs influence our actions for good or bad. Depending on the believer's perception of God, the effect of this influence can vary from glorifying to destructive. In other words, not all beliefs are equal. For example, a sincerely held belief that God wants us to kill our neighbors, which is directly contrary to His true command to love our neighbors, is destructive and evil. It is a counterfeit of God's will for us. Religion, therefore, can be found at both ends of the spectrum of good and evil, and everywhere in between.

Yet the importance of this religious context can be lost in faithlessness. Much is made of the saying that religion "is the opium of the people."[3] Karl Marx coined it, and many have repeated it since. Characterizing religion as a reality-altering and pain-killing drug marginalizes religion, reducing it to a caricature of its social function, as if it had no other purpose than to pacify the oppressed. It also completely avoids the questions that religion seeks to address: Why are we here? Is there life after this life? Is there a God?

If there is no God, religion as opium is a reasonable position. If there is no God, there is no danger in failing to discover Him and worship Him or failing to somehow give Him His due. If there is no God, there is no danger in attempting to find meaning in life by applying reason alone to the search.

Trying to convince a determined atheist that our relationship with God is important is difficult—like trying to convince a skydiver who does not believe in gravity to wear a parachute. The result is the same. The failure to wear the parachute, or to believe in God and treat our relationship with Him as important, will hurt.

If there is a God, our relationship with Him, acknowledged or unacknowledged, is the most important relationship in our lives; it matters for us to know Him and know His desires. If there is a God, it is unreasonable to dismiss all religion as the opium of the masses or the weak without due investigation. If there is a God, we must take Him into account if we are to discover the meaning of our mortal lives, cradle to grave.

For these reasons, whether there is a God is the first question we should answer—or, if we don't go directly to that question, it is the question we must eventually get around to answering. Rejecting the existence of God, if there is a God, is dangerous to our souls, leaving the potential that we are forfeiting something important that He offers us. Failing to resolve the question is no better than rejecting the existence of God outright because any benefit we might derive from acknowledging and worshiping God must come as a result of our belief in Him, not our indifference to the question of His existence.

We cannot blissfully deny God's existence or the importance of His commands. Nephi summed up that attitude: "And there shall also be many which shall say: Eat, drink, and be merry; nevertheless, fear God—he will justify in committing a little sin; yea, lie a little, take the advantage of one because of his words, dig a pit for thy neighbor; there is no harm in this; and do all these things, for tomorrow we die; and if it so be that we are guilty, God will beat us with a few stripes, and at last we shall be saved in the kingdom of God" (2 Nephi 28:8). Nephi's response to that attitude was unequivocal: "O the wise, and the learned, and the rich, that are puffed up in the pride of their hearts, and all those who preach false doctrines, and all those who commit whoredoms, and pervert the right way of the Lord, wo, wo, wo be unto them, saith the Lord God Almighty, for they shall be thrust down to hell!" (2 Nephi 28:15).

However, it does injustice to the whole subject of the existence of God to couch the possibilities only in the negative. Knowing there is a God opens an eternity of possibilities. It provides a perspective infinitely broader and clearer than our own navel-gazing attempt to give meaning to life without allowing for greater possibilities than those available to the physical senses. This is not a tension between science and religion. Science allows that there are truths out there as yet undiscovered. Science can declare that God is unproven, but it cannot prove that God does not exist.

While it may sound pithy, even learned in a worldly sense, to declare that religion is the opium of the people, it can be just as easily said that doubt is the opium of the amoral; doubt allows the amoral to live without regard to God's laws because the doubter believes there is a chance that living a moral life will do them no good in this life or afterward. We decide for ourselves our own approaches to religion and the existence of God. But reducing the subjects to a social function does no better than to limit the power that religion has in our lives.

The desire to avoid the question of whether God exists does not eliminate the question; it only delays it. Sooner or later, we each must decide.

And if we come to the false conclusion that there is no God, we will be forced again to deal with the question. Eventually, everyone will know. "Every knee shall bow . . . , and every tongue shall confess to God. So then every one of us shall give account of himself to God" (Romans 14:11–12).

Not only is it critical to determine for ourselves whether there is a God, but we must also discover His true nature and desires. Anything short of that discovery is risky because it may lead us into destructive conduct, thinking it is the will of God. As our knowledge of His true nature and desires grows, we are better able to do His will and become what He wants us to become. This conception of God allows that He is omniscient and omnipotent but also allows that we are agents unto ourselves, free to choose, free to succeed or fail at becoming what God wants us to become.

Elder Robert D. Hales explained the importance of believing in God:

> Some wonder, why is belief in God so important? Why did the Savior say, "And this is life eternal, that they might *know* thee the only true God, and Jesus Christ, whom thou hast sent"? [John 17:3; emphasis added]. Without God, life would end at the grave and our mortal experiences would have no purpose. Growth and progress would be temporary, accomplishment without value, challenges without meaning. There would be no ultimate right and wrong and no moral responsibility to care for one another as fellow children of God. Indeed, without God, there would be no mortal or eternal life.[4]

If this question of the existence of God is so important to us, how do we come to believe in God? Simply by study and prayer, with faith. There is no shortcut past study and prayer; there is no substitute for faith. And faith requires action. The Lord said: "If any man will do [God's] will, he shall know of the doctrine" (John 7:17).

President Joseph Fielding Smith explained that everyone is capable of learning whether there is life after death, and we may apply his explanation to gaining a knowledge of all saving truths. He said:

> There is no need for any man being in darkness or declaring that he has no evidence of life after death, and that no one has ever returned. Instead of being the statement of someone wise and learned, such statement as that is a statement of ignorance. We may all know the truth; we are not helpless. The Lord has made it possible for every man to know the truth by observance of these laws, and through the guidance of his Holy Spirit—who is sent purposely to teach us when we comply with the law, so that we may know that truth which makes us free. So

this is the best way in which to learn the truth of immortality and the resurrection of the dead.[5]

Those who declare that God is unknowable are simply declaring that they are not observing the laws whose observance lead to knowledge. Or the more charitable way of looking at it is that those who persistently doubt God and His truths have not yet learned about this key of knowledge.

Elder Hales identified the source of our knowledge, once obtained: "We know He lives because we believe the testimonies of His ancient and living prophets, and we have felt God's Spirit confirm that the testimonies of these prophets are true."[6]

Moroni provided the template for knowing truth, which also applies to our question of whether God exists. First, we must "receive" truth, such as by reading the Bible or Book of Mormon or hearing the testimony of a prophet. Second, we must sincerely ask God with faith and with the intent to act upon an answer. Third, we will receive the testimony, the assurance of truth, in our hearts by the power of the Holy Ghost.

Moroni used these words: "And when ye shall *receive these things*, I would exhort you that ye would *ask God*, the Eternal Father, in the name of Christ, if these things are not true; and if ye shall ask *with a sincere heart, with real intent, having faith in Christ*, he will *manifest the truth* of it unto you, by the *power of the Holy Ghost*" (Moroni 10:4; italics added).

Asking God whether God exists is not as circular as it first sounds. We are asking God to reveal Himself. When we do this with a hope that He exists and a desire to be acquainted with Him, He will reveal Himself. We can begin with merely "a particle of faith, . . . no more than desire to believe" (Alma 32:27). That particle or seed of faith will grow within us, if we allow it to. And, by this means, we eventually receive the full testimony of divine truth (see Alma 32:28–43).

Comprehending God's Character

After we have established for ourselves that God exists, the next question should be whether He has a plan for us. Understanding God's true nature—His character and desires—answers that question. He is a loving God who wants the best for His children. He wants for us nothing less than all He has and is. His work and His glory are to bring to pass our immortality and eternal life (see Moses 1:39). He is immortal, and eternal life is the life that He lives.

Joseph Smith encapsulated our need to know the character of God: "If men do not comprehend the character of God, they do not comprehend themselves."[7] This principle came from a discussion by Joseph on the ability and need to know God, an ability and need that is uniquely human. About this human trait, the Prophet taught: "If a man learns nothing more than to eat, drink and sleep, and does not comprehend any of the designs of God, the beast comprehends the same things. It eats, drinks, sleeps, and knows nothing more about God; yet it knows as much as we, unless we are able to comprehend by the inspiration of Almighty God."[8]

Misconceptions about God can inhibit our ability, and our willingness, to believe in God and have faith in Him. If we do not understand what He is and who He is, we cannot completely know Him.

An example of a misconception that may inhibit a belief in God is the misunderstanding of the source of good and evil. One of the arguments against a belief in God is that, if He is the Creator of all things, He created evil.[9] That is simply not true. God created neither evil nor good. They are part of the eternal, uncreated nature of agency. Jesus Christ is the personification of good because of His perfectly right choices. Lucifer is the personification of evil because of his own wrong choices. While it is true that God created Lucifer in the sense that He begat him spiritually, God did not force him to make evil choices. That was Lucifer's own doing. Each individual is accountable before God for choices made.

The context for understanding our covenants with God lies in belief in God and knowledge of His purpose for us. Joseph Smith taught:

> In the first place, I wish to go back to the beginning—to the morn of creation. There is the starting point for us to look to, in order to understand and be fully acquainted with the mind, purposes and decrees of the Great Elohim [God the Father], who sits in yonder heavens as he did at the creation of this world. It is necessary for us to have an understanding of God himself in the beginning. If we start right, it is easy to go right all the time; but if we start wrong, we may go wrong, and it be a hard matter to get right.[10]

Joseph also identified knowledge of God as our key to approaching Him: "Having a knowledge of God, we begin to know how to approach him, and how to ask so as to receive an answer. When we understand the character of God, and know how to come to him, he begins to unfold the heavens to us, and to tell us all about it. When we are ready to come to him, he is ready to come to us."[11]

Without knowledge of the character of God and His purpose for us, we are figuratively blind, unable to discern what God wants for us. "How blind and impenetrable are the understandings of the children of men; for they will not seek wisdom, neither do they desire that she should rule over them! Yea, they are as a wild flock which fleeth from the shepherd, and scattereth, and are driven, and are devoured by the beasts of the forest" (Mosiah 8:20–21).

Our God, as revealed through Joseph, differs in important respects from the creeds of the world. This is both a distinguishing point between The Church of Jesus Christ of Latter-day Saints and most of the rest of Christianity and, at times, a source of criticism from other denominations.

During Christ's mortal ministry, He taught His disciples concerning the true character of God—for example, that God the Father, God the Son, and the Holy Ghost are three distinct personages. Jesus, the Apostles, and early Christian writers taught that the members of the Godhead are separate personages, but They are perfectly unified in purpose. Thus, when Jesus declared that "I and my Father are one" (John 10:30), He meant one in purpose, and it was consistent with His other teachings, such as His Great Intercessory Prayer, in which He prayed concerning His disciples "that they all may be one; as thou, Father, art in me, and I in thee, that they also may be one in us" (John 17:21). He meant one in purpose, not merged into one being.

In the centuries after the death and resurrection of Jesus Christ and the loss of the Apostles, the truths taught by Jesus and His Apostles were confused and disputed. No single authority was the ultimate source for resolving questions of theological importance. The books we Christians now call the Bible were not compiled and canonized until about four hundred years after Christ.

To make matters worse, the truth concerning the character of God became a philosophical debate. The Christian doctrine of a Godhead comprised of three separate and distinct personages contradicted the Greek philosophical teaching that there is only one cause to all being. A compromise between the two positions was eventually reached, a compromise in which both incompatible truths (the one cause and the three personages) were accepted. The compromise was called the Athanasian Creed and stated that God the Father, God the Son, and the Holy Ghost are the same substance, three in one, a Trinity. Thus, God was deemed incomprehensible—a mystery. This creed has been used in most Christian churches since the sixth century after Christ.[12]

After many years of spiritual darkness during which the character of God was considered unknowable, the truth was restored, beginning in 1820. Over a period of several years, the doctrine of the character of God, including the true doctrine of the Godhead, was given to Joseph by divine revelation.

In 1820, Joseph sought guidance on which church to join. He had read from the Bible and had listened to the various ministers. While they all preached from the Bible, they came to different conclusions about what the Bible meant (see Joseph Smith—History 1:12). After reading in the Bible that a person could ask God for himself (see James 1:5), fourteen–year-old Joseph went into a grove of trees and prayed. He received what members of The Church of Jesus Christ of Latter-day Saints refer to as the First Vision. He recalled: "I saw a pillar of light exactly over my head, above the brightness of the sun, which descended gradually until it fell upon me. . . . When the light rested upon me I saw two Personages, whose brightness and glory defy all description, standing above me in the air. One of them spake unto me, calling me by name and said, pointing to the other—*This is My Beloved Son. Hear Him!*" (Joseph Smith—History 1:16–17).

Thus began the restoration of the knowledge of God's nature. Two personages, separate and distinct, appeared to Joseph, identifying Themselves as Father and Son. The Church of Jesus Christ of Latter-day Saints is a restored church, meaning it is a restoration of the church established by Jesus Christ during His earthly ministry. It is not a protest against or reformation of any church extant in the 1800s. Thus, Latter-day Saints refer to the organization of the Church in 1830, and related events, as the restoration of the Church of Jesus Christ or the restoration of the gospel of Jesus Christ.

A prime feature of the restoration of the gospel of Jesus Christ became revelations given to Joseph concerning the nature of God the Father and His Son, Jesus Christ: "The Father has a body of flesh and bones as tangible as man's; the Son also; but the Holy Ghost has not a body of flesh and bones, but is a personage of Spirit. Were it not so, the Holy Ghost could not dwell in us" (D&C 130:22). "And now, after the many testimonies which have been given of him, this is the testimony, last of all, which we give of him: That he lives! For we saw him, even on the right hand of God; and we heard the voice bearing record that he is the Only Begotten of the Father—That by him, and through him, and of him, the worlds are and were created, and the inhabitants thereof are begotten sons and daughters unto God" (D&C 76:22–24).

With the knowledge that God the Father and His Son Jesus Christ are two separate and distinct personages, Joseph received the further knowledge that God the Father is an exalted man:

> God himself was once as we are now, and is an exalted man, and sits enthroned in yonder heavens! That is the great secret. If the veil were rent today, and the great God who holds this world in its orbit, and who upholds all worlds and all things by his power, was to make himself visible—I say, if you were to see him today, you would see him like a man in form—like yourselves in all the person, image, and very form as a man; for Adam was created in the very fashion, image and likeness of God, and received instruction from, and walked, talked and conversed with him, as one man talks and communes with another.[13]

Our Co-eternal Nature with God

As God is eternal, so are we. It is true that we were born into this mortal life from a forgotten premortal life. It is also true that we were begotten spirit sons and daughters of God. But even before that, we existed as intelligence, already capable of exercising agency. Joseph Smith taught that "intelligence is eternal."[14] And intelligence is "independent in that sphere in which God has placed it, to act for itself" (D&C 93:39). This explains (1) how God could be our "creator" and still be perfect, despite the evil choices we, His "creations," sometimes make, and (2) how truly meaningful are agency and the covenants we make with God.

Along with knowledge of the character of God goes knowledge of the nature of creation. As the creeds of Christendom have departed from the true character of God, defining Him as incomprehensible and unattainable, so they have redefined creation as the illogical act of creating something out of nothing. But the theory of creation from nothing has logical difficulties. The problem of evil and evildoers is the most troublesome. If God alone is eternal and He created everything else from nothing, why did He allow evil to exist? Why would He create from nothing a person who chooses evil over good? If God is the sole cause of our existence, why is He not responsible for every outcome—both good and bad?

Elder B.H. Roberts identified these theoretical difficulties:

> As matters now stand, the usually accepted Christian doctrine on the matter of man's origin is that God of His free-will created men. That they are as He would have them, since in His act of creation He

could have had them different if He had so minded. Then why should He—being infinitely wise and infinitely powerful, and infinitely good—for so the creeds represent Him—why should He create by mere act of volition, beings such as men are, not only capable of, but prone to, moral Evil? Which, in the last analysis of things, in spite of all special pleadings to the contrary, leaves responsibility for moral Evil with God? God's creative acts culminating thus, the next pertinent questions are: Then what of the decreed purpose of God to punish moral Evil? And what of the much-vaunted justice of God in that punishment? Wherein lies the just responsibility of man if he was so created as to love Evil and to follow it?[15]

The difficulties inherent in the theory of creation out of nothing cannot be resolved because the theory of creation out of nothing is wrong. Free from the influences of Greek philosophy and the theorizing of earlier Christians trying to harmonize theology and philosophy, Joseph Smith received revelation on our nature and specifically rejected the theory of creation out of nothing.

Joseph taught that intelligence, or the mind, is self-existing, uncreated. In that way we are equal with God. "Man was also in the beginning with God. Intelligence, or the light of truth, was not created or made, neither indeed can be" (D&C 93:29). We are of the same species as God. Granted, our station is lower because our intelligence has not progressed to the extent God's has, but we are nonetheless of His species with the potential to become as He is. This is another testimony that He is our Father in a real sense, not merely in some metaphorical sense.

With this knowledge of our co-eternal nature with God, we can better understand our relationship with Him. Our loving Heavenly Father, having gained higher intelligence, regarded us with our lower intelligence and desired to provide a path for us to His higher intelligence. Joseph taught: "The first principles of man are self-existent with God. God himself, finding he was in the midst of spirits and glory, because he was more intelligent, saw proper to institute laws whereby the rest could have a privilege to advance like himself. The relationship we have with God places us in a situation to advance in knowledge."[16]

Not only does knowledge of our nature as co-eternal beings with God help us better understand our relationship with Him, but it also helps us understand our covenants with Him. If God created us from nothing, then covenants have little meaning. Under those circumstances, our destiny was determined when God created us, and we are powerless to change that destiny. But He did not create us out of nothing. We were begotten spirit sons and daughters of God from self-existent intelligence that already had agency. As spirit sons and daughters of God, we chose to follow Jesus Christ and continue to gain higher intelligence by experiencing mortality. Here in mortal life we still continue to choose our path, that choice being whether we will continue to gain higher intelligence by obeying God. His desire is for us to continue in our progression, and His commandments are directions on how to progress.

We don't have to continue on this journey toward higher intelligence. But whether we do is up to us. And making covenants with God is how we assent to His help and guidance. The prophet Lehi taught, "Wherefore, the Lord God gave unto man that he should act for himself" (2 Nephi 2:16). "And they are free to choose liberty and eternal life, through the great Mediator of all men" (2 Nephi 2:27), by making and keeping sacred covenants. So covenants are an act of free will of a being equal with God when it comes to the exercise of agency.

Make no mistake: God is omnipotent and omniscient; we are not. He is a higher intelligence than we are. He determines the terms of the covenants; there is no arms-length negotiation over their terms, which is fortunate because only God's terms can exalt us. Yet, in the matter of whether or not to enter into and abide by the covenants, we are God's equals. He will not overcome our will and impose a covenant on us, just as He will not break the covenant He makes with us.[17] For that reason, covenants truly are our agreement to be exalted. If we were to arrive at exaltation by any other means, it would be against our will, or without our having exercised our will. That cannot be. We are free to choose.

This knowledge of our co-eternal nature with God and our co-equal agency with Him also emphasizes the tragedy of damnation, which is the choice to stop progressing by disobeying God and either refusing to make covenants with Him or making and then breaking those covenants. We are free "to choose captivity and death, according to the captivity and power of the devil; for he seeketh that all men might be miserable like unto himself" (2 Nephi 2:27).

The wisdom of Lehi's final plea to his sons, then, is self-evident: "And now, my sons, I would that ye should look to the great Mediator, and hearken unto his great commandments; and be faithful unto his words, and choose eternal life, according to the will of his Holy Spirit; and not choose eternal death, according to the will of the flesh and the evil which is therein, which giveth the spirit of the devil power to captivate, to bring you down to hell, that he may reign over you in his own kingdom" (2 Nephi 2:28–29).

Exaltation

In a nutshell, our purpose, and God's desire for us, is to gain exaltation. If exaltation is our goal, understanding exaltation is essential to understanding God, His plan for us, and our relationship with Him. Without that understanding, every theory about the purpose of life falls short. We comprehend exaltation when we comprehend God and our co-eternal relationship with Him.

An exalted individual is a god who inhabits the highest degree of the celestial kingdom. An exalted individual has eternal increase by spiritually begetting sons and daughters and providing them the opportunity also to inherit the celestial kingdom.

Eternal life is another name for exaltation. It is different from immortality, which is the condition of all humans after the resurrection. "Immortality" means that the spirit and the body will never again be separated as they are at death. After resurrection, they are inseparably connected. Eternal life includes immortality but is much more; it is to inherit all that our exalted Father possesses. "Endless" or "Eternal" is the Father's name, and "eternal life" is the life that He lives (see D&C 19:10–12; Moses 1:3).

It is with this exalted Father that we seek to have a covenant relationship. He is perfect but understands imperfection. He is exalted and perfectly understands the process of exaltation. He is real and tangible. And He loves us perfectly. We came from Him, and He wants us to return to Him of our own free will.

Ultimately, knowing God goes well beyond being acquainted with Him. Joseph taught this extension of knowing God when he said: "Here, then, is eternal life—to know the only wise and true God; and you have got to learn how to be Gods yourselves, and to be kings and priests to God, the same as all Gods have done before you."[18]

Endnotes

1. Widtsoe, *A Rational Theology as Taught by the Church of Jesus Christ of Latter-day Saints*, 2.
2. Ibid.
3. Van der Hoeven, *Karl Marx: The Roots of His Thought*, 35. One can imagine that Marx would not agree with King Benjamin that submission, even to God, is a virtue (see Mosiah 3:19).
4. Hales, "Seeking to Know God, Our Heavenly Father, and His Son, Jesus Christ," 29.
5. Smith, *Doctrines of Salvation*, 1:295–296; italics omitted.
6. Hales, "Seeking to Know God, Our Heavenly Father, and His Son, Jesus Christ," 30.
7. *Teachings of the Prophet Joseph Smith*, 343.
8. Ibid.
9. The God-and-evil problem "remains the strongest secular objection to belief in a purposive and worthy Deity" (Madsen, *Eternal Man*, 27, n. 13).
10. *Teachings of the Prophet Joseph Smith*, 343.
11. Ibid., 350.
12. See Talmage, *Jesus the Christ*, 745–757, for an overview of the apostasy.
13. *Teachings of the Prophet Joseph Smith*, 345.
14. Ibid., 354.
15. Roberts, *Joseph Smith: The Prophet-Teacher, A Discourse*, 57–58.
16. *Teachings of the Prophet Joseph Smith*, 354.
17. See chapter 15 for additional discussion on covenanting with God as equals.
18. *Teachings of the Prophet Joseph Smith*, 346.

Chapter 4

PREMORTAL COVENANTS

For behold, this is my work and my glory—
to bring to pass the immortality and eternal life of man.

—Moses 1:39

We began making covenants with God before this life. The most basic premortal covenant we made with God was that we would obey Him, and, in return, He would provide a Savior. Those who made this covenant kept their first estate and have come or will come to the earth as mortals with the potential to become like God. Those who did not make this covenant and followed Lucifer became his angels, forever damned.

Premortal Life

Before we came to this mortal life, we lived with God. We could see that He had a resurrected and exalted body of flesh and bone, and we wanted to be like Him. Exaltation was not for us an imaginary goal during our premortal life. God was our Exemplar and was a tangible representation of our goal.

In the premortal realm, we were begotten spirit sons and daughters of Heavenly Father. This process was a creation in the general sense of the term, but it was more accurately and specifically a *procreation*—the bringing together of elements to compose a being that has the potential to become like the parents.[1] Before that spirit birth, we existed as intelligence. That intelligence was brought together with spirit matter to make our spirits. Our spirit birth allowed us to participate in God's plan of salvation, giving us the potential to eventually become like Him.

The Apostle Paul, in fact, attributed our divine potential to our status as children of God: "Ye have received the Spirit of adoption, whereby we cry, Abba, Father. The Spirit itself beareth witness with our spirit, that we are the children of God. And if children, then heirs; heirs of God, and joint-heirs with Christ; if so be that we suffer with him, that we may be also glorified together" (Romans 8:15–17).

Putting the creation of our spirits in these terms of procreation naturally raises the question of whether it is analogous to our mortal birth and whether it involves man and woman. The answer is an emphatic yes! In fact, there is no other way.

We are, male and female, spirit sons and daughters of Heavenly Parents. Our status as spirit sons and daughters of Heavenly Parents not only defines our relationship to them but also defines our potential. Brigham Young explained that the logical conclusion from our status as sons and daughters of Heavenly Parents is that we can become like Them: "We are the sons and daughters of celestial Beings, and the germ of the Deity dwells within us."[2] Brigham Young also said: "We were created upright, pure, and holy, in the image of our father and our mother, the image of our God."[3]

The truth that we have both a Heavenly Father and a Heavenly Mother also implies that exaltation is for couples. There is no Heavenly Father without a Heavenly Mother, and vice versa. "Neither is the man without the woman, neither the woman without the man, in the Lord" (1 Corinthians 11:11).

An enlightened reading of the Bible, as we know it today, reveals a few gems of knowledge concerning our premortal life. The Lord told Jeremiah that Jeremiah was known to the Lord before birth: "Before I formed thee in the belly I knew thee; and before thou camest forth out of the womb I sanctified thee, and I ordained thee a prophet unto the nations" (Jeremiah 1:5).

The Book of Mormon also offers glimpses of premortal life. Alma said that priesthood holders were "called and prepared from the foundation of the world according to the foreknowledge of God, on account of their exceeding faith and good works" (Alma 13:3). Alma also taught that we had agency in the premortal life and implied that some exercised that agency more righteously than others: "In the first place [in the premortal life] being left to choose good or evil; therefore they having chosen good, and exercising exceedingly great faith, are called with a holy calling, yea, with that holy calling which was prepared with, and according to, a preparatory redemption for such" (Alma 13:3).

While these Bible and Book of Mormon glimpses of the premortal life are inspiring, a greater knowledge of premortal life is to be found in the Pearl of Great Price—in the books of Moses and Abraham. There, we learn that we are spirit sons and daughters of God who lived with God in a premortal life where we indeed had agency and, using that agency, made eternally significant choices.

Joseph Smith's translation of the Bible, and specifically his translation of Genesis, gives us a better understanding of agency and covenants in the premortal life. The first eight chapters of the translation of Genesis are contained in the book of Moses in the Pearl of Great Price. Unlike the vaguer references in the Bible and Book of Mormon, the book of Moses educates us plainly on our premortal life and our role in the events that transpired before we came to earth.

Right from the start of the book of Moses, our relationship with God was emphasized as God told Moses, "Thou art my son" (Moses 1:4). The Lord continued with this parentage theme: "And I have a work for thee, Moses, my son; and thou art in the similitude of mine Only Begotten" (Moses 1:6). Immediately after Moses's conversation with the Lord, Satan appeared to Moses, calling him "son of man" and imploring Moses to worship him (see Moses 1:12). It is telling that God referred to Moses as His own son, acknowledging and implying Moses's divine parentage and potential, and Satan tried to minimize Moses's potential and his relationship with God by emphasizing Moses's mere-mortal status.

Moses recognized that God was glorified, while Satan was full of darkness. Based on that difference Moses rejected Satan, telling Satan that Moses was "after the similitude" of God (Moses 1:15–16). "For his glory has been upon me, wherefore I can judge between him and thee" (Moses 1:18). Apparently understanding that he had power over Satan, he commanded Satan to "depart hence" (Moses 1:18). When Satan refused, Moses invoked the authority of the priesthood: "In the name of the Only Begotten, depart hence, Satan" (Moses 1:21). Then, Satan had no choice. He wept and wailed and gnashed his teeth but departed (see Moses 1:22).

After Satan departed, Moses called upon the Lord again, and he again enjoyed the Lord's glory. This time, Moses witnessed great visions and spoke to the Lord face to face. The Lord informed Moses that Israel was chosen, as was Moses (see Moses 1:24–31). The Lord showed Moses the work of His hands and revealed to Moses the Lord's work and glory: "For behold, this is my work and my glory—to bring to pass the immortality and eternal life of man" (Moses 1:39).

The Lord taught Moses about the creation of this earth and formation of man. While Adam was the first man on the earth, Adam was created spiritually before that, as were all things (see Moses 3:7).

The First Presidency, in 1912, reaffirmed these truths from the Pearl of Great Price. In an official statement, the First Presidency said, referring to the book of Moses: "The written standards of scripture show that all people who come to this earth and are born in mortality, had a pre-existent, spiritual personality, as the sons and daughters of the Eternal Father. Jesus Christ was the first-born. A spirit born of God is an immortal being. When the body dies, the spirit does not die. In the resurrected state the body will be immortal as well as the spirit."[4]

Later in the book of Moses, the Lord continued Moses's education on eternal matters. Not only was Moses God's son and all men were created spiritually before they were created physically, but Satan also existed before the creation of the earth.

God instructed Moses that Satan and Jehovah (Jesus Christ) existed "from the beginning"—in a time preceding the creation of this world (see Moses 4:1). There was a contest of sorts for the favor of God. I say "of sorts" because Jehovah had already been chosen and, in reality, championed the Father's plan, not His own. Nonetheless, Satan challenged Jehovah, asking God to choose Satan. He offered: "Behold, here am I, send me, I will be thy son, and I will redeem all mankind, that one soul shall not be lost, and surely I will do it; wherefore give me thine honor" (Moses 4:1).

Satan's plan was to take God's honor for himself. But that wasn't the extent of his deviousness. He also wanted to take away our agency and force us to obey. Moses recorded that God rejected Satan's plan and cast him out of heaven not only because he rebelled but also because he "sought to destroy the agency of man" (Moses 4:3). Note that Satan did not seek to prevent man from obtaining agency; he sought to destroy man's agency, implying we already had agency in the premortal life.

Three great principles are established in these chapters of the book of Moses: (1) we were created spiritually in a premortal life before we were created physically in this life, (2) God is the Father of our spirits, and (3) our spirits had agency before we were born in mortality.

These truths extracted from the book of Moses, including the essential truth that Satan's evil plan was to take away the agency of man, were restored through Joseph Smith. They were originally included in the text of Moses's book, but they were taken out by men who "esteem [the Lord's] words as naught and take many of them from the book" (Moses 1:41). The Lord told Moses that the Lord would "raise up another like unto [Moses]; and [the Lord's revelations to Moses] shall be had again among the children of men—among as many as shall believe" (Moses 1:41).

Moses knew that some of the truths revealed to him by the Lord would be lost, and another prophet, Joseph Smith, would be raised up to restore those truths. The Book of Mormon is more specific on this subject, explaining that not just *truths* but *covenants* were also lost. Lehi said that the Lord told Joseph of Egypt: "A choice seer [Joseph Smith] will I raise up out of the fruit of thy loins [a descendant of Joseph of Egypt]. . . . And unto him will I give commandment that he shall do a work . . . , even to the bringing of them to the knowledge of the *covenants* which I have made with thy fathers" (2 Nephi 3:7; italics added).

The book of Abraham also provides knowledge about premortal life and premortal covenants—knowledge not clearly imparted in the Bible, or even the Book of Mormon. The Lord appeared to Abraham and pronounced great blessings on Abraham and his future seed. The great Abrahamic covenant, the covenant between Abraham and the Lord, promised that the earth would be blessed through Abraham's seed (see Abraham 2:6–11). The Lord gave Abraham the Urim and Thummim, an instrument for receiving revelation, and Abraham received advanced knowledge concerning God's creations (see Abraham 3:1–17).

In the course of this divine instruction concerning God's creations, the Lord revealed to Abraham the eternal nature of spirits or intelligences: "If there be two spirits, and one shall be more intelligent than the other, yet these two spirits, notwithstanding one is more intelligent than the other, have no beginning; they existed before, they shall have no end, they shall exist after, for they are gnolaum, or eternal" (Abraham 3:18).

From the Doctrine and Covenants we learn: "Man was also in the beginning with God. Intelligence, or the light of truth, was not created or made, neither indeed can be" (D&C 93:29). Thus, we existed as intelligence, co-eternal with God, before we became spirit sons and daughters of Heavenly Parents, through a procreative process.

The Lord made it clear to Abraham that these spirits of which He spoke included those that would inhabit mortal bodies and live on this earth. Abraham was specifically named as one of them. It is here that the Lord instructed on the existence of noble and great spirits, which is evidence that the spirit sons and daughters made choices in the premortal life that resulted in varying degrees of progress, according to the value of the choices made.

Abraham wrote: "Now the Lord had shown unto me, Abraham, the intelligences that were organized before the world was; and among all these there were many of the noble and great ones; And God saw these souls that they were good, and he stood in the midst of them, and he said: These I will make my rulers; for he stood among those that were spirits, and he saw that they were good; and he said unto me: Abraham, thou art one of them; thou wast chosen before thou wast born" (Abraham 3:22–23).

The revelation continued with a description of the council in heaven, where the spirits were put to the choice of following Jehovah or Satan. Without agency, there could have been no such choice. We know that we chose to follow Jehovah because the book of Abraham informs that only those who followed Him came to this earth to be tested—"we will prove them herewith"—and to have the opportunity to progress toward eternal life (see Abraham 3:24–28).

In summary, the book of Abraham establishes that (1) our spirits are co-eternal with God, (2) we are spirit sons and daughters of Heavenly Parents, (3) we had agency before we came to this life, and (4) we exercised that agency by following Jehovah and coming to this earth to be tested.

Finally, President Joseph F. Smith's Vision of the Redemption of the Dead in section 138 of the Doctrine and Covenants reaffirms that some of God's spirit children rose to the stature of noble and great ones in the premortal life and were chosen "to be rulers in the Church of God" (D&C 138:55): "Even before they were born, they, with many others, received their first lessons in the world of spirits and were prepared to come forth in the due time of the Lord to labor in his vineyard for the salvation of the souls of men" (D&C 138:56).

Agency and Progress in Premortal Life

We all started our spirit lives innocent (see D&C 93:38). We progressed in intelligence and righteousness according to our choices. Some chose better than others and gained more intelligence because of that righteousness.

Latter-day prophets have described this premortal agency. President Joseph Fielding Smith taught:

> The spirits of man had their free agency, some were greater than others, and from among them the Father called and foreordained his prophets and rulers. Jeremiah and Abraham were two of them. . . . The spirits of men were not equal. They may have had an equal start, and we know they were all innocent in the beginning; but the right of free agency which was given to them enabled some to outstrip others, and thus, through the eons of immortal existence, to become more intelligent, more faithful, for they were free to act for themselves, to think for themselves, to receive the truth or rebel against it.[5]

Elder LeGrand Richards confirmed the conclusion that we had agency as spirits in the premortal life. He said: "We read in the Book of Abraham that the Lord stood in the midst of the spirits, and among them there were noble and great ones—and they couldn't be noble and great if they hadn't done something to make them noble and great."[6]

Thus, even before we exercised our agency in the council in heaven to follow Jesus Christ, we exercised agency through which some of us, the spirit children of God, became noble and great ones.

We know that one of our brothers exceeded all of us in quality premortal decision making, in His exercise of His moral agency, because He became our Savior and the cornerstone of Heavenly Father's plan to provide us with the opportunity to reach exaltation. Jehovah, the Son of God whom we call Jesus Christ, did not become a God by some unnatural agency. He became a God by being perfectly obedient to His Father and bending His will to the Father's will, thus qualifying for eternal life even before He came to this earth.

Understanding premortal agency also helps us understand God's dealings with His children in this life. The justice of God is perfect. It must be, or God is not perfect. Yet we see so many inequities that cannot be attributed to a person's actions in this life. Children are the easiest example: some are born free; some are born in slavery; some have physical deformities; some are mentally challenged. There is no end to the variety of conditions into which children are born, yet they have done *nothing* in this life, let alone anything that would merit such different treatment by God.

The answer is that this life is a continuation of life from the premortal realm. We are born into this life in circumstances we (1) merited because of our premortal choices, (2) needed in order to have the experiences and growth necessary to eventually reach exaltation, or (3) both. Mind you, this does not fit nicely with worldly notions of justice and fairness. And we cannot tell for sure why we are subjected to certain mortal conditions, seemingly through no fault of our own, because we cannot remember the premortal life and we cannot therefore judge the justice and fairness meted out to us here, at least to the extent that justice and fairness relates to our premortal choices. This is another place where faith comes in. We have faith that God is perfect and, therefore, places us in conditions that we either merit or need.

It cannot be said that more challenges in mortality and more intense mortal suffering are necessarily a result of bad premortal choices. Jesus Christ is the perfect rebuttal to that argument. He was born into lowly circumstances and suffered more than anyone else, yet He came here perfect and remained perfect. We know that He volunteered for mortal suffering. We know why Jesus was born humbly and suffered so greatly because we know of His premortal calling, but we don't know our own, unless that premortal calling is somehow revealed to us. So the correlation between mortal suffering and premortal choices is mostly beyond our current knowledge, hidden from us by the veil of forgetfulness.

We are not born equal into this life. That is hard for me to say, as a lawyer, because it does not seem fair to our limited, mortal minds. However, it is the only position that accounts for agency in the premortal life and the different conditions we are born into. And it is the correct position. Each individual is a unique premortal spirit. Elder Bruce R. McConkie said that we are not born equal because we "enter this life with the talents and capacities developed" in the premortal life.[7]

We all must attain perfection to return to live with our Father, and mortality is an opportunity to progress in that direction. Because God loves us, He provides the opportunities in mortality that we can get in no other way. Each of us comes to mortality with a different set of imperfections, traits that must be polished and prepared for perfection. With that in mind, it makes sense that God gives us different challenges and obstacles. It requires faith to believe He gives us those challenges and obstacles that will help us prepare for exaltation.

Because of the choices each of us made in the premortal life, our challenges and obstacles will be different here. This is not a matter of being blessed or cursed. Mortality is a blessing, even if it is difficult. We can have faith that the challenges and obstacles that we do not bring upon ourselves through sin are preparing us for exaltation.

The differences in mortal experience can be explained by the process of acquiring a skill. If everyone's goal were to become a left-handed pitcher in the major leagues, I would have to begin by learning how to throw left-handed. My left-handed son, Joe, already has that skill mastered, so his first task might be to develop more strength in his left arm or to learn how to throw a curve ball. Even though we cannot remember the skills and characteristics we developed by our choices in premortal life, the Lord knows them, and He knows which experiences we need in this life "to progress toward perfection and ultimately realize [our] eternal destiny as heirs of eternal life."[8]

The story of Saul of Tarsus illustrates that what may seem unfair in this life is actually not only fair but part of God's plan to help us return to Him. Saul was an evil man, or at least a man doing evil things. He had a religious fervor—not a fervor of true religion but of persecution of the true religion, ostensibly in the name of God. A prominent Pharisee, he was educated at the feet of the famous and influential rabbi Gamaliel. Saul became one of the chief persecutors of the early Christians, those who followed Jesus Christ. When the Jews stoned Stephen, a disciple of Christ and passionate defender of the Christian faith, Saul stood by, holding the killer's coats for them (see Acts 7; 8:1–3; 22:3).

Continuing his campaign against the Christians, Saul went to the Jewish high priest and obtained authority to go to Damascus, arrest any Christians he found there, and bring them bound to Jerusalem (see Acts 9:1–2). Despite his active wrongdoing, however, Saul was personally visited by the Lord Jesus Christ, who was by then a resurrected being. Saul was on his way to Damascus to arrest Christians when an event changed his mortal life. As he approached Damascus, a light from heaven appeared. He fell to the ground and heard a voice say, "Saul, Saul, why persecutest thou me?" Identifying Himself as "Jesus whom thou persecutest" (Acts 9:4–5), the Lord commanded Saul to go into Damascus and do as he was instructed there.

Physically blinded by the experience, Saul went to Damascus. There, the Lord had prepared Ananias for Saul's arrival, instructing Ananias to go find Saul and administer to him. But Ananias feared Saul, telling the Lord he knew of "how much evil he hath done to thy saints in Jerusalem" (Acts 9:13).

Why would the Lord give such a great advantage to Saul, who was actively opposing the Lord's work? Why would He appear to Saul and set him on the right path? In the Lord's response to Ananias's fear lies the answer: "[Saul] is a chosen vessel unto me, to bear my name before the Gentiles, and kings, and the children of Israel" (Acts 2:15).

Saul was "chosen." Once converted to the gospel of Jesus Christ, he responded to the call with a righteous zeal that outpaced even his earlier enthusiastic offenses. He became an Apostle, known as Paul, and served the Lord the remainder of his life until his blood was shed as a testimony of Jesus Christ.

If Saul was chosen, then he must have been chosen in the premortal life. Any other conclusion would require a random act of favoritism on God's part, a violation of eternal law because "God is no respecter of persons" (Acts 10:34). If God is perfectly just, and we did not make premortal choices the consequences of which followed us into this life, then there is no adequate explanation for God's favored treatment of Saul. His conduct in this life before the incident on the road to Damascus did not merit a life-changing visitation from the Lord Himself. Instead, he deserved condemnation.

Only one explanation for the Lord's visit to Paul accounts for God's perfectly just and fair treatment of his children: Paul, through his premortal choices, had become a person who merited the trust and confidence of God. He was chosen premortally. God knew of Paul's premortal valiance and acted to salvage and use Paul for His own purposes.

Elder John A. Widtsoe attributed our mortal callings to our premortal choices: "It is not unthinkable that, in a plan governed by a supreme intelligent Being, since there are differences of advancement, the spirits who come on earth are placed frequently in positions for which they are best fitted. An intelligent ruler would probably use ability where it is most needed. To some extent, therefore, men may have been chosen for this or that work on earth."[9]

We as individuals and a society do not have the advantage of remembering a person's premortal character and conduct. Therefore, to be fair, we must act as if there is no in-born difference. Acting on this principle, the framers of the U.S. Bill of Rights required government to treat similarly situated people similarly, basing different treatment only on mortal actions that merit different treatment—at least that is the theory.

While, for the most part, we do not understand the effect our premortal life had on our mortal condition, God reveals that connection in some instances. As Latter-day Saints, we believe that God has revealed that connection to us, to some extent. For example, we know that we have come to this earth in the days preceding the Second Coming of Jesus Christ because of our valiance in the premortal life.

Touching on this subject, Elder David B. Haight said: "Most of us have wondered about what occurred in the premortal world and how it relates to our existence here. We should be acquainted with the truth that knowledge of the premortal life was restored that we might fulfill our responsibilities as children of God."[10]

Council in Heaven

With agency, we have the chance to make covenants. That is true in mortality, where we have agency and the opportunity to make covenants such as those we make when we are baptized. The same was true of premortal life. We had agency, and we had opportunities to covenant.

After an eternity of experience with our Heavenly Parents in the premortal life, it came time for us to leave the nest, to move on toward becoming more like Them. In this wrapping up of our premortal experience, we faced the most momentous of choices—whether to accept or reject God's plan for our continuing progress.

To prepare and unveil that plan, God called a council. Joseph Smith described this council: "In the beginning, the head of the Gods called a council of the Gods; and they came together and concocted a plan to create the world and people it."[11]

The champion of God's plan was Jehovah. Every reasonable and logical argument pointed to Him as the One who would faithfully and effectively carry out God's plan. As He told Abraham, "These two facts do exist, that there are two spirits, one being more intelligent than the other; there shall be another more intelligent than they; I am the Lord thy God, I am more intelligent than they all" (Abraham 3:19). Elder Neal A. Maxwell added that "what the Lord knows is, fortunately, *vastly* more—not just *barely* more—than the combination of what all mortals know."[12]

Jehovah stood, rightfully higher, among the noble and great ones, and He said: "We will go down, for there is space there, and we will take of these materials, and we will make an earth whereon these may dwell" (Abraham 3:24). Jehovah also explained the plan, in summary: "We will prove them [God's children] herewith, to see if they will do all things whatsoever the Lord their God shall command them" (Abraham 3:25).

The test of mortality is simple: will we obey? The reward for obedience, for passing the test, is also simple: we "shall have glory added upon [our] heads for ever and ever" (Abraham 3:26). We will be exalted.

But, as we learned from Abraham, an alternative to God's plan was proposed. Lucifer, one of the most influential of God's spirit children, advocated his own plan.

Even though reason and logic dictated following Jehovah, we were then, as we are now, not completely reasonable and logical beings. Multiple motivators pull us in different directions. Love is the purest of motivators and is powerful; therefore, hate—love's opposite—is also powerful. Duty, fear, and force can also motivate formidably. Because of these countervailing motivators, we sometimes ignore reason and logic.

In opposition to Jehovah, Lucifer sought to draw God's spirit children away from God's plan.

Returning to the knowledge of our premortal life imparted through Moses, we see that Lucifer's plan was also simple. He proposed to God: "Send me, I will be thy son, and I will redeem all mankind, that one soul shall not be lost, and surely I will do it; wherefore give me thine honor" (Moses 4:1).

"One soul shall not be lost" sounds like a good plan. By the terms of God's plan, there is opposition and agency. Each chooses whether to obey. In other words, exaltation is not assured for everyone because some, for whatever reason, may choose not to obey. We can see why some of the defiantly disobedient, some of the weak-minded, or some of the laziest would choose to follow Lucifer and accept his guarantee of exaltation.

The problem with Lucifer's plan was that it was a lie. He could not deliver on the promise. He could not exalt anyone by forcing them to be obedient. We progressed in the premortal life by exercising our agency in favor of good moral choices, and the same process would allow us to progress toward God in mortality. There must be opposition and agency or there is no progress. Without opposition and agency, Lucifer could not exalt his followers and receive the glory he so craved.

The difference between Heavenly Father's plan and Satan's plan, as they were presented to us in the premortal council, can be compared to our exercise regimen. Imagine that you and I are working on getting in shape, so we go to a mile-long track. There are two coaches there, each offering promises of fitness and health.

If you give your allegiance to the first coach, he helps you warm up, makes sure you are sufficiently hydrated, teaches you proper technique to gain strength and avoid injury, gives you encouragement, and makes sure you know where to go. He promises to help you along the way, but you must be the one who puts in the effort to run the track and to stay on the track to the end because the journey along the track is more important to your strength and conditioning than simply arriving at the finish line. The first coach assures you that if you complete the run and cross the finish line, he will be there to welcome you. You can choose at any time to ignore the first coach's instructions and leave the track, but the only way to become healthier and stronger is to complete the entire course according to the instructions given.

The second coach offers an alternate plan. He proposes to take the effort and the uncertainty out of the activity. Instead of having you run the track, he will drive you around the track in a golf cart. To make sure you don't fall out (or escape), he will tie you into your seat. With the second coach, there is no doubt that you will complete the course and cross the finish line. But the unfortunate result of following the second coach's plan is that when you cross the finish line you will not be healthier or stronger.

It is easy to understand why the second coach's exercise regimen is undesirable. It fails to provide the benefits of physical strength and conditioning. Crossing the finish line is assured, but the benefits of having run the course are absent.

On the other hand, the first coach's exercise regimen is harder, but it is the only way to achieve the desired results of strength and conditioning. There is no guarantee of reaching the finish line because that is up to the person who is running.

Like the second coach's exercise regimen, Lucifer's plan in the premortal life was a lie. He promised to get us all into the celestial kingdom, but under his plan we would not arrive with the experiences and progression that would allow us to become like our Heavenly Father. And under Lucifer's plan, covenants were pointless. Once accepted, Lucifer's plan demanded that we be bound, like being tied into the golf cart for the journey along the track. With no agency and with no ability to fail, we could not make valid and elevating covenants.

Like the first coach's exercise regimen, the plan of our Heavenly Father, as presented by our Savior Jesus Christ, provided the freedom and opportunity to grow spiritually stronger and prepare for eternal life. He helped us before this life by committing to preserve our agency and provide the Atonement. Here, He teaches us the proper technique to gain spiritual strength and avoid spiritual injury. He encourages us and makes sure we have the knowledge and understanding to succeed and has provided the way to return to the track if we wander, but only if we choose to return. He assures us that, if we complete this mortal life having followed the proper path, He will be there to welcome us and eventually usher us into the celestial kingdom. In this system, covenants are paramount. They represent our decision to stay the course and obtain the reward offered by our Heavenly Father to be like Him and live the life He lives—eternal life.

Under Lucifer's plan there would have been no covenants. With no opposition or agency, we would have had no choice whether to obey. Our promise to obey, under those conditions, would have been empty. Likewise, Lucifer's promise to exalt us was empty because it would not work. Ultimately, he would abandon us, as Korihor learned (see Alma 30:60).

By proposing his plan and gathering followers, Lucifer committed the most egregious sin against God—open rebellion. Again we learn from Moses why Satan was cast out: "Wherefore, because that Satan rebelled against me, and *sought to destroy the agency of man*, which I, the Lord God, had given him, and also, that I should give unto him mine own power; by the power of mine Only Begotten, I caused that he should be cast down. And he became Satan, yea, even the devil, the father of all lies, to deceive and to blind men, and to lead them captive at his will, even as many as would not hearken unto my voice" (Moses 4:3–4; italics added).

And God lamented: "How art thou fallen from heaven, O Lucifer, son of the morning! how art thou cut down to the ground, which didst weaken the nations! For thou hast said in thine heart, I will ascend into heaven, I will exalt my throne above the stars of God. . . . I will ascend above the heights of the clouds; I will be like the most High. Yet thou shalt be brought down to hell, to the sides of the pit" (Isaiah 14:12–15).

Lucifer did not fall alone. He took with him "a third part of the hosts of heaven" (D&C 29:36–38)—those who chose to follow Lucifer rather than Jehovah—and they were cast "out into the earth" (Revelation 12:9). According to Brigham Young, this group comprised "one-third part of the spirits who were prepared to take tabernacles upon this earth, and who rebelled against the other two-thirds of the heavenly host."[13]

The knowledge we have of the loss of one-third of the heavenly host is both a comfort and a caution to us: a comfort because our presence here on earth as mortals proves that we followed Jehovah in the premortal life and preserved our opportunity to continue progressing toward exaltation; a caution because the loss of the one-third proves that our Father will not take from us our agency, even if our choices lead to damnation. Whether we actually achieve exaltation is therefore an open question.

Premortal Covenants

Keeping our first estate—following Jehovah in accepting our Father's plan—required faith on our part (see Alma 13:3). Although we had a perfect knowledge of the existence of Heavenly Father, we had to have faith in Him that He would hold up His end of the bargain. Although we could also see Jehovah, keeping our first estate required us to have faith that He would do as He promised—that is, accomplish the Atonement, saving us from death and hell.

In Moses 5 we learn that these promised blessings were revealed to Adam and Eve. Having fallen, they showed their obedience to the Lord's commandment to worship the Lord and offer sacrifice (see Moses 5:5). An angel appeared and explained to them that the sacrifice was to remind them of the promised sacrifice of the Lord, by which Heavenly Father would provide a Savior (see Moses 5:6–7). And then the Holy Ghost bore witness to Adam and Eve of the blessings that would be theirs as followers of the Lord. Specifically, the Holy Ghost revealed to them that the Father would provide a Redeemer. Through the Holy Ghost, the Lord assured them: "I am the Only Begotten of the Father from the beginning, henceforth and forever, that as thou hast fallen thou mayest be redeemed, and all mankind, even as many as will" (Moses 5:9).

Because of Adam's fall, which was part of the plan, Adam's eyes were opened, meaning he had knowledge of good and evil. It was revealed to him that he would have joy in this mortal life and then, again in the flesh, as a resurrected being, He would see God (see Moses 5:10).

Eve also understood that without the Fall, she would not have had children. She would not have known the difference between good and evil. She would not have experienced the joy of redemption. And she would not have had the opportunity to be exalted (see Moses 5:11).

Adam and Eve understood all of these blessings to be a part of God's promise to them because they had followed God's plan in the premortal life. These are the blessings and opportunities that are promised and will be provided to all those who kept their first estate.

Lucifer's followers did not enter into this basic premortal covenant with Heavenly Father. They did not accept His plan. They did not keep their first estate, and, as a result, will not—cannot—receive the blessings promised to those who kept their first estate. They cannot receive a physical body and mortal life. They cannot receive a perfect physical body through resurrection. And they cannot obtain eternal life through obedience.

The most basic premortal covenant we made with our Heavenly Father was to accept His plan for us and obey Him. Lucifer opposed that plan and offered us an alternative. Therefore, we had a real choice—follow Jehovah, who championed the Father's plan, or follow Lucifer. Because we are here, we know that we chose to follow the Lord; we accepted Heavenly Father's plan. We not only promised to accept the Lord's plan, but we also fulfilled that promise. We performed our part of the bargain. Heavenly Father, therefore, is bound to provide the promised blessing (see D&C 82:10). In other words, the promised blessing is sealed upon us.

President Henry B. Eyring outlined the terms of this basic premortal covenant: "The central element of this plan was the promise that Jesus Christ would offer Himself as a sacrifice, to rescue us from sin and death. Our task in that plan is to accept the Savior's sacrifice by obeying the laws and ordinances of the gospel. You and I accepted this plan. In fact, we rejoiced in it, even though it would mean that we would leave the presence of our Father and forget what we had experienced there with Him."[14]

What is the promised blessing for fulfilling our end of this basic premortal covenant? It is nothing less than receiving (1) a physical body and mortal life, (2) a perfect body through resurrection, and (3) the opportunity to qualify for eternal life.

When we came to this mortal life, this basic premortal covenant remained in force. We remain under covenant to obey the Lord, even if we do not accept any further covenants in this life, even if we reject baptism and refuse to repent of our sins. Our mortal birth neither fulfilled nor nullified our end of the premortal bargain.

President Boyd K. Packer taught that we accepted the law, as well as the punishment for breaking the law: "We may not live perfect lives, and there are penalties for our mistakes, but before we came to earth, we agreed to be subject to His laws and to accept the punishment for violating those laws."[15]

President Spencer W. Kimball couched this basic premortal covenant in contract terms:

> When we were spiritual beings, fully organized and able to think and study and understand with him, our Heavenly Father said to us, in effect: "Now, my beloved children, in your spirit state you have progressed about as far as you can. To continue your development, you need physical bodies. I intend to provide a plan whereby you may continue your growth. As you know, one can grow only by overcoming.

"Now," said the Lord, "we shall take of the elements at hand and organize them into an earth. . . . This will be your proving ground. . . . We shall see if you will prove true and do the things that are asked of you. I will enter into a contract with you. If you will agree to exercise control over your desires and continue to grow toward perfection and godhood by the plan which I shall provide, I will give to you a physical body of flesh and bones and a rich and productive earth. . . . In addition to this, I will make it possible for you to eventually return to me as you improve your life, overcoming obstacles and approaching perfection."[16]

We remain obligated to obey the Lord. But our premortal covenants were not just to obey Heavenly Father and return to his presence. We also took upon ourselves the responsibility to assist others to achieve the same goal. When Moroni appeared to Joseph Smith to prepare him to get the hidden plates and translate them for the world, Moroni referred to Malachi's prophecy that the prophet Elijah would return to "plant in the hearts of the children the promises made to the fathers" (Joseph Smith—History 1:39). Referring to Moroni's statement to Joseph about these promises, Elder Jeffrey R. Holland said that "we undoubtedly made them to our own lineal fathers and mothers, those who came to earth before the gospel was restored but whom we promised to provide its saving ordinances."[17]

Elder John A. Widtsoe reminded the Latter-day Saints of the covenant they made concerning the eternal welfare of all of the sons and daughters of the Eternal Father:

> In our preexistent state, in the day of the great council, . . . we made a certain agreement with the Almighty. The Lord proposed a plan. . . . We accepted it. Since the plan is intended for all men, we became parties to the salvation of every person under that plan. We agreed, right then and there, to be not only saviors for ourselves but . . . saviors for the whole human family. We went into a partnership with the Lord. The working out of the plan became then not merely the Father's work, and the Savior's work, but also our work. The least of us, the humblest, is in partnership with the Almighty in achieving the purpose of the eternal plan of salvation.
>
> That places us in a very responsible attitude towards the human race. By that doctrine, with the Lord at the head, we become saviors on Mount Zion, all committed to the great plan of offering salvation to the untold numbers of spirits. To do this is the Lord's self-imposed duty, this great labor His highest glory. Likewise, it is man's duty, self-imposed, his pleasure and joy, his labor, and ultimately his glory.[18]

We are therefore a people chosen to work with the Lord in partnership to help save His children, both living and dead. "For we without them cannot be made perfect; neither can they without us be made perfect" (D&C 128:18).

Lucifer's plan was rejected; God's was accepted. Lucifer and his followers were cast out of heaven down into earth, and we were sent to this earth for our mortal opportunity to fulfill the covenants we made in the premortal life.

Endnotes

1. Madsen, *Eternal Man*, 34–35.
2. *Discourses of Brigham Young*, 50.
3. Ibid., 51.
4. First Presidency, "Pre-existent States," 417.
5. Smith, *Doctrines of Salvation*, 1:59.
6. Richards, in Conference Report, Apr. 1981, 41.
7. McConkie, *A New Witness for the Articles of Faith*, 34.
8. "The Family: A Proclamation to the World" (1995).
9. Widtsoe, *A Rational Theology as Taught by the Church of Jesus Christ of Latter-day Saints*, 137.
10. Haight, in Conference Report, Oct. 1990, 73.
11. *Teachings of the Prophet Joseph Smith*, 349.
12. Maxwell, *All These Things Shall Give Thee Experience*, 22, emphasis in original.
13. *Discourses of Brigham Young*, 54.
14. Eyring, "Gathering the Family of God," 20.
15. Packer, "The Reason for Our Hope," 6.
16. Kimball, "Absolute Truth," BYU Devotional, Sept. 6, 1977.
17. Holland, *Christ and the New Covenant*, 297.
18. Widtsoe, "The Worth of Souls," 131–32.

PART II

THE DOCTRINE OF CHRIST

Chapter 5

THE GATE AND PATH
TO ETERNAL LIFE

Wherefore, ye must press forward with a steadfastness in Christ, having a perfect brightness of hope, and a love of God and of all men. Wherefore, if ye shall press forward, feasting upon the word of Christ, and endure to the end, behold, thus saith the Father: Ye shall have eternal life.

—2 Nephi 31:20

The purpose of mortal life is to obtain a physical body, have earthly experiences, and receive ordinances. The ordinances are outward manifestations of sacred covenants with God, and these sacred covenants set us on the path toward exaltation. This is the doctrine of Christ, that we may progress through this mortal life and return to our Heavenly Father.

Mortal Life

We arrived in mortality from an enlightening and productive premortal life. But we don't remember. We don't even know what it was like to be born. Both a veil of forgetfulness over our premortal life and the cognitive fog of early mortality have placed those memories in a corner of our minds where they are irretrievable—for now. The distance from heaven can therefore seem great.

President Thomas S. Monson described this veil of forgetfulness as a blessing: "How grateful we should be that a wise Creator fashioned an earth and placed us here, with a veil of forgetfulness of our previous existence so that we might experience a time of testing, an opportunity to prove ourselves in order to qualify for all that God has prepared for us to receive."[1]

Another reason for the veil of forgetfulness, beyond the building of faith, may be that we would be mesmerized and paralyzed by our memory of living in God's presence. We came from a celestial presence into a telestial world, having never before experienced mortal hunger and pain. Would it be too difficult if we could see what we left behind at birth? At that critical point of entering this harsh world, would we be willing to accept our mortal probation and the pains, trials, and imperfections of life?

I trust in the wisdom of the veil. Birth might be more terrible than its twin death if it weren't for the veil of forgetfulness. But in His wisdom, our Father smoothed the path and allowed us to begin the proving ground of mortality in an innocent, forgetful state. Praise be to Him!

The prophets have taught clearly that birth is a *blessing* made possible by the Fall of Adam, not a *curse* caused by the Fall. Brigham Young responded to the argument that birth is a curse. He taught that spirits were willing to "come to the meanest, lowest and humblest of the human race to obtain [a mortal body] rather than run any risk of not doing so."[2]

Brigham Young continued: "I have heard that the celebrated Mr. Beecher, of Brooklyn, once said that the greatest misfortune that could ever happen to man was to be born; but I say that the greatest good fortune that ever happened or can happen to human beings is to be born on this earth, for then life and salvation are before them; then they have the privilege of overcoming death, and of treading sin and iniquity under their feet, of incorporating into their daily lives every principle of life and salvation and of dwelling eternally with the Gods."[3]

Joseph Smith put into perspective the great blessing of receiving a mortal body: "We came to this earth that we might have a body and present it pure before God in the celestial kingdom. The great principle of happiness consists in having a body. The devil has no body, and herein is his punishment. He is pleased when he can obtain the tabernacle of man. . . . All beings who have bodies have power over those who have not."[4]

Although blessings, these mortal bodies are imperfect. They are subject to injury and disease, and over time they grow old and don't function as well as they did when we were younger. But injury, disease, and aging are not the only challenges resulting from our mortal condition. We also have to deal with what prophets have called the "natural man."

Though we are born innocent (see D&C 93:38), we eventually must face the influences of a mortal body and a telestial world. Because of the Fall of Adam, we live in a fallen state, distanced from God. Those who allow the natural urges of the flesh to dictate their actions become "carnal, sensual, devilish, knowing evil from good, subjecting themselves to the devil" (Mosiah 16:3). And we will remain in that state, unless we follow the Holy Ghost and put off the natural man (see Mosiah 3:19). We can put off the natural man only through the Atonement of Jesus Christ (see Mosiah 16:4) by submitting to the will of God—in King Benjamin's words, by "becom[ing] as a child, submissive, meek, humble, patient, full of love, willing to submit to all things which the Lord seeth fit to inflict upon [us], even as a child doth submit to his father" (Mosiah 3:19).

The prophet Abinadi gave a stern warning to those who fail to submit to God: "But remember that he that persists in his own carnal nature, and goes on in the ways of sin and rebellion against God, remaineth in his fallen state and the devil hath all power over him. Therefore he is as though there was no redemption made, being an enemy to God" (Mosiah 16:5).

It makes sense that submitting to God's will is central to the process of attaining eternal life because the goal is to become like Him. This is the process Jesus Christ referred to in His Intercessory Prayer on behalf of His disciples as He approached the time to atone for the pains and sins of mankind (see John 17).

In the prayer, Jesus identified "life eternal" as knowing God the Father and his Son, Jesus Christ (see John 17:3). He told the Father: "I have given unto them the words which thou gavest me; and they have *received* them" (John 17:8; italics added). *Receiving* God's words is more than just hearing them. Receiving them requires action on our part, finding a place for God's words in our hearts. Unlike most people of Jesus's time who heard His words and did not conform their lives to His teachings, the disciples for whom Jesus prayed in the Intercessory Prayer heard and hearkened. Jesus acknowledged and gave thanks for the fact that they were actively becoming like God by bending their wills to His.

Jesus then referred to the result of the process of coming to know God the Father and His Son. Keep in mind while reading this passage that we are exalted when we submit to the will of God—that is the oneness referred to. His will, alone, is the motivator leading to exaltation, and, therefore, we must adopt His will voluntarily (because it cannot be forced) to become like Him. Here are the words of the Intercessory Prayer:

> That they all may be one; as thou, Father, art in me, and I in thee, that they also may be one in us: that the world may believe that thou hast sent me.
>
> And the glory which thou gavest me I have given them; that they may be one, even as we are one:
>
> I in them, and thou in me, that they may be made perfect in one; and that the world may know that thou hast sent me, and hast loved them, as thou hast loved me. (John 17:21–23)

Our will—meaning our agency—is the only thing that is uniquely ours that God will never take away. Therefore, to become like Him, we must bend our own will to His; we must submit ourselves to Him by desiring what He desires. When we do that, we become like Him, and that is the objective of the plan of salvation.

In the Book of Mormon Jacob taught the importance of bending our will to God's, reminding us that, even after we have succeeded in doing so, we can be saved only through the grace of God: "Wherefore, my beloved brethren, reconcile yourselves to the will of God, and not to the will of the devil and the flesh; and remember, after ye are reconciled unto God, that it is only in and through the grace of God that ye are saved" (2 Nephi 10:24).

Covenants mark our submission to God's will. In making a covenant with God, we agree to give up the only thing we truly have to give. We make a binding agreement to exercise our agency in a certain way—a way that under eternal law will lead to becoming like our Father. God, without our consent, may take our wealth, our health, our friends, our family members—just ask Job—even our lives, but He cannot (because He perfectly will not) take away our agency. He allowed a third of the hosts of heaven to follow Lucifer because He would not force them to follow Him. Therefore, promising to exercise our agency consistent with God's plan for us, which is what we do when we make covenants, is all we have that we can give in return for His promise of eternal life.

Reconciling ourselves to God—submitting to His will—is our goal, and mortality is the time to do it. It is a probationary period. As the prophet Alma said, "this life is the time for men to prepare to meet God" (Alma 34:32). We must "repent while in the flesh" (2 Nephi 2:21). After we die, "then cometh the night of darkness wherein there can be no labor performed" (Alma 34:33). The moral of this story, then, is "do not procrastinate the day of your repentance" (Alma 34:33).

Those who accept the gospel in this life and either (1) fail to make the covenants for exaltation or (2) make them but break them have failed the test of mortality. They are "subjected to the spirit of the devil, and he doth seal [them] his" (Alma 34:35).

Speaking to those who had truth and rejected it, Samuel the Lamanite made it clear that there would be no second chance for exaltation: "Your days of probation are past; ye have procrastinated the day of your salvation until it is everlastingly too late, and your destruction is made sure" (Helaman 13:38).

That is not to say, however, that we mortals have the knowledge and capacity to judge whether someone has had a fair and full chance to accept the gospel. We don't know people's hearts, and God does. Therefore, judgment is in God's hands. President James E. Faust taught, "That judgment must . . . be left up to the Lord."[5]

Nevertheless, we who have received truth have a responsibility to make and keep the covenants of exaltation in this life. We don't know when death will come, when the probation will end. For this reason, death is daunting. But preparation brings peace. We can be like the Apostle Paul, who said, "The time of my departure is at hand. I have fought a good fight, I have finished my course, I have kept the faith" (2 Timothy 4:6–7).

The Gate and the Path

We are blessed in these latter days with a fulness of the gospel. We have the Bible, and that is a source of much guidance. But we also have living prophets who help us, and we have the Book of Mormon.

The Bible says: "Whosoever transgresseth, and abideth not in the doctrine of Christ, hath not God. He that abideth in the doctrine of Christ, he hath both the Father and the Son" (2 John 1:9). The doctrine of Christ isn't clearly defined in the Bible. In the Book of Mormon, it is. President Henry B. Eyring said: "All of us feel . . . a desire to return home to live with God. . . . [The Book of Mormon] is our sure guide on the way home to God. . . . The Book of Mormon gives us the Savior's example to increase our faith and determination to obey His command to follow Him. The book is filled with the doctrine of Christ to guide us."[6]

We know Nephi as a young, strong, faithful man. As the years passed he led his people well. He taught them the gospel. Imagine Nephi as an older man—gray hair probably, possibly stooped a little—but very wise. He wants to teach his people one last time and tells them, "The things which I have written sufficeth me, save it be a few words which I must speak concerning the doctrine of Christ" (2 Nephi 31:2).

He then talks about Jesus Christ and our reliance on Him. He calls Him the Lamb of God and explains that Jesus Christ was baptized. Then he says to his people: "If the Lamb of God, he being holy, should have need to be baptized by water, to fulfill all righteousness, O then, how much more need have we, being unholy, to be baptized, yea, even by water!" (2 Nephi 31:5).

But baptism by water is not enough, and Nephi knows that, so he tells his people that "after [Jesus] was baptized with water the Holy Ghost descended upon him in the form of a dove. . . . And he said unto the children of men: Follow thou me" (2 Nephi 31:8, 10).

The Lord commands: "Repent ye, repent ye, and be baptized in the name of my Beloved Son. And also, the voice of the Son came unto [Nephi], saying: He that is baptized in my name, to him will the Father give the Holy Ghost, like unto me; wherefore, follow me, and do the things which ye have seen me do" (2 Nephi 31:11–12).

Nephi was eager for his people to have faith, repent, be baptized, and receive the Holy Ghost. This is the doctrine of Christ found in the third and fourth articles of faith:

> We believe that through the Atonement of Christ, all mankind may be saved, by obedience to the laws and ordinances of the Gospel. (Articles of Faith 1:3).
>
> We believe that the first principles and ordinances of the Gospel are: first, Faith in the Lord Jesus Christ; second, Repentance; third, Baptism by immersion for the remission of sins; fourth, Laying on of hands for the gift of the Holy Ghost. (Articles of Faith 1:4).

Any one of these principles and ordinances without the others is insufficient. We must have all four—faith, repentance, baptism, and the Holy Ghost.

Nephi then teaches his people about the doctrine of Christ using a metaphor: a gate and a path. A gate swings open, and you can go through that gate onto the path. "For the gate by which ye should enter is repentance and baptism by water; and then cometh a remission of your sins by fire and by the Holy Ghost" (2 Nephi 31:17).

We know that we need to be baptized, and we are fond of saying that when we are baptized our sins are washed away. But that is not what Nephi taught. When we are confirmed and receive the Holy Ghost our sins are burned away. "Then cometh a remission of our sins by fire and by the

Holy Ghost" (2 Nephi 31:17). The cleansing doesn't come by literal water; it comes by figurative fire.

Jesus Christ taught that after we are baptized we may be "sanctified by the reception of the Holy Ghost, that [we] may stand spotless before [Him] at the last day" (3 Nephi 27:20). Moroni echoed that teaching. He said that after we are baptized we may be "wrought upon and cleansed by the power of the Holy Ghost [and] numbered among the people of the church of Christ" (Moroni 6:4).

If you were baptized in The Church of Jesus Christ of Latter-day Saints, you were also confirmed by the laying on of hands. When you were confirmed, you were commanded—directed—to receive the Holy Ghost. Whether you receive the Holy Ghost is up to you. If you do, then your sins are burned away. But if you do not receive the Holy Ghost, your sins are not remitted. It is effective only if you have the Holy Ghost. And that process continues throughout our lifetimes. When we have the Holy Ghost, our sins are remitted.

Elder D. Todd Christofferson described this cleansing power of the Holy Ghost: "[The] 'power of godliness' comes in the person and by the influence of the Holy Ghost. The gift of the Holy Ghost is part of the new and everlasting covenant. It is an essential part of our baptism, the baptism of the Spirit. It is the messenger of grace by which the blood of Christ is applied to take away our sins and sanctify us (see 2 Nephi 31:17)."[7]

Nephi said: "Then are ye in this strait and narrow path which leads to eternal life" (2 Nephi 31:18). We go through the gate of faith, repentance, baptism, and the gift of the Holy Ghost. Then we are on the path, and that path leads to eternal life. We have not arrived at eternal life yet, but we're on the path.

Elder L. Tom Perry explained why baptism is a gate:

> It is an ordinance denoting entry into a sacred and binding covenant between God and man. Men promise to forsake the world, love and serve their fellowmen, visit the fatherless and the widows in their afflictions, proclaim peace, preach the gospel, serve the Lord, and keep His commandments. The Lord promises to "pour out his Spirit more abundantly upon [us]" (Mosiah 18:10), redeem His Saints both temporally and spiritually, number them with those of the First Resurrection, and offer life eternal.[8]

Now let's return to Nephi's last discourse: "And now, my beloved brethren, after ye have gotten into this strait and narrow path, I would ask if all is done? Behold, I say unto you, Nay; for ye have not come thus far save it were by the word of Christ with unshaken faith in him, relying wholly upon the merits of him who is mighty to save" (2 Nephi 31:19).

Nephi died more than five hundred years before Jesus Christ was even born. But he understood that Jesus would suffer and die for our sins, and that it was only through Jesus Christ that our sins could be remitted and we could be ushered into the celestial kingdom.

One verse in Nephi's discourse (2 Nephi 31:20) encapsulates the essence of the plan of salvation. Nephi said: "Wherefore, ye must press forward with a steadfastness in Christ." Nephi knew, and we must know, that Christ is our Savior and Redeemer. He is the Lamb of God. He is the Only Begotten of the Father. He is our Mediator with God.

We must press forward "having a perfect brightness of hope." Hope comes because of our faith. When we have faith in Jesus Christ, we can have an optimistic view that, even though we are imperfect now, we can strive to be perfect and through the Atonement of Jesus Christ can be saved. We can be exalted.

We must press forward having "a love of God and of all men." We love our Heavenly Father—and that is essential—but we also love our neighbor. That is also essential.

"Wherefore, if ye shall press forward"—always moving forward, following the path—"feasting upon the word of Christ." We have been taught to read the scriptures every day. The days when we could get enough spiritual nourishment just by going to church on Sunday, if those days ever existed, are past. We are bombarded the rest of the week with the world. And the world does not want us to believe in Jesus Christ; it does not want our minds to be centered on Him. So we must study the scriptures, feast upon them, be edified by them every day. And we must "endure to the end." That doesn't mean to just hang around to the end. We must travel on the path, magnify our callings, fulfill our responsibilities, and keep our covenants. President Russell M. Nelson includes the endowment and sealing in the temple as elements of enduring to the end.[9]

Nephi, in this great verse of chapter 31, wraps up by saying, "Behold, thus saith the Father: Ye shall have eternal life." Life with our Heavenly Father is celestial life—the life He lives. That is where this path leads.

Nephi testified: "And now, behold, my beloved brethren, this is the way; and there is none other way nor name given under heaven whereby man can be saved in the kingdom of God. And now, behold, this is the doctrine of Christ" (2 Nephi 31:21).

Because of the Book of Mormon, we have the opportunity to understand the doctrine of Christ, which is mentioned in the Bible but is not fully explained to us there.

The Foundation of Doctrine

The process of learning, teaching, and protecting the doctrine of Christ provides a foundation for making and keeping covenants in this life. Without such a foundation, there is no reason to make, let alone keep, eternal covenants. On the other hand, knowledge of the doctrine of Christ gives us not only a reason to make and keep covenants but also a heightened ability to do so faithfully.

Apostasy results in loss of the priesthood, the authority to provide the ordinances necessary to our covenants with God—thus preventing the people from making the covenants that will help them return to God. Just as important, apostasy results in loss of the doctrine of Christ. This darkness causes the people to wander in the wilderness of sin and to be washed away in the filthy waters of sin's consequences. If the doctrine is lost or corrupted, the people have no reason to covenant with God and their covenant relationship is lost.

The adversary knows that it can be more effective to attack the doctrine of Christ than it is simply to tempt good people who know the doctrine to do wrong knowingly. Whole populations fall into sin and suffer the consequences if he is successful in deceiving the people that either there is no God and no doctrine, or there is a God but his doctrine is some perversion of the truth.

One of the great themes of the Book of Mormon is the importance of learning, teaching, and protecting the doctrine of Christ. The iron rod is the word of God that safely guides us through to the tree of life (see 1 Nephi 11:25). Sherem, Nehor, and Korihor battled prophets, challenging the very existence of a Christ (see Jacob 7; Alma 1, 30). Zeezrom debated Amulek over the foundational doctrines of the gospel (see Alma 10:31, 11:20–46). These stories bring to life the everyday struggle between light and darkness, good and evil, knowledge and ignorance.

Lehi and his son Nephi saw in vision the iron rod (the word of God) that leads along the path to the tree of life (the love of God).[10] The path, however, is not easily discerned because it is enshrouded in mists of darkness. These "mists of darkness are the temptations of the devil, which blindeth the eyes, and hardeneth the hearts of the children of men, and leadeth them away into broad roads, that they perish and are lost" (1 Nephi 12:17). Some of those traveling on the path or eating from the tree are lost also because of the ridicule of those who watch from the great and spacious building (the pride of the world).

This representation of the interplay between good and evil accurately describes today's conditions. Truth is not readily discernible, and one must hold to the word of God. But while holding to that rod, we are accosted by those who mock and ridicule, who attempt to label our doctrine as out of the mainstream, backwards, risible, or immoral. The measure they use, of course, is the wisdom of man, largely untethered from the truths of God.

Thus, for example, the doctrine of the family as an eternal unit with a father and a mother who make eternal covenants is mocked as unmodern. The plan of salvation is disputed as unscientific. The doctrine of continuing revelation through modern-day prophets is shouted down as unbiblical. With these doctrines in worldly disrepute, the adversary holds sway. Many are not taught the true doctrine of Christ. As a consequence, they wander in the mists of darkness. Others learn truth but let go of the iron rod or wander away from the tree because of the world's temptations and ridicule. Few learn and teach and protect the doctrine, eating of the tree of life, unmoved by the adversary.

The story of Jacob and Sherem illustrates this tension and confrontation between good and evil. After Nephi died, Jacob, his younger brother, was the prophet who led the Nephites. While the Nephites fell into sin, Jacob warned them of the consequences of sin, denouncing pride and immorality (see Jacob 2). He testified of Christ, His Atonement, and His plan of salvation (see Jacob 4). Despite Jacob's earnest teaching, however, Satan had taken hold of many of the Nephites as they knowingly violated the commandments of God.

Into this environment arrived Sherem, who frontally challenged the doctrine of Christ. He was learned, with an understanding of the law of Moses, which governed the Nephites. He was a powerful speaker, impressing the people with flattery. He labored diligently to "lead away the hearts of the people" and "overthrow the doctrine of Christ" (Jacob 7: 2–3). He specifically taught that a doctrine that included a savior perverted the right way of God, and that it was blasphemy and false prophecy to suggest that anyone could tell the future (see Jacob 7:2, 6–7). Yet, while claiming that no one could tell the future, he declared that he knew that there would be no Christ (see Jacob 7:9).

Jacob confronted Sherem on these points of doctrine. Jacob testified that the scriptures and the prophets spoke of Christ. And he added his own testimony, which he obtained by the power of the Holy Ghost, that "if there should be no atonement made all mankind must be lost" (Jacob 7:12).

Sherem, as did Korihor later, then made the critical mistake of demanding a sign. He said to Jacob: "Show me a sign by this power of the Holy Ghost, in the which ye know so much" (Jacob 7:13). This unrighteous challenge was unlike the humble request of the sincere to receive from the Holy Ghost a testimony of the truth. Instead, Sherem must have expected that his challenge would go unanswered and that his fame and success in spreading the antithesis of the doctrine of Christ would be bolstered.

The Lord, however, had other plans for Sherem, this antichrist. As Sherem requested, he received a sign. He was struck down and eventually died as a result. But before he died, he confessed his error. He testified of Christ and the power of the Holy Ghost. He said that he had been deceived by the power of the devil and that he was afraid he had committed the unpardonable sin (see Jacob 7:14–20).

This drama astonished the multitude. They were overcome and fell to the earth (see Jacob 7:21). The result pleased Jacob because "peace and the love of God was restored again among the people; and they searched the scriptures, and hearkened no more to the words of this wicked man" (Jacob 7:22–23).

The LDS Bible Dictionary describes an antichrist in two ways. First, it is someone "who would assume the guise of Christ, but in reality would be opposed to Christ. Second, "in a broader sense it is anyone or anything that counterfeits the true gospel or plan of salvation and that openly or secretly is set up in opposition to Christ. The great antichrist is Lucifer, but he has many assistants both as spirit beings and as mortals."[11] In either sense, the antichrist is a function of the adversary in opposition to truth. Christ provides light and knowledge; the antichrist promotes darkness and ignorance.

If the doctrine of Christ prevails, the people are capable and free to have a covenant relationship with God because the truth makes them free (see John 8:32). If the adversary pollutes or destroys the doctrine of Christ in the minds of the people, the truth is lost and a covenant relationship with God, which must be based on truth, is impossible. When knowledge is lost, freedom is lost because "it is impossible for a man to be saved in ignorance" (D&C 131:6).

Despite Satan's efforts to take away our freedom to covenant with God, we know that we have the truth upon which we can base eternal covenants, and eventually all mankind will have the same. Everyone will have the opportunity to accept true doctrine and, with it, the saving grace of Christ, whether it be in this life or the next.

When Jesus appeared to the inhabitants of the American continent after His resurrection, He claimed the doctrine of Christ as His own. He taught: "I will declare unto you my doctrine. . . . The Father commandeth all men, everywhere, to repent and believe in me. And whoso believeth in me, and is baptized, the same shall be saved; and they are they who shall inherit the kingdom of God. . . . Whoso believeth in me believeth in the Father also; and unto him will the Father bear record of me, for he will visit him with fire and with the Holy Ghost. . . . Ye must repent, and become as a little child, and be baptized in my name. . . . This is my doctrine, and whoso buildeth upon this buildeth upon my rock, and the gates of hell shall not prevail against them" (3 Nephi 11:31–33, 35, 37, 39).

The Book of Mormon teaches the doctrine of Christ clearly and explicitly. And the scant references to the doctrine of Christ in the Bible are consistent with the Book of Mormon's teachings. Paul told the Hebrews: "Therefore leaving the principles of the doctrine of Christ, let us go on unto perfection" (Hebrews 6:1). Certainly, the doctrine of Christ, including the covenants associated with that doctrine, will allow us to go on to perfection and eternal life with our Heavenly Father.

Endnotes

1. Monson, "The Race of Life," 91.
2. *Discourses of Brigham Young*, 51.
3. Ibid.
4. *Teachings of the Prophet Joseph Smith*, 181.
5. Faust, in Conference Report, Apr. 2003, 68.
6. Eyring, "The Book of Mormon as a Personal Guide," 4.
7. Christofferson, "The Power of Covenants," 22.
8. Perry, "The Gospel of Jesus Christ," *Ensign*, 46.
9. Nelson, *Accomplishing the Impossible*, 42.
10. Lehi's vision is recorded in 1 Nephi 8. Nephi's vision and interpretation of the vision are recorded in 1 Nephi 11, 12, and 15.
11. LDS Bible Dictionary, s.v. "Antichrist," 609.

Chapter 6

BAPTISM BY IMMERSION FOR THE REMISSION OF SINS

We believe that the first principles and ordinances of the Gospel are: first, Faith in the Lord Jesus Christ; second, Repentance; third, Baptism by immersion for the remission of sins; fourth, Laying on of hands for the gift of the Holy Ghost.

—Articles of Faith 1:4

The grand issue of this mortal life is whether we will use our agency to choose the path to eternal life, the path Nephi talked about—the covenant path as President Russell M. Nelson calls it. The choice is whether to enter the path through the strait gate of baptism or follow the broad avenues of the natural man. Baptism is the first gateway ordinance of God's eternal plan.

Ordinances

Ordinances are outward acts that signify our covenant relationship with God. His house is a house of order, everything in its right place at its right time (see D&C 88:119). When we receive ordinances, we are putting ourselves in the right place and following the divine order. Knowing this, it is understandable that the word *ordinance* is rooted in "order." Order has two related meanings, both applicable to the ordinances of the gospel.

First, order denotes following the proper form or being done properly. And second, order denotes sequence. There is a sequence to the ordinances that lead to eternal life.

When the Lord instructed Joseph Smith on the restoration of the Church of Jesus Christ, He used the word *order* to project both senses of the word: propriety and sequence. For example, concerning the process to be followed after converts are baptized, the Lord said: "The elders or priests are to have a sufficient time to expound all things concerning the church of Christ to their understanding, previous to their partaking of the sacrament and being confirmed by the laying on of the hands of the elders, so that *all things may be done in order*" (D&C 20:68; italics added).

In this life, we make some of the most important covenants with God by performing ordinances. Not all ordinances involve covenants. For example, we do not make covenants when we bless a child and give the child a name or when we administer to the sick. But there is another class of ordinances, called the saving ordinances, in which we make the covenants leading to exaltation. These saving ordinances are (1) baptism by immersion for the remission of sins, (2) the laying on of hands for the gift of the Holy Ghost, (3) ordination to the Melchizedek Priesthood for men, (4) temple endowment, and (5) temple sealing. Every accountable person must receive these ordinances to be exalted.

The consequence of rejecting the saving ordinances is to be forever stopped in our progression. The Apostle Paul made it clear that whoever "resisteth the ordinance of God . . . shall receive to themselves damnation" (Romans 13:2). By refusing the ordinances, we forfeit the rights we have as heirs of God, as joint-heirs with Christ.

Receiving ordinances is one of the three primary purposes of mortality, along with receiving a mortal body and having mortal experiences. We gather Israel so that each person may receive ordinances. We build temples to make ordinances available to the living and the dead. Joseph Smith asked and answered why we gather Israel: "Why gather the people together in this place? For the same purpose that Jesus wanted to gather the Jews—to receive the ordinances, the blessings, and glories that God has in store for His Saints."[1] The Lord told Joseph to build a temple unto Him "that I may reveal mine ordinances therein unto my people" (D&C 124:40).

The saving ordinances must be performed in mortality. President Joseph Fielding Smith said that they must be performed here because they "pertain to this mortal life."[2] President Smith explained how the saving ordinances pertain to this mortal life by saying that "it would be inconsistent for a resurrected being to come and be baptized for the dead. The resurrected person has passed to another sphere where the laws and blessings do not pertain to this mortal life."[3]

Elder Orson Pratt, discussing the importance of temple marriage in this life, warned: "This is the world for all ordinances as well as the ordinance of marriage. If you want to be baptized, do it here. No such thing as being baptized for yourselves in that world. If you want to be confirmed, have it done here, for there is no confirming there. If you want to partake of any of the ordinances of the Lord our God, this is the place for us to attend to them."[4]

That mortal ordinances pertain to mortal life leads me to believe that other ordinances pertain to other stages of our eternal progression. Brigham Young taught this principle by comparing the saving ordinances performed in this mortal life to ordinances that will be performed after this mortal life. He said: "It is supposed by this people that we have all the ordinances in our possession for life and salvation, and exaltation, and that we are administering in these ordinances. This is not the case. We are in possession of all the ordinances that can be administered in the flesh; but there are other ordinances and administrations that must be administered beyond this world. I know you would ask what they are. I will mention one. We have not, neither can we receive here, the ordinance and the keys of the resurrection."[5]

Another ordinance that Brigham Young said pertains to a future existence is to receive the power to organize matter: "We cannot receive, while in the flesh, the keys to form and fashion kingdoms and to organize matter, for they are beyond our capacity and calling, beyond this world. In the resurrection, men who have been faithful and diligent in all things in the flesh, have kept their first and second estate, and worthy to be crowned Gods, even the sons of God, will be ordained to organize matter."[6]

And Brigham Young taught that there are "many more" ordinances that we cannot receive here and now. He said: "We will operate here, in all the ordinances of the house of God which *pertain* to this side of the veil, and those who pass beyond and secure to themselves a resurrection pertaining to the lives will go on and receive more and more, more and more, and will receive one after another until they are crowned Gods, even the sons of God."[7]

There may be ordinances that pertained to the premortal life. Perhaps foreordination is one of those premortal ordinances. But I think it is enough to understand that each ordinance *pertains* to a certain stage of progression toward eternal life. And the saving ordinances, from baptism to temple sealing, pertain to this mortal life and therefore must be performed in this mortal life. In God's orderly house, these ordinances pertain to mortal life.

An analogy from my life that helps me understand this concept of ordinances pertaining to stages in our eternal progression was an experience I had when I was preparing to go to law school. I heard that everyone had to take the law school admissions test, so I signed up and went to take it. I had not heard that people actually studied and took preparation courses for the test. I sat down to a test that was completely unfamiliar to me. On the test, there was an essay question about whether it should be legal for cars to have radar detectors so that drivers could detect when their speed was being measured by radar. I struggled with the question, and I'm sure the answer wasn't very coherent.

Now, after more than thirty years of writing about the law, I think I could write a much better answer. But I can't go back and answer that question now on the law school admissions test because it pertained to my preparation to go to law school. I am finished with that part of my life and can't go back to my pre-law self.

Another analogy from my life is perhaps better.

When I was in ninth grade, I ran in the city finals for the 100–yard dash. I prepared my starting blocks (or so I thought), and when the gun sounded I tried to push off for a good start. But I had not prepared the blocks well. The blocks gave way to the pressure I exerted against them and, rather than having my push against the blocks launch me into the race, I fell to my knees. I jumped up and ran as hard as I could, but my only satisfaction was that I did not come in last.

Today, if I ran that race, I would be sure to prepare the blocks properly. But even with my best effort at the start of such a race, I would surely come in last, by a wide margin. That race pertained to my ninth-grade self. I don't have the ability at this point in my life to compete in a sprint with ninth-graders. And I rightfully would be excluded from the race in any event.

Currently, we have mortal bodies and live in a mortal sphere. We must do now what can be done only in mortality, including receiving the saving ordinances for ourselves and for those who have passed on and no longer have that ability.

Like the requirement to receive the saving ordinances in mortality, the saving ordinances must also be performed under the direction and approval of priesthood keys. Without the proper authority and the proper authorization those saving ordinances are not done in the name of God and are not valid.

Finally, ordinances must be done properly and in the right sequence, which brings me back to the word *order*. A baptism performed by sprinkling water over the head of the person being baptized is not a baptism at all in the eyes of the Lord because immersion is the revealed and authorized mode. Sprinkling to baptize is like baking a cake without turning the oven on. No matter how much you want it to bake or believe that it will bake, it won't.

Similarly, an ordination to the priesthood before baptism has no effect because the saving ordinance of baptism must precede the saving ordinance of ordination to the priesthood. Performing the saving ordinances out of order is like putting the baking pan in the oven before putting the cake ingredients in the pan. If we turn the heat on, the pan will get hot, but the result will not be a baked cake.

But going through the motions of ordinances is not enough. We must internalize these outward commitments to God in the process of becoming like Him. Performed and received in propriety and order, ordinances lead to exaltation. "Let all things be done decently and in order" (1 Corinthians 14:40).

Baptism by Immersion for the Remission of Sins

One of the most recognizable and significant stories in the Bible is John's baptism of Jesus in the Jordan River. John, known to us as the Baptist, was seen by prophets long before his day as the forerunner of Jesus Christ. Isaiah referred to him as the prophet preaching in the wilderness, "Prepare ye the way of the Lord" (Isaiah 40:3). Lehi saw John in a vision, preaching the gospel and baptizing in the Jordan River (see 1 Nephi 10:7–10). Malachi prophesied of the messenger who would prepare the way for the Lord (see Malachi 3:1).

John's righteous parents, Elizabeth and Zacharias, had been childless into their old age when Gabriel, an angel from the presence of God, announced to Zacharias that they would have a son who was to be named John (see Luke 1:5–20). As the son of Elizabeth and Zacharias, who were both of the tribe of Levi and descendants of Aaron, John had the right to the Aaronic Priesthood. An angel bestowed on eight-day-old John the divine commission to be the forerunner of the Lord, and John later received necessary ordination to the priesthood. He held the authority and keys of baptism by immersion for the remission of sins. John was not ordained to the priesthood, as we would use the word "ordain," at the age of eight days but instead received the life calling to be the forerunner of the Lord.[8]

In a revelation to Joseph Smith on the priesthood, the Lord said that John held the keys of the Aaronic Priesthood. This included "the key of the ministering of angels and the preparatory gospel, which gospel is the gospel of repentance and baptism, and the remission of sins" (D&C 84:26–27). In John's preaching before the baptism of Jesus, he taught that he would "baptize you with water, upon your repentance; and when he of whom I bear record cometh, who is mightier than I, whose shoes I am not worthy to bear (or whose place I am not able to fill), as I said, I indeed baptize you before he cometh, that when he cometh he may baptize you with the Holy Ghost and fire" (JST, Matthew 3:11).

In preparation for Jesus's baptism, John was sent to preach and baptize in the wilderness of Judea, by the Jordan River. The Gospels do not say who sent John. It may have been an angel, or the Spirit by direct revelation, or some other messenger from God. But whoever it was, he told John that the Messiah would come to him for baptism and John would know it was the Messiah by the sign of the dove (see John 1:33).

When Jesus was thirty years old, he found this John, his cousin, baptizing by the Jordan River, in the wilderness of Judea. It was the moment more important than any other for which John had been prophesied, born, raised, preserved, prepared, and ordained.

John took Jesus down into the river and baptized Jesus (see JST, Matthew 3:44). After John baptized Jesus, John "saw the Spirit of God descending like a dove and lighting upon Jesus. And lo, he heard a voice from heaven, saying, This is my beloved Son, in whom I am well pleased. Hear ye him" (JST, Matthew 3:45–46). Having received the promised sign, John testified to his followers, "Behold the Lamb of God" (John 1:36).

Baptism is for the remission of sins, but Jesus was without sin. So there must be something more to baptism than just the remission of sins—not that remission of sins is a small thing.

Jesus explained to John why this baptism of the only sinless man was necessary. He said it was to "fulfill all righteousness" (Matthew 3:15). Even Jesus Christ, to be completely righteous and obedient to his Father, had to be baptized (see 2 Nephi 31:7).

While John's baptism of Jesus may have been the most notable, it was not the first baptism, not even for John, who had been baptizing before Jesus came. Yet there is a common misconception that John initiated the ordinance of baptism, that it did not exist before his time.

Baptism is as old as humanity, a lost truth restored to the earth through prophets in the latter days. Baptism dates back to Adam, which you would expect since it is a saving ordinance. It would defy logic (or, at least, any sense of fairness) to make baptism a saving ordinance and then to offer it only to those who lived during and after the time of Jesus Christ. Yet that is what some faith traditions teach.

Modern scripture tells us that "[Adam] was caught away by the Spirit of the Lord, and was carried down into the water, and was laid under the water, and was brought forth out of the water. And thus he was baptized" (Moses 6:64–65). And baptism continued in dispensations after Adam. The Old Testament, as we know it today, alludes to baptisms, even if it does not describe the ordinance clearly. For example, Ezekiel prophesied in the words of the Lord: "Then will I sprinkle clean water upon you, and ye shall be clean: from all your filthiness, and from all your idols, will I cleanse you. A new heart also will I give you, and a new spirit will I put within you: and I will take away the stony heart out of your flesh, and I will give you an heart of flesh. And I will put my spirit within you, and cause you to walk in my statutes, and ye shall keep my judgments, and do them" (Ezekiel 36:25–27).

At least one Old Testament prophet saw that basic ordinances of the gospel would be lost. Isaiah said that "the earth also is defiled under the inhabitants thereof; because they have transgressed the laws, *changed the ordinance, broken the everlasting covenant*" (Isaiah 24:5; italics added). And the Lord revealed to Joseph Smith that a restoration was necessary because "they have strayed from mine ordinances, and have broken mine everlasting covenant" (D&C 1:15).

Although there is no clear description of baptism in the Old Testament as we know it today, the Apostle Paul spoke of the ordinance being performed in Moses's day (see 1 Corinthians 10:2). The Book of Mormon, on the other hand, features baptism prominently. Nephi taught that baptism is the gate to the path that leads to eternal life (see 2 Nephi 31:17). And Alma baptized at the Waters of Mormon (see Mosiah 18:8–17). As noted, earlier John was baptizing in the Jordan River even before Jesus came to him, asking to be baptized (see Matthew 3:1–6). Thus, baptism predated the Savior's earthly ministry.

President Harold B. Lee commented on how important it is that baptism was performed anciently, before Christ. He said: "To suppose that God would initiate ordinances on which salvation would be conditioned, and then allow four thousand years to pass without any authority or any organization to administer those ordinances, is untenable to the thinking man. A thinking man would have to conclude with Napoleon, 'Unless a religion existed from the beginning, I cannot believe.'"[9]

When the Lord restored the gospel through Joseph Smith, He restored baptism first among the ordinances. John the Baptist, the keyholder, appeared to Joseph Smith and Oliver Cowdery and bestowed on them the authority to baptize. With this authority, Joseph and Oliver went immediately into the water of the Susquehanna River to baptize each other (see Joseph Smith—History 1:68–73). From that day, May 15, 1829, to today, the authority to baptize as Adam and Jesus Christ were baptized has remained on the earth.

In the Lord's church, baptism is performed by one holding the priesthood and authorized by one holding the keys of the priesthood. The priesthood holder and the person to be baptized both change out of their everyday clothing and into white apparel. They go down into the water together, where the priesthood holder, raising his right arm to the square, recites the baptismal prayer verbatim. Calling the person by name, he says: "Having been commissioned of Jesus Christ, I baptize you in the name of the Father, and of the Son, and of the Holy Ghost. Amen." The priesthood holder then immerses the person briefly but fully in the water, and the ordinance is complete (see D&C 20:72–74).

This baptism, though simple and straightforward, is rich in symbolism and sacred in effect. We take off our street clothes and put on all-white clothing. Symbolically, we throw off the natural man as represented by the street clothes we wear, and we put on the white clothing of purity and covenant.

The Apostle Paul said: "But now ye also put off all these; anger, wrath, malice, blasphemy, filthy communication out of your mouth. Lie not one to another, seeing that ye have put off the old man with his deeds; And have put on the new man, which is renewed in knowledge after the image of him that created him" (Colossians 3:8–10).

Paul also said: "That ye put off concerning the former conversation the old man, which is corrupt according to the deceitful lusts; And be renewed in the spirit of your mind; And that ye put on the new man, which after God is created in righteousness and true holiness" (Ephesians 4:22–24).

We must put off the natural man and become saints through the Atonement of Jesus Christ (see Mosiah 3:19), as King Benjamin taught, and taking off our street clothes and putting on white clothing reminds us of that commitment—a commitment we make as part of our baptismal covenants.

We descend into the baptismal font, which is traditionally below floor-level in our meetinghouses. In making His atoning sacrifice, the Lord descended below all so that He might comprehend all things (see D&C 88:6). Elder Neal A. Maxwell said: "How deep that descent into despair and abysmal agony must have been! He did it to rescue us and in order to comprehend human suffering."[10]

We are buried in the water, as Jesus was buried in the tomb and the natural man is symbolically laid to rest. We are "baptized after the manner of his burial, being buried in the water in his name, and this according to the commandment which he has given" (D&C 76:51).

And after we are buried in the water as Jesus was buried in the tomb, we reemerge as a new person in Christ. Again, Paul explained the analogy: "Know ye not, that so many of us as were baptized into Jesus Christ were baptized into his death? Therefore we are buried with him by baptism into death: that like as Christ was raised up from the dead by the glory of the Father, even so we also should walk in newness of life. For if we have been planted together in the likeness of his death, we shall be also in the likeness of his resurrection" (Romans 6:3–6).

Inversely, Jesus used the imagery of baptism to describe His suffering and death. Referring to His coming atoning sacrifice, which was on His mind well before the night in Gethsemane and the day of the cross, He said, "I have a baptism to be baptized with; and how am I straitened till it be accomplished!" (Luke 12:50). When James and John asked if they could sit down with the Lord in His glory, Jesus answered: "Ye know not what ye ask: can ye drink of the cup that I drink of? and be baptized with the baptism that I am baptized with?" (Mark 10:38). The ministry of Jesus Christ was to be bookended by literal immersion in water and figurative immersion in suffering.

The most recognizable symbolism of baptism is the washing away of sins. We wash our bodies, our food, our clothing, and so many other things in water to eliminate impurities. Soon after his blinding vision on the road to Damascus, Saul received instruction from Ananias, who told Saul to "arise, and be baptized, and wash away thy sins, calling on the name of the

Lord" (Acts 22:16). Baptism by immersion in water truly is for the remission of sins, but the process must also include the baptism by fire.

Baptismal Covenants

Through baptism we reaffirm in mortality the covenant relationship we had with our Father in the premortal life. We already covenanted with God to obey Him when we decided to follow Jehovah in the premortal life. The council in heaven was not a casual picking of teams or a random assignment to sides. No, it was a conscious decision to covenant with God or with the adversary, an act of free will. And by virtue of the fact that we are here as mortals, we know that we chose to follow Jehovah and obey God. That is what following Jehovah consisted of.

But we do not remember that covenant. The veil of forgetfulness gives us the opportunity and privilege of establishing our allegiance to God anew. The test of mortality begins with birth. Then we are given an eight-year training period before we are responsible for making and keeping covenants with God. When we have reached the point of accountability, baptism is a momentous act of agency that ties us again to our Heavenly Father, from Whom we came.

Obedience to our Father is the preeminent covenant we make at baptism. Elder D. Todd Christofferson said: "For our turning to the Lord to be complete, it must include nothing less than a covenant of obedience to Him. We often speak of this covenant as the baptismal covenant since it is witnessed by being baptized in water (see Mosiah 18:10). The Savior's own baptism, providing the example, confirmed His covenant of obedience to the Father."[11]

Whether we were baptized when we were eight years old or come to those waters later in life, the covenant of obedience is the same. President M. Russell Ballard provided this reminder:

> Many of you were baptized when you were eight years old, and you may not realize that this is the promise you made to your Heavenly Father when you were baptized. Always remember that you are under this covenant. Your Heavenly Father has promised in return that He will give marvelous blessings to those who honor their covenants, keep His commandments, and endure faithfully to the end. They will be sealed by the Holy Spirit of promise and will be "given *all* things" (D&C 76:55; emphasis added; see also D&C 76:50–54, 70), including an inheritance in the celestial kingdom (see 2 Nephi 31:16–20).[12]

As baptism is a covenant of obedience, it is also our covenant of rebirth—spiritual rebirth. When we agreed to come to this earth and to be tested, we agreed to a test of our will that included becoming subject to a fallen state. We were cut off temporally and spiritually from the presence of the Lord, a condition called spiritual death. Two circumstances bring spiritual death: (1) Adam's fall and (2) our own sins. The first is no fault of our own and *is* remedied by the Atonement of Jesus Christ. The second is all our own fault and *may be* remedied by the Atonement of Jesus Christ.

Because our own sins cause spiritual death, we must seek a remedy to return to live with God. "Remember," warned Abinadi, "that he that persists in his own carnal nature, and goes on in the ways of sin and rebellion against God, remaineth in his fallen state and the devil hath all power over him" (Mosiah 16:5).

To be reconciled with God, we must experience a mighty change in our hearts—a spiritual rebirth (see Alma 5:14). It is a change from a "disposition to do evil" to a desire to "do good continually" (Mosiah 5:2). And Jesus taught unmistakably that this mighty change in our heart requires baptism.

Nicodemus, a Jewish ruler, sought out Jesus at night. He expressed his respect for Jesus and acknowledged the miracles Jesus had performed. Recognizing Nicodemus's curiosity and seizing the missionary opportunity, Jesus said: "Except a man be born again, he cannot see the kingdom of God" (John 3:3). Nicodemus wondered how a person could be born again, and Jesus answered: "Except a man be born of water and of the Spirit, he cannot enter the kingdom of God" (John 3:5). No one should doubt that Jesus, who was Himself baptized to fulfill all righteousness and declared the necessity of baptism to Nicodemus, requires of us baptism and spiritual rebirth as a condition of exaltation.

In addition to obedience to our Father, our baptismal covenants include those that accompany joining the community of saints. We commit to "come into the fold of God, and to be called his people, [to be] willing to bear one another's burdens, that they may be light; . . . [to be] willing to mourn with those that mourn; yea, and comfort those that stand in need of comfort, and to stand as witnesses of God at all times and in all things, and in all places that ye may be in, even until death" (Mosiah 18:8–9).

Elder Joseph B. Wirthlin explained this responsibility to others as a result of baptism: "We cannot work out our salvation alone. We cannot return to the presence of our Father in Heaven without helping our brothers and sisters. Once we understand that we are all literally brothers and sisters in the family of God, we should also feel an obligation for one another's welfare and show our love through deeds of kindness and concern."[13]

We take upon ourselves the name of Jesus Christ when we are baptized. President Dallin H. Oaks said that "we take upon us the name of Christ when we are baptized in his name, when we belong to his Church and profess our belief in him, and when we do the work of his kingdom. There are other meanings as well, deeper meanings that the more mature members of the Church should understand and ponder as he or she partakes of the sacrament."[14] This taking upon us the name of Jesus Christ pertains to all of our covenants with God.

Baptismal covenants are serious and obligating covenants, but God's promises are sure. President George Q. Cannon said: "When we went forth into the waters of baptism and covenanted with our Father in Heaven to serve Him and keep His commandments, He bound Himself also, by covenant to us, that He would never desert us, never leave us to ourselves, never forget us; that in the midst of trials and hardships, when everything was arrayed against us, He would be near unto us and would sustain us. That was His covenant, and He has fulfilled it up to the present time, and has shown that we can tie to the promises that He has made."[15]

Accountability

In chapter 2, I described the relationship among agency, accountability, and covenants. Agency makes covenants possible, and accountability makes covenants significant. Under most mortal circumstances, accountability naturally follows agency. Because we are free to choose, we are responsible for the consequences that naturally follow from our choices. In this chapter, I continue the discussion of accountability: When do we become accountable for our sins? What happens to those who do not have the capacity to make the decisions for which we are normally accountable? The answers are simple in God's plan, but the adversary has sought to complicate, and in many ways succeeded in complicating, the issue beyond recognition. We are accountable for our sins if we are at least eight years old and are not intellectually disabled. Any other definition overcomplicates the matter and mocks the Lord's Atonement and His perfect plan of fairness and justice.

The most common example of the absence of accountability is infancy. By revelation, we know that children are not accountable until they turn eight years old. That age is not an arbitrary line drawn by administrators of the gospel. Instead, it is a truth known anciently and restored in the latter days. Children under the age of eight do not need baptism.

The prophet Mormon gave a comprehensive critique of infant baptism. A controversy concerning infant baptism had arisen amidst the apostasy taking place before Mormon's dismayed eyes. Why, with all that evil around him, would Mormon care that much about infant baptism? Simply because it is a "gross error" and a "solemn mockery before God," because it "setteth at naught the atonement of [Christ]" (Moroni 8:6, 9, 20). Mormon couldn't just stand by and do nothing in the face of such contempt for the Atonement of Jesus Christ.

Mormon reminded his son that "little children are alive in Christ" (Moroni 8:22). He quoted the Lord, saying: "I came into the world not to call the righteous but sinners to repentance; the whole need no physician, but they that are sick; wherefore, little children are whole, for they are not capable of committing sin; wherefore the curse of Adam is taken from them in me, that it hath no power over them" (Moroni 8:8).

The adversary has no power over children under eight. Because they cannot sin, they are not accountable. They cannot repent, and they do not need baptism. "Little children need no repentance, neither baptism. Behold, baptism is unto repentance to the fulfilling the commandments unto the remission of sins" (Moroni 8:11).

These simple truths have been lost as intelligent but uninspired analysts have tried to understand the relationship between the Fall of Adam and the Atonement of Jesus Christ. Many have reconciled these two events by concluding that, as a result of the Fall of Adam, all are subject to "original sin." This theory posits that we are all sinners because Adam sinned. Even little children are tainted by sin and need to be baptized to remove that taint.

Elder Bruce R. McConkie explained that this theory is false:

> There is no such thing as original sin as such is defined in the creeds of Christendom. Such a concept denies the efficacy of the atonement. Our revelation says: "Every spirit of man was innocent in the beginning"—meaning that spirits started out in a state of purity and innocence in preexistence—"and God having redeemed man from the fall, men became again, in their infant state, innocent before God" (D&C 93:38)—meaning that all children start out their mortal probation in purity and innocence because of the atonement. Our revelations also say, "The Son of God hath atoned for original guilt, wherein the sins of the parents cannot be answered upon the heads of the children, for they are whole from the foundation of the world." (Moses 6:54.)[16]

Once we let go of the original-sin theory and recognize the Atonement of Jesus Christ for what it is—an infinite recompense that provides that children are born innocent—the importance of whether a person is accountable for sin is obvious. Only those who are accountable need to repent and need to be baptized. And the revealed word is that children under eight are not accountable.

As a core doctrine of salvation associated with agency and Atonement, the age of accountability must have been revealed to Adam—the first man, the first prophet, and the first mortal administrator of the gospel of Jesus Christ. We have evidence that it was revealed before Abraham's time. On the occasion when the Lord changed Abram's name to Abraham, the prophet fell on his face and called upon the Lord. The Lord spoke to His prophet and warned him that the saving ordinances had been corrupted. The Lord said: "My people have gone astray from my precepts, and have not kept mine ordinances, which I gave unto their fathers; and they have not observed mine anointing, and the burial, or baptism wherewith I commanded them; but have turned from the commandment, and taken unto themselves the washing of children, and the blood of sprinkling; and have said that the blood of the righteous Abel was shed for sins; and have not known wherein they are accountable before me" (JST, Genesis 17:4–7). The Lord then told Abraham, clearly and unmistakably, that "children are not accountable before me until they are eight years old" (JST, Genesis 17:11).

This decree from the Lord to Abraham correcting the false practices that had crept into the doctrines originally given to Adam was lost at some point from Moses's books, but the decree was restored to the holy writ through Joseph Smith in the latter days. We now know what the Lord revealed to Abraham—that, in the two millennia since the Fall of Adam, the people had corrupted the saving ordinances. They had "not observed . . . baptism wherewith I commanded them." They had "taken upon themselves the washing of children," and they no longer understood "wherein they are accountable before [the Lord]."

The Lord revealed to Joseph Smith that "children shall be baptized for the remission of their sins when eight years old, and receive the laying on of the hands" (D&C 68:27) and that we need not worry about the welfare of a child under eight who dies unbaptized because "all children who die before they arrive at the years of accountability are saved in the celestial kingdom of heaven" (D&C 137:10).

It has been the experience of Christians of all eras, when in apostasy, to adopt the unchristian practice of infant baptism. Isaiah prophesied that the wicked would defile the earth "because they have transgressed the laws, changed the ordinance, broken the everlasting covenant" (Isaiah 24:5).

The Lord's covenant people in ancient times, before Abraham, had already fallen into the practice of infant baptism, the "washing of children" (JST, Genesis 17:6).

Infant baptism became the norm in the old world after the death of the Apostles. Around the end of the second century after Christ, men who had no doctrinal guidance from authorized and inspired leaders began to hypothesize that infants needed baptism because of Adam's transgression. Eventually, this led to widespread acceptance of the false doctrine of original sin and the corrupt practice of infant baptism.

The covenant people also adopted infant baptism in the new world as wickedness began to creep in among them, as the people gradually became so totally corrupt that they were ripe for destruction. Those were the circumstances that prompted Mormon to rail against that particular mockery of God (see Moroni 8:9).

Why has the Lord chosen the age of eight? Wisdom is in the omniscience of God. He knows all perfectly and knowing all has set an age threshold for accountability.

Why doesn't the Lord leave to His commissioned servants the task of determining when a child has sufficient knowledge and experience and the capacity to choose between right and wrong to be held accountable? This, like many other questions involving judgment, is not well-suited to our mortal minds. Judgment belongs to the Lord (see Hebrews 10:30). In limited circumstances, the Lord has allowed His servants who are authorized as common judges in Israel to help individuals repent and to protect the Church and victims from harmful conduct. But the judgment of the cognitive and spiritual development of a child under eight has been reserved by the Lord for Himself.

In providing a bright-line rule (a clearly defined limit based on an objective standard, such as age), the Lord has exercised the discretion accorded Him as the Redeemer. He paid the price for sin, and as a result has the right to establish this bright-line rule.

Consider the state of affairs if it were left to us to determine when each child has developed sufficiently to be accountable and, thus, to be baptized. Everyone knows that some six-year-olds, for example, are more advanced than others. In some instances, a six-year-old may be more capable of choosing between right and wrong than some eight-year-olds. It doesn't take much imagination to recognize that the baptismal age would creep down over time. Fearing that we would leave an accountable child unbaptized, we would err on the side of caution and baptize them younger and younger. Finally, we would engage in what Mormon identified as mocking God by baptizing infants. God's wisdom in establishing eight as the age of accountability is apparent.

Anyone who has had dealings with a seven-year-old knows that a child of that age is well along in learning the difference between right and wrong and does not always choose the right. Even at a very early age, an infant has to begin dealing with the natural-man aspect of mortality. I have held a newborn granddaughter in my arms, for example, and watched as she goes from sleeping peacefully, to waking up, to feeling hunger, to crying, as the demands of mortality and the appetites of the flesh come to bear. Certainly, we would not fault a newborn for crying out in hunger, and neither does the Lord fault a seven-year-old for yielding to the natural man and making the wrong choice. It is not that the seven-year-old has not learned the difference between right and wrong; instead, it is that the Lord does not hold the seven-year-old accountable. And the Lord can make that allowance because of His infinite Atonement. But when we turn eight, the training wheels come off, and we are responsible for our own sins, at least to the extent we truly understand the difference between right and wrong.

Even though the Lord has exercised His divine discretion in behalf of children under the age of eight and does not allow us to alter that judgment, He has allowed, even required, us to use judgment when it comes to some who have reached the age of eight but do not have the intellectual capacity to effectively repent—who remain unaccountable even though they have reached the age of accountability. The justice and mercy of God, along with the power of the Atonement of Jesus Christ, work to exalt these innocent children of God in the same way they work to save children under eight.

Whether an adult has the capacity to choose right from wrong may be difficult. For the purpose of determining whether a person eight years of age or older with an intellectual disability is accountable and therefore requires baptism, a bishop, as a common judge in Israel, along with the person's parents, must seek inspiration from the Lord and may seek guidance from other priesthood leaders. If the person is worthy and willing and has sufficient understanding to make and keep the associated covenants, baptism, as well as other ordinances, should not be withheld. But the Lord has taught that those with the intellectual capacity of little children, with "no understanding," are saved through the Atonement of Jesus Christ (see D&C 29:50).

Baptism for the remission of sins is for those who are accountable for their own sins. For that reason, most of us must be baptized to be forgiven of our sins and qualify for eternal life. It is a gate on the path to exaltation.

Endnotes

1. *Teachings of the Prophet Joseph Smith*, 312.
2. Smith, *Doctrines of Salvation*, 2:178.
3. Ibid.
4. Pratt, in *Journal of Discourses*, 20:157.
5. Young, in *Journal of Discourses*, 15:137.
6. Ibid.
7. Ibid.; italics added.
8. Matthews, *A Burning Light: The Life and Ministry of John the Baptist*, 21–23.
9. Lee, in Conference Report, Oct. 1953, 24–25.
10. Maxwell, in Conference Report, Apr. 2001, 77.
11. Christofferson, "The Divine Gift of Repentance," 39.
12. Ballard, in Conference Report, Apr. 1993, 5.
13. Wirthlin, in Conference Report, Apr. 1998, 16.
14. Oaks, in Conference Report, Apr. 1985, 102.
15. Cannon, "Discourse by President George Q. Cannon," 670.
16. McConkie, "The Salvation of Little Children," 4; quoted in *Doctrine and Covenants Student Manual*, 221.

Chapter 7

THE LAYING ON OF HANDS FOR THE GIFT OF THE HOLY GHOST

And when Paul had laid his hands upon them, the Holy Ghost came on them.

—Acts 19:6

Baptism by water is essential and meaningful, but without baptism by fire it is incomplete. Baptism by water must be followed by the baptism of fire and the Holy Ghost. Together, these two baptisms provide new birth—conversion.

Confirmation

When John preached repentance and baptized in the Jordan River, he taught the law unabashedly, which led the people to wonder whether he was the Christ foretold by the prophets. But he answered them clearly and unmistakably that, although he baptized with authority, "one mightier than I cometh, the latchet of whose shoes I am not worthy to unloose; he shall baptize you with the Holy Ghost and with fire" (Luke 3:16).

John wasn't teaching his followers only that Jesus was greater than he was, although that was part of his message. He was also teaching that baptism by water alone is not enough. They also needed what Jesus would bring—that is, the baptism of fire and the Holy Ghost. So when Jesus began His ministry, John told his own disciples, "Behold the Lamb of God!" (John 1:36), signaling to them to follow Jesus.

For the disciples of John the Baptist, his baptism was in preparation for the higher authority that would baptize with fire and the Holy Ghost, by the laying on of hands. This laying on of hands after baptism is what we call confirmation. We are confirmed members of The Church of Jesus Christ of Latter-day Saints and receive the gift of the Holy Ghost. "And whoso having faith you shall confirm in my church, by the laying on of the hands, and I will bestow the gift of the Holy Ghost upon them" (D&C 33:15). The ordinance is performed either right after baptism or in the next sacrament meeting.

The Light of Christ

The baptism by fire and the Holy Ghost is rooted in light and truth. Without divine guidance, our hope for eternal life is dim. We need that guidance to lead us to covenants, to encourage us to accept them, and to help us to live and honor them. Our Heavenly Father is always willing to give that guidance. If we are willing to receive it, He shares light and truth with us by the power of the Holy Ghost.

Ancient and modern revelations are full of references to light and truth. "The glory of God is intelligence, or, in other words, light and truth. Light and truth forsake that evil one" (D&C 93:36–37). "Intelligence, or the light of truth, was not created or made, neither indeed can be" (D&C 93:29). "Whatsoever is light, is good, because it is discernible, therefore ye must know that it is good" (Alma 32:35).

Darkness, the opposite of light, is the absence of light and is found in those who reject the light. "And the light shineth in darkness; and the darkness comprehended it not" (John 1:5).

God is the source of light, and light is the means by which He governs. "God is light, and in him is no darkness at all" (1 John 1:5). "The Lord shall be unto thee an everlasting light, and thy God thy glory" (Isaiah 60:19). "Light proceedeth forth from the presence of God to fill the immensity of space. The light which is in all things, which giveth life to all things, which is the law by which all things are governed, even the power of God who sitteth upon his throne, who is in the bosom of eternity, who is in the midst of all things" (D&C 88:12–13). Jesus said: "I am the light of the world: he that followeth me shall not walk in darkness, but shall have the light of life" (John 8:12).

We are responsible to receive and retain light and to reject darkness. "And every man whose spirit receiveth not the light is under condemnation" (D&C 93:32). "That wicked one cometh and taketh away light and truth, through disobedience, from the children of men" (D&C 93:39). We are warned not to "transgress contrary to the light" (Alma 9:23).

We are also responsible to share the light. During His Sermon on the Mount, the Savior said, "Let your light so shine before men, that they may see your good works, and glorify your Father which is in heaven" (Matthew 5:16).

Our goal is to have the light within us grow until we are like God. "That which is of God is light; and he that receiveth light, and continueth in God, receiveth more light; and that light groweth brighter and brighter until the perfect day" (D&C 50:24).

So light is essential in our lives. But how do we receive it? Mainly by two means: (1) the Light of Christ and (2) the Holy Ghost.

While God is a physical being and cannot be everywhere at once, His power, will, and word permeate the universe. Elder John A. Widtsoe described this influence, which we call the Light of Christ, as "the chief agent employed by God to communicate his will to the universe."[1] This godly influence is different from the Holy Ghost, who is a personage of spirit. The Light of Christ is sometimes referred to as the Spirit of Christ or the Spirit of God. According to the LDS Bible Dictionary, the Light of Christ "is preliminary to and preparatory to one's receiving the Holy Ghost. The Light of Christ will lead the honest soul who 'hearkeneth to the voice' to find the true gospel and the true Church and thereby receive the Holy Ghost (see D&C 84:46–48)."[2]

In its permeation, influence, and effect, the Light of Christ may be compared to wireless technology. In fact, Elder Widtsoe made that comparison a hundred years ago, comparing the Light of Christ to a wireless telegraph. He wrote that the Light of Christ "may be called the great wireless system of communication among the intelligent beings of the universe. The holy spirit vibrates with intelligence; it takes up the word and will of God as given by him or by his personal agents, and transmits the message to the remotest parts of space. By the intelligent operation and infinite extent of the holy spirit, the whole universe is held together and made as one unit. By its means there is no remoteness into which intelligent beings may escape the dominating will of God. By the holy spirit, the Lord is always with us, and 'is nearer than breathing, and nearer than hands and feet.'"[3]

Each of us is one of those intelligent beings referred to by Elder Widtsoe who communicate by the Light of Christ. We receive information from God directly to our spirits in a way that "transcend[s] the ordinary methods of acquiring knowledge."[4] If we want it to be, the Light of Christ will be a source of enlightenment and knowledge that uplifts us and helps us to persevere. It can be that guiding intuition we call conscience. On the other hand, we can also tune out the Light of Christ because we have agency.

Everyone has access to the Light of Christ. And everyone can benefit from the Light of Christ if they respond positively to its influence. "The Spirit giveth light to every man that cometh into the world; and the Spirit enlighteneth every man through the world, that hearkeneth to the voice of the Spirit" (D&C 84:46). The Light of Christ "is given to every man, that he may know good from evil" (Moroni 7:16).

When George Washington was sixteen years old, he copied into his school writing book this quote: "Labour to keep alive in your Breast that Little Spark of Celestial fire Called Conscience."[5] The influence of the Light of Christ is truly a spark, compared to the fire of the Holy Ghost.

But it can be rejected. Nephi's older brothers, Laman and Lemuel, were unfortunate examples of what happens when someone casts off the Light of Christ. They were privileged to receive the guidance of prophets who were members of their own family—their father Lehi and their brother Nephi. And an angel appeared to them. But they rejected the godly influence that was all around them. Nephi rebuked them for this rejection: "Ye are swift to do iniquity but slow to remember the Lord your God. Ye have seen an angel, and he spake unto you; yea, ye have heard his voice from time to time; and he hath spoken unto you in a still small voice, but ye were past feeling, that ye could not feel his words" (1 Nephi 17:45).

The Holy Ghost

While the Light of Christ is God's influence that permeates the universe and allows everyone to know good from evil, the Holy Ghost has a more focused role—He bears testimony of truth, but only to those who are sincerely seeking it. President Dallin H. Oaks distinguished the Light of Christ from the Holy Ghost: "The Light of Christ is given to all men and women that they may know good from evil; manifestations of the Holy Ghost are given to lead sincere seekers to gospel truths that will persuade them to repentance and baptism."[6]

The Holy Ghost is the third member of the Godhead, separate and distinct from God the Father and His Son Jesus Christ. Unlike the Father and the Son, who have exalted and perfect bodies of flesh and bone, the Holy Ghost does not have a tangible body, but instead is a personage of Spirit. "Were it not so, the Holy Ghost could not dwell in us" (D&C 130:22).

Joseph Smith taught that the Holy Ghost imparts pure intelligence; it expands the mind, enlightens the understanding, and "stor[es] the intellect with present knowledge."[7] He said that "a person may profit by noticing the first intimation of the spirit of revelation; . . . and thus by learning the Spirit of God and understanding it, you may grow into the principle of revelation, until you become perfect in Christ Jesus."[8]

The manifestations of the Holy Ghost are many, but one public manifestation and one private manifestation, each recounted in the Bible, deserve special notice for what they teach us—the first on the day of Pentecost (and particularly its influence on Peter) and the second to Cornelius the first Gentile to be baptized into the ancient church. The first shows the presence and power of the Holy Ghost to guide the leaders of God's church on the earth, and the second shows the influence of the Holy Ghost on a sincere seeker for truth who has not received the gift of the Holy Ghost.

First, let's examine Peter and the Pentecost. During His last days in mortality, Jesus told His Apostles that He would have to leave them. Even though they did not fully understand this warning, Jesus said: "It is expedient for you that I go away: for if I go not away, the Comforter will not come unto you; but if I depart, I will send him unto you" (John 16:7). This promised Comforter is the Holy Ghost (see John 14:26).

Before the crucifixion and resurrection of Jesus, Peter faithfully followed the Lord. He was inexperienced and deeply dependent on Jesus. He had a steep learning curve. In three years, he was to go from lowly fisherman to earthly leader of the kingdom of God. President Spencer W. Kimball said that, when Jesus called Peter, the fisherman was "a diamond in the rough."[9]

After denying he knew Jesus, but notably not denying that Jesus was the Savior, Peter heard the cockcrow and recognized the fulfillment of Jesus's prophecy that the Apostle would deny Him three times before that signal. President Kimball reflected on the emotion of that occasion: "[Peter] was humbled to the dust. Hearing the bird's announcement of the dawn reminded him not only that he had denied the Lord but also that all the Lord had said would be fulfilled, even to the crucifixion. He went out and wept bitterly."[10]

After the crucifixion, the resurrected Lord appeared to Peter and his associates. As a testimony of His sacrifice and His resurrection, Jesus showed them the marks of the injuries on His hands and in His side. And, perceiving that these followers were in turmoil, Jesus blessed them: "Peace be unto you: as my Father hath sent me, even so send I you. And when he had said this, he breathed on them, and saith unto them, *Receive ye the Holy Ghost*" (John 20:21–22; italics added).

After the crucifixion and resurrection, Peter was left without the familiar and comforting direction of the Lord. With no better idea of how to proceed, he reverted to his former profession; he went fishing, and he took other Apostles with him (see John 21:3). But the Lord had other activities in mind for the lead Apostles. Jesus appeared on the shore and told them to cast their net on the right side of the boat. Obeying, they caught a "multitude of fishes." As the Apostles then recognized Jesus, irrepressible Peter dove into the water to be the first to approach his beloved Master (see John 21:6–7). After the joyful meal of fish and bread that followed, Jesus charged Peter to feed the Lord's sheep (see John 21:15–17).

For forty days after His resurrection, Jesus continued to appear to His Apostles, reminding them that they would "receive power, after that the Holy Ghost is come upon you" (Acts 1:8). He told them to remain in Jerusalem "until ye be endued with power from on high" (Luke 24:49). Finally, Jesus physically left them, ascending into heaven from the Mount of Olives (see Acts 1:9–12).

Obediently remaining in Jerusalem, the Apostles met ten days later with some of the other faithful. Luke described what happened next: "Suddenly there came a sound from heaven as of a rushing mighty wind, and it filled all the house where they were sitting. And there appeared unto them cloven tongues like as of fire, and it sat upon each of them. And they were all filled with the Holy Ghost, and began to speak with other tongues, as the Spirit gave them utterance" (Acts 2:2–4).

After these miraculous manifestations, Peter bravely stood with the other Apostles and lifted up his voice: "Ye men of Judea, and all ye that dwell at Jerusalem, be this known unto you, and hearken to my words" (Acts 2:14). Forever after that moment, Peter was more confident, more decisive, more courageous, and divinely inspired in his leadership of the Lord's church.

President Kimball felt an affinity to Peter, which is understandable in light of their similarities. They both forsook their early careers to dedicate their lives to the Lord. They both rose to the role of senior Apostle in the

Lord's church. And they both received revelation to share gospel blessings with those to whom the blessings had previously been denied.

Of Peter, President Kimball said: "Peter was a man of faith. He healed the sick by their merely passing through his shadow. Prison walls could not hold him. Because of him, the dead came back to life."[11]

Elder LeGrand Richards squarely attributed the obvious spiritual growth in Peter to the Holy Ghost:

> Now one of the finest illustrations we have in holy writ of what the Holy Ghost can do for a man is in the case of Peter. You remember when Jesus met with them in the last supper and told them that there was one among them who would betray him, Peter said something like this: "Though all men shall be offended because of thee, yet will I never be offended.
>
> "Though I should die with thee, yet will I not deny thee." And Jesus said: "Before the cock crow, thou shalt deny me thrice." (See Matthew 26:3–35.) Then when Jesus was taken prisoner and Peter sat in the outer room, two different women came up to him and said: "Thou also wast with Jesus" (Matthew 26:69); and he denied it emphatically. Then a man came, and he even denied it with curses. And when he was through, he heard the cock crow, "and he went out and wept" (Matthew 26:75). Now that was Peter before he received the Holy Ghost. . . .
>
> Now look at Peter after he received the Holy Ghost and when he was commanded by the chief priests not to preach Christ in the streets of Jerusalem. He said: "We ought to obey God rather than men" (Acts 5:29). He was as fearless as a lion.[12]

The influence of the Holy Ghost on Peter produced a powerful, inspired, dedicated, fearless, compassionate leader. The lowly fisherman of Galilee rose to his full statute as Apostle of Jesus Christ.

Now let's turn to Cornelius and the Gentiles. When Jesus first sent His Apostles out to preach the gospel, He "commanded them, saying, Go not into the way of the Gentiles" (Matthew 10:5). Their time was not yet. But after the resurrection and ascension of Jesus, the Lord alerted Peter in a revelatory dream that it was time to share the gospel and the saving ordinances with the Gentiles.

Cornelius was a Roman centurion stationed at Caesarea. As a centurion, he was a senior officer who commanded at least eighty men and probably more as shown by the prominence of his household, with family and servants. Luke tells us that Cornelius was "a devout man, and one that feared God with all his house, which gave much alms to the people, and prayed to God alway" (Acts 10:2). After Cornelius had fasted and prayed to know God's will, an angel appeared to him in the afternoon one day and commended Cornelius for his alms and his prayers. The angel told Cornelius to send for Peter to come to his house because Peter would tell him what to do. Cornelius obeyed the angel and sent for Peter.

The Lord had prepared Peter through revelation, telling him not to call the Gentiles, or at least this one Gentile, unclean, so Peter went to Cornelius and asked him what he wanted. Wisely, Cornelius, who had gathered his family and friends, turned the question back to the prophet: "Now therefore are we all here present before God, to hear all things that are commanded thee of God" (Acts 10:33). And Peter did what prophets do—declared the mind and will of God, bearing witness of the sacrifice and divinity of the Son of God and teaching the doctrine of Christ.

As Cornelius and his guests listened intently to Peter, the influence of the Holy Ghost fell upon them and they spoke in tongues and magnified God. This amazed Peter's companions because they had never seen the Holy Ghost fall upon Gentiles. Knowing that Cornelius and his guests received the witness of the Holy Ghost, Peter commanded them to be baptized.

Peter's and Cornelius's experiences of the Holy Ghost strengthening them and testifying to them illustrate the two types of influence the Holy Ghost exercises. In Peter's case, the Holy Ghost influenced one who had already made baptismal covenants and had received the laying on of hands for the gift of the Holy Ghost. In Cornelius's case, the Holy Ghost influenced a sincere seeker to make those baptismal covenants.

"There is a difference," said Joseph Smith, "between the Holy Ghost and the gift of the Holy Ghost. Cornelius received the Holy Ghost before he was baptized, which was the convincing power of God unto him of the truth of the Gospel, but he could not receive the gift of the Holy Ghost until after he was baptized. Had he not taken this sign or ordinance upon him, the Holy Ghost which convinced him of the truth of God, would have left him."[13]

Cornelius's experience was the result of his sincere search for truth with a real intent to act on the truth when he found it. With this formula, anyone can be touched by the convincing power of the Holy Ghost. Indeed, it is the formula taught by missionaries of The Church of Jesus Christ of Latter-day Saints when they preach the gospel and invite women and men to come unto Christ through baptism. Jacob told the Nephites that "the Spirit speaketh the truth and lieth not. Wherefore, it speaketh of things as they really are, and of things as they really will be" (Jacob 4:13).

Moroni said: "When ye shall receive these things, I would exhort you that ye would ask God, the Eternal Father, in the name of Christ, if these things are not true; and if ye shall ask with a sincere heart, with real intent, having faith in Christ, he will manifest the truth of it unto you, by the power of the Holy Ghost. And by the power of the Holy Ghost ye may know the truth of all things" (Moroni 10:4–5).

Anyone can receive the testimony of the Holy Ghost concerning truth if, as President Oaks taught, the person is a sincere seeker, if the seeker *intends* to act on the revelation received.

The principle of intent applies in many aspects of life. For example, intent is crucial in criminal law. Imagine that you and I live next door to each other. You are gone on vacation, and I discover that your back door is unlocked. If I enter your house to steal your jewelry, I have committed burglary, whether or not I actually steal the jewelry. Just by entering your house with the intent to steal I have committed a crime that, in California, can earn me a six-year visit to state prison. On the other hand, if my intent is to water your houseplants when I enter your house, I have not committed a serious crime. At most, I have committed a minor trespass, and most probably I have merely been a helpful neighbor.

Intent is even more relevant when someone is killed. If the killer intended to kill, it may be murder. But if the killer did not intend to kill, it may be no more than a terrible accident.

When we approach God in prayer, asking Him to reveal truth to us, our intent matters. If our intent is, using Moroni's word, "real," then we may receive the answer we are looking for—in the Lord's time and in His way, of course. President Russell M. Nelson said that real intent means that you really intend to follow the guidance you receive.[14] It means that you really intend to change.

On the other hand, seeking the guidance of the Holy Ghost without intending to follow through on the revealed course of action will not produce a positive response from the Holy Ghost. God does not satisfy idle curiosity.

The Gift of the Holy Ghost

Sincere repentance and worthy baptism qualify us for the gift of the Holy Ghost and the constant companionship and influence of the Holy Ghost. Feeling the influence of the Holy Ghost helps us maintain righteousness. And righteousness qualifies us for the continued companionship and influence of the Holy Ghost. So it becomes a favorable cycle of godly influence followed by righteousness followed by more godly influence and righteousness. The cycle is broken only when we reject the godly influence and willfully sin.

This cycle and its upward trajectory are expressed in the revelation Joseph Smith received in 1831 about light, saying that when we receive light and continue in God, the light will grow brighter "until the perfect day" (D&C 50:24).

I saw a similar cycle with an upward trajectory in nature. When my children were growing up, each year we went to eastern Oregon to visit my father-in-law. He would close up his barber shop and take us fishing. One summer he took us to Unity Reservoir. As we were fishing I looked over a little bit beyond the lake and saw two golden eagles. They were down pretty close to the ground, but they were just soaring in circles—around and around in circles. I thought it was odd. They weren't flapping their wings. They were just soaring. And it didn't look like they were looking for food; they were just following each other around in circles.

Golden eagles are fascinating birds. They're huge. They can be up to three feet tall, and a three-foot-tall bird can have up to a seven-foot wingspan. You could probably imagine with wings that big it takes a lot of energy to flap them, so golden eagles don't flap their wings a lot. They flap their wings to take off. Once in the air, they flap their wings a few times and then glide and then flap their wings again and glide. Gaining altitude takes much energy, so they look for wind currents to help them.

Golden eagles have been clocked flying up to two hundred miles per hour. But that is only when they are heading straight down—when they're doing their best imitation of a ten-pound rock. But they're not very fast flyers otherwise. When they desire to stay aloft, gravity is their enemy. And they have to find ways to use the wind currents and their big wings to overcome gravity.

I was watching these eagles, and my father-in-law noticed. He said, "They're catching a thermal." That didn't really mean anything to me, so he explained: "When there's warm air close to the ground and colder air above it, the warm air rises, and it can rise thousands of feet into the atmosphere. The eagles start soaring in this warm air close to the ground. As the warm air rises the eagles rise."

I thought that was very interesting and went back to fishing. A while later I looked for the eagles again. I didn't see them at first, but then I realized they were much higher in the air, still soaring around in circles. Now I was really interested, so I didn't do much fishing. I just watched the eagles. When they finally got so high that they were just two little dots in the sky, they flew off across the sky in a high-altitude air current, still soaring.

Just as gravity is the enemy of the eagle, the natural man is the enemy of what God wants for us. It's like gravity holding us down. We eventually need to find that air current way up in the atmosphere where we can soar toward our eternal destination of the celestial kingdom. But how do we get there? How do we get that high in the atmosphere? We can't do it alone. We can't flap our figurative wings enough to get that high in the atmosphere. We need to find a thermal. We need to find an updraft of air. And we have enough energy to exercise our agency (flap our wings) to go find that updraft. Once we get in that updraft, we need to stay in it. We can soar in that updraft until we make it to that high-altitude air current.

Think of the soaring eagles and their thermal as they relate to this scripture: "For the natural man (gravity) is an enemy to God, and has been from the Fall of Adam, and will be, forever and ever, unless (here's the thermal) he yields to the enticings of the Holy Spirit, and putteth off the natural man and becometh a saint through the atonement of Christ the Lord" (Mosiah 3:19).

The thermal is yielding to the enticings of the Holy Ghost. We can't be exalted on our own power. We need something that will help us rise. To do that, we make a life plan to have the companionship of the Holy Ghost by making and keeping sacred covenants. We also seek the companionship of the Holy Ghost on a daily basis by praying, studying the scriptures, keeping the commandments, and ministering to others. We renew our covenants with God every Sunday by partaking of the sacrament.

President Henry B. Eyring explained how to keep the Holy Ghost with us:

> For those who are struggling with the high standard needed to qualify for the gift of the Spirit's companionship, I offer this encouragement. You have had times when you have felt the influence of the Holy Ghost. It may have happened for you today. You can treat those moments of inspiration like the seed of faith that Alma described (see Alma 32:28). Plant each one. You can do that by acting on the prompting you felt. The most valuable inspiration will be for you to know what God would have you do. If it is to pay tithing or to visit a grieving friend, you should do it. Whatever it is, do it. When you demonstrate your willingness to obey, the Spirit will send you more impressions of what God would have you

do for Him. As you obey, the impressions from the Spirit will come more frequently, becoming closer and closer to constant companionship.[15]

The golden eagles soaring around and around in the thermals and rising higher symbolize our rise to our Heavenly Father. On the other hand, there is another animal that also goes around and around. The wildebeest, in Africa, runs in very large herds. They're large animals. But they have no natural leaders. The wildebeest migrates, but in doing so it tends to follow the wildebeest right in front of it, which can cause problems. For example, if several wildebeests are going through an area with large bushes, one of them might circle a bush. Other wildebeests behind the bush-circler will follow, and soon there may be ten wildebeests circling a bush, getting nowhere.

When we yield to the enticings of the natural man, rather than to the enticings of the Spirit, we're just following whoever or whatever is in front of us. We do what we do or act how we act because that is what others do or how our friends act, or it is simply what is easiest to do. But that may not be what helps us to ascend. It may be sin, or it may be just the distractions of a telestial world. Many times, instead of willfully applying gospel principles to have the constant companionship of the Holy Ghost, we're just following that wildebeest right in front of us. And the wildebeest does not ascend as it goes around and around and around. It gets nowhere. Gravity prevails.

Are you an eagle? Or are you a wildebeest?

We are all both. That's why this world is so hard—this telestial world where the natural man in us is at home. It's hard to have the constant companionship of the Holy Ghost. We need to work on getting it right every day. If we worked on it yesterday, it won't do us any good if we don't work on it again today. And, if we work on it today, we're going to have to work on it again tomorrow. We have to make the constant decision to stay in the ascending air of the thermal. If we don't, we will end up following the other wildebeests around the worldly bushes.

The gift of the Holy Ghost is a feature of the covenant relationship between individuals and God. While everyone has the Light of Christ and honest seekers can be influenced by the power of the Holy Ghost to accept truth, only those who have made baptismal covenants with God have the gift of the Holy Ghost. And those who have the gift of the Holy Ghost have its influence only when they choose to have it.

The influence of the Holy Ghost is never forced on anyone. If we choose, by our actions and thoughts, not to feel the influence, it will not bother us. We are free to have it or to reject it. Once again, in matters of eternal significance, it is our choices, not some supreme whim, that determine our destiny.

The gift of the Holy Ghost brings the potential for personal revelation—that is, divine guidance. It also provides comfort and sanctification. If that gift were the only benefit of repentance and baptism, it would be worth the effort. If the pursuit of eternal life were a competition and the playing field had to be level for everyone at all times, having the gift of the Holy Ghost would be an unfair advantage. Repentance and baptism, along with the gift of the Holy Ghost, give us the opportunity to always have the uplifting, inspiring, sanctifying influence of the Holy Ghost. And the constant companionship of the Holy Ghost helps us keep the sacred covenants we have made.

The companionship of the Holy Ghost inspires peace and comfort and can lead to deliverance from bondage, both physical and spiritual. This loving influence from the Lord comes in many variations: "Come unto me, all ye that labour and are heavy laden, and I will give you rest" (Matthew 11:28). "And it came to pass that the Lord did visit them with his Spirit, and said unto them: Be comforted. And they were comforted" (Alma 17:10). "Peace I leave with you, my peace I give unto you: not as the world giveth, give I unto you. Let not your heart be troubled, neither let it be afraid" (John 14:27).

Mortal life is meant to be hard, but we need not walk this difficult path alone. We need not make it any harder than it has to be.

Alma the Elder and his people learned that, even under some of the most difficult circumstances, we can have the comfort of the Spirit. Living in the land of Nephi under the wicked rule of a king named Noah, Alma found truth in the otherwise unappreciated ministry of Abinadi. Although Noah and the other priests rejected Abinadi's call to repentance, Alma responded by repenting and gathering others who likewise were touched by Abinadi's message. They gathered first at the Waters of Mormon, where they made covenants with God by being baptized. Then they escaped into the wilderness.

Believing they were out of the reach of King Noah's army, they settled in a land they called Helam. But a Lamanite army found them and eventually, joined by the wicked priests of Noah, placed heavy burdens on them. Even though Alma's people had been righteous, "the Lord seeth fit to chasten his people; yea, he trieth their patience and their faith" (Mosiah 23:21). In response to their earnest prayers, the Lord told them, "Lift up your heads and be of good comfort, for I know of the covenant which ye have made unto me; and I will covenant with my people and deliver them out of bondage. And I will also ease the burdens which are put upon your shoulders, that even you cannot feel them upon your backs, even while you are in bondage" (Mosiah 24:13–14). Relying on this promise and exercising their faith, they "submit[ted] cheerfully and with patience to all the will of the Lord" (Mosiah 24:15). And sooner than later they were led out of bondage.

Alma's people received comfort in their afflictions because (1) they made covenants with God, (2) they kept those covenants, (3) they humbled themselves, and (4) they called upon God for help, with faith and patience. Elder L. Tom Perry said that this covenant righteousness "made it appropriate and fair that the Lord would deliver them quickly in a miraculous way from the hand which kept them in bondage. These scriptures teach us of the Lord's power of deliverance."[16]

Elder Neal A. Maxwell summed up the importance of the comforting power of the Holy Ghost: "God will give us priceless, personal assurances through the Holy Ghost (see John 14:26; D&C 36:2). Whether in tranquil or turbulent times, our best source of comfort is the Comforter."[17]

Baptism by Fire and by the Holy Ghost—Conversion

When King Benjamin gave the closing speech of his life to his Nephite people, he pleaded with them to take upon themselves the name of Christ because there is no other name under which they can be exalted (see Mosiah 5:8). After hearing their beloved king's sermon, the Nephites felt so strongly that they made "a covenant with our God to do his will, and to be obedient to his commandments in all things that he shall command us, all the remainder of our days" (Mosiah 5:5). They had "no more disposition to do evil, but to do good continually" (Mosiah 5:2).

What caused this "mighty change" in the Nephites' hearts (see Mosiah 5:2), influencing them to make lifelong covenants of obedience? They experienced a mighty change because they received the Holy Ghost into their hearts. This is the process by which we are born again, the process by which we are converted to the gospel. It is the baptism of fire and by the Holy Ghost spoken of by Jesus Christ and His prophets.

We are born again as children of Jesus Christ, spiritually begotten of Him. We become His sons and daughters because He is the author of eternal life.

King Benjamin explained this relationship to his subjects: "And now, because of the covenant which ye have made ye shall be called the children of Christ, his sons, and his daughters; for behold, this day he hath spiritually begotten you; for ye say that your hearts are changed through faith on his name; therefore, ye are born of him and have become his sons and his daughters" (Mosiah 5:7).

Baptism by fire is more than just being confirmed a member of the Church and being given the gift of the Holy Ghost. To receive the baptism by fire, we must *receive* the Holy Ghost, as we are directed in the confirmation ordinance.

Elder David A. Bednar described this relationship between confirmation and receiving the Holy Ghost: "The Holy Ghost does not become operative in our lives merely because hands are placed upon our heads and those four important words [receive the Holy Ghost] are spoken. As we receive this ordinance, each of us accepts a sacred and ongoing responsibility to desire, to seek, to work, and to so live that we indeed 'receive the Holy Ghost' and its attendant spiritual gifts."[18]

Elder Heber C. Kimball, an early Apostle and loyal friend and counselor to Brigham Young, keenly felt the influence of the Holy Ghost. He said: "Under the ordinances of baptism and the laying on of hands, I received the Holy Ghost, as the disciples did in ancient days, which was like a consuming fire. I felt as though I sat at the feet of Jesus, and was clothed in my right mind, although the people called me crazy. I continued in this way for many months, and it seemed as though my body would consume away; at the same time the scriptures were unfolded to my mind in such a wonderful manner that it appeared to me, at times, as if I had formerly been familiar with them."[19]

Alma the Younger pleaded with his people to receive the Holy Ghost. He asked: "Have ye spiritually been born of God? Have ye received his image in your countenances? Have ye experienced this mighty change in your hearts? Do ye exercise faith in the redemption of him who created you?" (Alma 5:14–15).

The difference between the ordinance of the laying on of hands for the gift of the Holy Ghost and the desired result of baptism by fire and by the Holy Ghost, actual conversion, is an example of how all ordinances are effective only through the faithfulness of the person making the covenant. President Marion G. Romney explained the concept of conversion to the gospel. He said that conversion "generally implies not merely mental acceptance of Jesus and his teachings but also a motivating faith in him and in his gospel—a faith which works a transformation, an actual *change* in one's understanding of life's meaning and in his allegiance to God—in interest, in thought, and in conduct. While conversion may be accomplished in stages, one is not really converted in the full sense of the term unless and until he is at heart a new person. 'Born again' is the scriptural term."[20]

Notice that President Romney's description of conversion did not include baptism. Yet, later in his discourse on conversion, he taught that baptism is critical to conversion because it embodies the covenants that bind the convert to the Lord. Unrepentant baptism, unworthy baptism, unconverted baptism avails the person nothing because it is not the ordinance alone, the outward manifestation of the covenant, that saves but instead the blessing of conversion is the change of heart that accompanies baptism in one who is repentant, worthy, and converted.

Even a testimony of the truthfulness of the gospel is not conversion, but like baptism it is essential to conversion. President Romney related testimony to conversion:

> Being converted, as we are here using the term, and having a testimony are not necessarily the same thing. . . . A testimony comes when the Holy Ghost gives the earnest seeker a witness of the truth. A moving testimony vitalizes faith; that is, it induces repentance and obedience to the commandments. Conversion, on the other hand, is the fruit of, or the reward for, repentance and obedience. (Of course one's testimony continues to increase as he is converted.) Conversion is effected by divine forgiveness, which remits sins. The sequence is something like this. An honest seeker hears the message. He asks the Lord in prayer if it is true. The Holy Spirit gives him a witness. This is a testimony. If one's testimony is strong enough, he repents and obeys the commandments. By such obedience he receives divine forgiveness which remits sin. Thus he is converted to a newness of life. His spirit is healed.[21]

This change of one's very character, made possible by the Atonement of Jesus Christ, moves our spirits closer to God and His kingdom. This concept of conversion and continued faithfulness applies to every covenant. By making and keeping the covenant, even honoring it, we change and become more like our Heavenly Father and His Son Jesus Christ. This process of becoming is also closely tied to the Holy Ghost because He seals those covenants—makes them eternally effective. In this role, the Holy Ghost is referred to as the Holy Spirit of Promise.

The Holy Spirit of Promise

Our covenants are made effective for eternity through the power of the Holy Ghost: "All covenants . . . that are not made and entered into and sealed by the Holy Spirit of promise . . . are of no efficacy, virtue, or force in and after the resurrection from the dead; for all contracts that are not made unto this end have an end when men are dead" (D&C 132:7).

The function of this sealing power exercised by the Holy Ghost is to provide blessings only to those who merit them. While a person may deceive a Church leader and by that deception obtain an ordinance unworthily, no one can fool the Holy Ghost. In other words, it is conceivable that a man could lie about his worthiness and be ordained to the Melchizedek Priesthood, which ordination he must receive to enter into the celestial kingdom, but that ordination will avail him nothing—indeed, will be to his condemnation—because it will not be sealed by the Holy Spirit of Promise.

If one is worthy of the saving ordinance when it is received, that ordinance will be sealed by the Holy Spirit of Promise. But the sealing is conditional—that is, the sealing will be withdrawn and the ordinance will no longer be effective if the covenant is broken. President Joseph Fielding Smith said: "The Holy Spirit of Promise is the Holy Ghost who places the stamp of approval upon every ordinance that is done righteously; and when covenants are broken he removes the seal."[22] Fortunately, we can repent of our sins and recover the sealing of the Holy Spirit of Promise through the Atonement of Jesus Christ.

The ultimate influence of the Holy Spirit of Promise is to guarantee that one is sealed up unto eternal life, that one's exaltation is no more conditioned on continued faithfulness but, because of demonstrated, undeviating faithfulness, eternal life is assured. This is different from the conditional sealing of an ordinance on a person; the sealing of the person, not just an ordinance, is, except for one rare exception, unconditional. Everyone who seriously and sincerely makes and keeps covenants does so with the hope of eternal life. We want to return to our Father to live with Him and to be like Him; that is the goal, the ultimate blessing. Some have the assurance, the unconditional promise, of this ultimate blessing before they leave this mortal life.

To make your calling and election sure is to receive in this life the promise of eternal life. Elder Bruce R. McConkie described the effect of making your calling and election sure: "To have one's calling and election made sure is to be sealed up unto eternal life; it is to have the unconditional guarantee of exaltation in the highest heaven of the celestial world; it is to receive the assurance of godhood; it is, in effect, to have the day of judgment advanced, so that the inheritance of all the glory and honor of the Father's kingdom is assured prior to the day when the faithful actually enter into the divine presence to sit with Christ in his throne."[23]

The Lord revealed to Joseph Smith the conditions for this blessing of receiving the assurance of exaltation while still in mortality:

> After a person has faith in Christ, repents of his sins, and is baptized for the remission of his sins and receives the Holy Ghost, (by the laying on of hands), which is the first Comforter, then let him continue to humble himself before God, hungering and thirsting after righteousness, and living by every word of God, and the Lord will soon say unto him, Son, thou shalt be exalted. When the Lord has thoroughly proved him, and finds that the man is determined to serve Him at all hazards, then the man will find his calling and his election made sure, then it will be his privilege to receive the other Comforter, which the Lord hath promised the Saints.[24]

Jesus told His disciples: "I will pray the Father, and he shall give you another Comforter, that he may abide with you for ever" (John 14:16).

Joseph Smith identified this other Comforter as Jesus Christ: "Now what is this other Comforter? It is no more nor less than the Lord Jesus Christ Himself. . . . When any man obtains this last Comforter, he will have the personage of Jesus Christ to attend him, or appear unto him from time to time, and even He will manifest the Father unto him, and they will take up their abode with him, and the visions of the heavens will be opened unto him, and the Lord will teach him face to face, and he may have a perfect knowledge of the mysteries of the Kingdom of God."[25]

About making your calling and election sure, Peter testified: "We have also a more sure word of prophecy" (2 Peter 1:19). "The more sure word of prophecy means a man's knowing that he is sealed up unto eternal life, by revelation and the spirit of prophecy, through the power of the Holy Priesthood" (D&C 131:5–6).

The possibility of making your calling and election sure has an opposite possibility that is just as disturbing and devastating in its effect as making your calling and election sure is assuring and exhilarating. That opposite is becoming a son of perdition, eventually to be consigned to outer darkness where there is no glory. Cain is the prototype.

Cain loved Satan more than God (see Moses 5:18). Cain knew God, but he willfully rebelled by making an unworthy offering and murdering his innocent brother. So God cursed him: "I will deliver thee up, and it shall be unto thee according to [Satan's] desire. And thou shalt rule over him; for from this time forth thou shalt be the father of his lies; thou shalt be called Perdition; for thou wast also before the world" (Moses 5:23–24).

Becoming a son of perdition begins by having the same knowledge necessary to make your calling and election sure, but it goes seriously wrong after that. Paul wrote to the Hebrews: "For it is impossible for those who were once enlightened, and have tasted of the heavenly gift, and were made partakers of the Holy Ghost, and have tasted the good word of God, and the powers of the world to come, if they shall fall away, to renew them again unto repentance; seeing they crucify to themselves the Son of God afresh, and put him to an open shame" (Hebrews 6:4–6).

This concept is further explained in the Doctrine and Covenants:

> Thus saith the Lord concerning all those who know my power, and have been made partakers thereof, and suffered themselves through the power of the devil to be overcome, and to deny the truth and defy my power— they are they who are the sons of perdition, of whom I say that it had been better for them never to have been born; for they are vessels of wrath, doomed to suffer the wrath of God, with the devil and his angels in eternity; concerning whom I have said there is no forgiveness in this world nor in the world to come—having denied the Holy Spirit after having received it, and having denied the Only Begotten Son of the Father, having crucified him unto themselves and put him to an open shame. These are they who shall go away into the lake of fire and brimstone, with the devil and his angels. (D&C 76:31–36)

"If a man gets knowledge enough to have the companionship of the Son of God, the chances are his call and election would be sure," wrote President Joseph Fielding Smith. But he added that those who receive this knowledge will not be pardoned if they turn away.[26]

The existence of sons of perdition is evidence of agency, opposition, and accountability. That some of God's children who kept their first estate can be left with no glory after the resurrection shows that (1) God will not take away our agency, (2) there is an opposite of those who receive the fulness of the Father's glory, and (3) we all will ultimately be held accountable for whether we accept the redeeming sacrifice of the Savior.

Sons of perdition are those who have committed the unpardonable sin. According to Joseph Smith, they (1) receive the Holy Ghost, (2) have the heavens opened to them, (3) know God (have their calling and election made sure), and then (4) sin against the Holy Ghost. "After a man has sinned against the Holy Ghost, there is no repentance for him. He has got to say that the sun does not shine while he sees it; he has got to deny Jesus Christ when the heavens have been opened unto him, and to deny the plan of salvation with his eyes open to the truth of it."[27]

Sons of perdition are the ultimate covenant breakers. They have made the covenants of exaltation and received the saving ordinances, but they have altogether turned from those covenants (see D&C 84:41). They deny God's truth and defy God's power (see D&C 76:31). In doing so, they have rebelled from and turned against the very covenants and ordinances that would have brought them eternal glory in the celestial kingdom.

Unlike everyone else who kept their first estate, sons of perdition will never be forgiven of their sins but must pay for them eternally (see D&C 76:34). Speaking of everyone who will receive a portion of God's glory short of exaltation, the Lord revealed to President Joseph F. Smith that "the dead who repent [as opposed to the living who repent] will be redeemed, through obedience to the ordinances of the house of God. And after they have paid the penalty of their transgressions, and are washed clean, shall receive a reward according to their works, for they are heirs of salvation" (D&C 138:58–59). But the sons of perdition have sinned beyond the point of repentance and redemption, even redemption after death.

Having agency means that we can make poor decisions if we want. God will not stop us. He will mourn for us, but He will not stop us. God will not save us in our sins. If we reject the redeeming sacrifice of the Savior, we will receive no glory. Only those who ultimately accept the Atonement of Jesus Christ, whether in this life or in the hereafter, can receive a kingdom of glory, whether it be celestial, terrestrial, or telestial. Our desires will be fulfilled.

The existence of the sons of perdition also teaches us that the opposite of fulness is absence. The sons of perdition have no glory.[28] They are the opposite of those who are exalted. Both the sons of perdition and the heirs of exaltation have (1) kept their first estate, (2) received the Holy Ghost, (3) had the heavens opened to them, and (4) seen God. But the critical, defining difference between the sons of perdition and the heirs of exaltation is that the heirs of exaltation have remained faithful to the sure word of prophecy, while the sons of perdition have knowingly turned against it. As Jesus said, "All sins shall be forgiven unto the sons of men, and blasphemies wherewith soever they shall blaspheme. But he that shall blaspheme against the Holy Ghost hath never forgiveness, but is in danger of eternal damnation" (Mark 3:28–29). As a result, the heirs of exaltation enjoy a fulness of the Father's light and glory, while the sons of perdition have darkness, a complete absence of light and glory.

The sons of perdition are also in opposition to the unembodied spirits who rebelled in the premortal life and followed Satan, himself forever an unembodied spirit, rather than accepting the Father's plan and following Jesus Christ. Both the sons of perdition and Satan's followers in the council in heaven (1) are spirit children of God, (2) had agency, and (3) chose to rebel. The critical, defining difference is that the sons of perdition kept their first estate and will have immortal bodies, while the followers of Satan in the council in heaven will forever remain unembodied. Because of this difference, and the preeminence of the spirit joined with a body of flesh and bone over an unembodied spirit, Cain, the one known son of perdition, will rule over Satan in outer darkness.

Making your calling and election sure preliminary to exaltation, on the one hand, and becoming a son of perdition and enjoying no eternal glory, on the other, are the two extreme outcomes for those who have kept their first estate and have come to mortality. Making your calling and election sure assures an eventual fulness of glory, celestial glory, while becoming a son of perdition dooms the person to a complete absence of glory. Between those two extremes are glories lesser than exaltation. As Jesus said, in His Father's house are many mansions (see John 14:2).

Making your calling and election sure is not a saving ordinance in the sense that it must happen in mortality. Those who hear the word must have faith, repent, be baptized by water and by the Spirit, receive the temple endowment, and, if the appropriate opportunity presents itself, be sealed to a spouse in the temple. But the final requirement on this covenant path offered by the doctrine of Christ is to endure to the end. If you stay on the covenant path to the end of your life, it doesn't matter whether you have yet made your calling and election sure. It will come at the appropriate time for you, and that may be in the next life.

Robert L. Millett confirmed this when he said:

> Latter-day Saints who have received the ordinances of salvation—
> including the blessings of the temple—may press forward in the work of
> the Lord and with quiet dignity and patient maturity seek to be worthy
> of gaining the certain assurance of salvation before the end of their

mortal lives. But should one not formally receive the more sure word of prophecy in this life, he or she has the scriptural promise that faithfully enduring to the end—keeping the covenants and commandments from baptism to the end of their lives (see Mosiah 18:8–9)—leads one to the promise of eternal life, whether that promise be received here or hereafter (see D&C 14:7; 53:7; 2 Nephi 31:20; Mosiah 5:15).[29]

God's promise to us concerning making our calling and election sure is that if we do what we need to do and become what we need to become, it will happen. But when it will happen is left to God's perfect discretion: "It shall be in his own time, and in his own way, and according to his own will" (D&C 88:68). God promised through Nephi that if we press forward with a steadfastness in Christ and endure to the end, the Father will say: "Ye shall have eternal life" (2 Nephi 31:20). That declaration may come here in mortality or it may come in the next life, but it will come. God is bound when we obey (see D&C 82:10).

In the meantime, our focus should be on actively serving God and seeking to fulfill His purposes, not on passively pining for exaltation, because active service results in growth and mistakes and further growth. Alma the Elder's experience is a guide. As the high priest over the Church in Zarahemla, Alma battled the tendency of the rising generation to reject the teachings of King Benjamin. This rising generation was too young to fully understand and embrace the covenants made by their parents at the time King Benjamin preached from the tower. "Their hearts were hardened" (Mosiah 26:3). Dissensions arose in the Church, and many were led astray by the flattering words of the dissenters. King Mosiah refused to judge these dissenters and turned them over to Alma, probably because the matter was one of standing in the Church, not violation of law. Alma was troubled, and he did what a troubled Church leader must do in such times—he "inquired of the Lord what he should do concerning this matter, for he feared that he should do wrong in the sight of God" (Mosiah 26:13). Doing the Lord's will was his chief concern. He "poured out his whole soul," and "the voice of the Lord came to him saying: Blessed art thou, Alma. . . . Thou art my servant, and I covenant with thee that thou shalt have eternal life" (Mosiah 26:14–15, 20).

Alma the Elder, who had been a priest of the wicked King Noah, but who had repented and led many to the waters of baptism and had committed his life to the work of the Lord, received the promise of eternal life—not by seeking it, but by seeking to do the Lord's will and by seeking to align his own will to the Lord's in all things.

Brother Millett made this point that Alma's calling and election was made sure as he was diligently serving: "Alma was not seeking to be truer than true when this glorious assurance came to him. He was not on a calling and election crusade. Rather, he was busily engaged in doing his duty, striving with all his heart to bless, lift, and strengthen his brothers and sisters. There's a message there for us."[30]

Nevertheless, Peter implored us to "give diligence to make your calling and election sure" (2 Peter 1:10). And Joseph Smith agreed: "I would exhort you to go on and continue to call upon God until you make your calling and election sure for yourselves, by obtaining this more sure word of prophecy, and wait patiently for the promise until you obtain it."[31]

As did Alma, we must fulfill our covenant duties—the duties we took upon us when we were baptized and confirmed, when we received the priesthood, when we were endowed and sealed in the temple. Ultimately, making our calling and election sure is a blessing associated with the ordinances of the Melchizedek Priesthood. Without the ordinances of the Melchizedek Priesthood, "no man can see the face of God, even the Father, and live" (D&C 84:22).

"The power and authority of the . . . Melchizedek Priesthood, is to hold the keys of all the spiritual blessings of the church, to have the privilege of receiving the mysteries of the kingdom of heaven, to have the heavens opened unto them, to commune with the general assembly and church of the Firstborn, and to enjoy the communion and presence of God the Father, and Jesus the mediator of the new covenant" (D&C 107:18–19).

Thus, the relationship between agency and covenants, on one hand, and the Atonement of Jesus Christ and the companionship of the Holy Ghost, on the other, gives us the opportunity and the ability to choose eternal life and to succeed. Before we make covenants, our role is to be like Cornelius—to sincerely seek with faith and real intent. After we make covenants, our role is to be like Peter—continuing in righteousness so that we can have the Holy Ghost as our constant companion to reveal truth and imbue us with power, until we are sealed up to eternal life.

Endnotes

1. Widtsoe, *A Rational Theology as Taught by the Church of Jesus Christ of Latter-day Saints*, 72.
2. LDS Bible Dictionary, s.v. "Light of Christ," 725.

3. Widtsoe, *A Rational Theology as Taught by the Church of Jesus Christ of Latter-day Saints*, 73.

4. Ibid., 19.

5. Washington, *George Washington's Rules of Civility and Decent Behavior in Company and Conversation*, 19.

6. Oaks, in Conference Report, Oct. 1996, 80.

7. *Teachings of the Prophet Joseph Smith*, 149.

8. Ibid., 151.

9. Kimball, "Peter My Brother," 485.

10. Ibid., 488.

11. Ibid.

12. Richards, in Conference Report, Oct. 1979, 111–12.

13. *Teachings of the Prophet Joseph Smith*, 199.

14. Nelson, in Conference Report, Oct. 2009, 80.

15. Eyring, "The Holy Ghost as Your Companion," 105.

16. Perry, "The Power of Deliverance," 95.

17. Maxwell, in Conference Report, Oct. 2002, 15.

18. Bednar, in Conference Report, Oct. 2010, 95.

19. Whitney, *Life of Heber C. Kimball, an Apostle*, 38–39.

20 Romney, in Conference Report, Oct. 1963, 23, italics in original.

21. Ibid., 24.

22. Smith, *Doctrines of Salvation*, 1:55; see also 2:98.

23. McConkie, *Doctrinal New Testament Commentary*, 3:330–31.

24. *Teachings of the Prophet Joseph Smith*, 150.

25. Ibid., 150–51.

26. Smith, *Doctrines of Salvation*, 1:55.

27. *Teachings of the Prophet Joseph Smith*, 358.

28. Kimball, *The Miracle of Forgiveness*, 125–27.

29. Millet, "Make Your Calling and Election Sure," 280.

30. Ibid., 279.

31. *Teachings of the Prophet Joseph Smith*, 299.

Chapter 8

PRIESTHOOD AUTHORITY

---

*We believe that a man must be called of God, by prophecy,
and by the laying on of hands by those who are in authority,
to preach the Gospel and administer in the ordinances thereof.*

—Articles of Faith 1:5

Some of the most important covenants we make with the Lord accompany ordinances such as baptism. And only authorized agents of the Lord can validly perform these sacred ordinances. These authorized agents are priesthood holders who act on behalf of the Lord. Without priesthood authority, there could be no valid ordinances because, if the ordinance is not performed by someone acting on behalf of the Lord, it is ineffective.

Priesthood includes power, authority, and keys. A man gets authority when he is ordained. He gets power when he is righteous. And he gets keys when he is called to preside.

Priesthood and Ordinances

Brigham Young explained what the priesthood is:

> If anybody wants to know what the priesthood of the Son of God is, it is the law by which the worlds are, were, and will continue for ever and ever. It is that system which brings worlds into existence and peoples them, gives them their revolutions—their days, weeks, months, years, their seasons and times and by which they are rolled up as a

scroll, as it were, and go into a higher state of existence; and they who believe in the Lord Jesus Christ—the maker, framer, governor, dictator and controller of this earth—they who live according to his law and priesthood will be prepared to dwell on this earth when it is brought into the presence of the Father and the Son.[1]

In the Doctrine and Covenants we learn more about the Melchizedek Priesthood: "The power and authority of the higher, or Melchizedek Priesthood, is to hold the keys of all the spiritual blessings of the church—To have the privilege of receiving the mysteries of the kingdom of heaven, to have the heavens opened unto them, to commune with the general assembly and church of the Firstborn, and to enjoy the communion and presence of God the Father, and Jesus the mediator of the new covenant" (D&C 107:18–19).

The three aspects of priesthood (power, authority, and keys) can be compared to driving a car. The driver's license is the authority; it allows the person to validly drive the car. The steering wheel, accelerator, and brake are the keys. Without them, there is no direction, no order to the experience. And the motor is the power. We pour righteousness, like gas, into our tanks to have power.

When the Apostle Paul arrived in Ephesus, he found some who claimed to have been baptized but had not received the Holy Ghost. Paul asked: "Have ye received the Holy Ghost since ye believed?" They responded: "We have not so much as heard whether there be any Holy Ghost." This response raised Paul's suspicion that, if they had been baptized, it was done without the proper authority. He continued his interrogation: "Unto what then were ye baptized?" "Unto John's baptism," they responded (Acts 19:2–3). This response validated Paul's suspicion that they had been baptized without proper authority because an authorized baptism is done in the name of Jesus Christ and is followed by the laying on of hands for the gift of the Holy Ghost, a Melchizedek Priesthood ordinance.

Paul then instructed these disciples on the preeminence of Jesus Christ over John the Baptist and the necessity of being baptized in the name of Jesus Christ: "John verily baptized with the baptism of repentance, saying unto the people, that they should believe on [Jesus Christ] which should come after [John the Baptist]" (Acts 19:4). The disciples were immediately "baptized in the name of the Lord Jesus" (Acts 19:5). After they were baptized, Paul laid his hands on them and they received the Holy Ghost (see Acts 19:6).

Joseph Smith recounted this story and commented: "It seems from the reasoning above that some sectarian Jew had been baptizing like John, but had forgotten to inform them that there was one to follow by the name of Jesus Christ, to baptize with fire and the Holy Ghost:—which showed these converts that their first baptism was illegal, and when they heard this they were gladly baptized, and after hands were laid on them, they received the gifts, according to promise, and spake with tongues and prophesied."[2]

Thus the need, not only for baptism, but for baptism by one who holds the proper authority.

What right does a missionary have to take a convert into a baptismal font and baptize that convert by immersion for the remission of sins?

Where does a father get the authorization to lay his hands on the head of his son and ordain him to the Aaronic Priesthood?

When a sealer marries a couple in the temple, why would the Lord recognize that marriage as sealing the couple not only for time but also for eternity?

These questions, and many more like them, are answered by a study of priesthood authority, along with power and keys.

Our opportunity to make and keep essential covenants today would be impossible without the proper authority to provide the corresponding ordinances. And that authority had been lost from the earth when Jesus's Apostles died off. Oliver Cowdery recounted: "Darkness covered the earth and gross darkness the minds of the people. . . . Amid the strife and noise concerning religion, none had authority from God to administer the ordinances of the Gospel" (Joseph Smith—History 1:71, fn). The absence of priesthood authority on the earth required a heavenly restoration, which began on a spring day in 1829.

Joseph and Oliver went into the woods near the Susquehanna River in Pennsylvania on May 15, 1829, to pray about something they had learned from the work of translating the gold plates. Joseph had been translating for several months, but the work had gone faster since Oliver had arrived in early April and took up the position of scribe. They learned from the plates about the ordinance of baptism by immersion for the remission of sins. When Alma left the court of wicked King Noah, he went into the wilderness and baptized unto repentance. When Jesus visited the Nephites, He commanded them to be baptized. With this commandment in mind, Joseph and Oliver felt the need to ask the Lord for a better understanding of this baptism (see Joseph Smith—History 1:68).

But Joseph and Oliver had more than just the concept of baptism on their minds when they went into the woods. After all, many of the sects of the day performed baptism. What the translator and scribe went to find out was where the authority existed to perform valid baptisms.

Joseph's visit to the woods with Oliver in 1829 came nine years after Joseph's experience in the sacred grove as a fourteen-year-old boy when he inquired of the Lord concerning which church he should join. In that grove, God the Father and Jesus Christ appeared to Joseph, opening the dispensation of the fulness of times, the last time that the gospel would be dispensed or revealed to God's children on earth before the Second Coming of the Lord in his glory. Since that First Vision, Moroni, the last ancient prophet to write on the plates before depositing them in the ground, had appeared to Joseph several times to give him instruction and encouragement and to guide Joseph to the hiding place of the plates.

In 1829, it was time for the restoration of gospel principles and authority to rise to a new level, to take on a new momentum that would carry through to the restoration of the Lord's church within a year and on to the many developments that characterized Joseph's short life as a prophet, seer, and revelator and the head of the dispensation of the fulness of times.

To fully understand what happened that long-ago May day, we must go back even further to the mortal life of Jesus Christ and to three events that set the stage for Joseph and Oliver's inquiry.

The first event was John the Baptist's baptism of Jesus Christ. Although Jesus was without sin, He directed John to baptize Him to fulfill all righteousness. John possessed the authority to baptize because he had been ordained to the Aaronic Priesthood. He was entitled to the ordination because he was a descendant of Aaron, the brother of Moses, through whose posterity the Aaronic Priesthood was passed down. He was therefore a legal administrator of the priesthood, an authorized agent of the Lord, commissioned of God to perform the ordinances of the Aaronic Priesthood.[3]

The second event was Jesus's ordination of His Apostles. During His mortal ministry, many people heard His teaching, saw His miracles, and followed Him. A few, however, were chosen not only to follow Him but also to receive authority from Him—authority that was meant to remain in force after the Lord's crucifixion and resurrection. To some, twelve in number, He specifically extended the invitation to "follow" so that He could make them "fishers of men" (Matthew 4:19). To them, He gave "power" to cast out unclean spirits and heal sickness and disease—in other words, authority to do the same things Jesus, Himself, had been doing (Matthew 10:1; Luke 9:1).

Jesus gave these disciples this authority by ordination, telling them: "Ye have not chosen me, but I have chosen you, and ordained you, that ye should go and bring forth fruit, and that your fruit should remain: that whatsoever ye shall ask of the Father in my name, he may give it to you" (John 15:16). After His crucifixion and resurrection, Jesus commissioned these disciples, the Apostles, to continue His work: "Go ye therefore, and teach all nations, baptizing them in the name of the Father, and of the Son, and of the Holy Ghost" (Matthew 28:19).

The death of Judas Iscariot left a vacancy in the Quorum of the Twelve Apostles, a vacancy that Peter and the other ten remaining Apostles filled by calling Matthias "to be a witness with us of his resurrection" (Acts 1:22). Later, others were ordained apostles—Paul (see Romans 1:1; 1 Corinthians 9:1–2), James, the Lord's brother (see Gal. 1:19), and Barnabas (see 1 Corinthians 9:5–6).

The importance of Apostles to the true church of Jesus Christ cannot be understated. They are "special witnesses of the name of Christ in all the world" (D&C 107:23). Joseph Smith taught: "The fundamental principles of our religion are the testimony of the Apostles and Prophets, concerning Jesus Christ, that He died, was buried, and rose again the third day, and ascended into heaven; and all other things which pertain to our religion are only appendages to it."[4]

The third event was the bestowal of the keys of the kingdom on Peter, James, and John. Late in His earthly ministry, Jesus promised to bestow the keys of the kingdom on Peter, saying to Peter, "I will give unto thee the keys of the kingdom of heaven: and whatsoever thou shalt bind on earth shall be bound in heaven: and whatsoever thou shalt loose on earth shall be loosed in heaven" (Matthew 16:19).

Not long after this promise was made, Jesus took Peter, James, and John up into a mountain and was transfigured before them. Two translated beings were also present there on the mountain—Moses and Elijah[5] (see Matthew 17:3–4). Both Moses and Elijah had been taken up into heaven without tasting death. During their stay on the mountain, Peter, James, and John received the promised keys of the kingdom.[6]

Restoration of the Priesthood

As Joseph and Oliver prayed in the woods next to the Susquehanna River that spring day in 1829, a heavenly messenger appeared in a cloud of light. The angel said he was John, who was called John the Baptist in the New Testament (see Joseph Smith—History 1:68, 72).

When John the Baptist appeared to Joseph and Oliver, he greeted them by calling them his "fellow servants." This must have been thrilling, comforting, and reassuring to Joseph and Oliver to receive such a greeting from one so honored and recognizable from the New Testament—the one who had baptized Jesus and the one about whom Jesus had said: "Among them that are born of women there hath not risen a greater than John the Baptist" (Matthew 11:11). For their whole lives to that age, Joseph and Oliver had read about John the Baptist, heard sermons about him, learned from his exhortations to repent and be baptized. And now he blessed them with his bodily, angelic presence.

John's appearance to Joseph and Oliver was certainly impressive to Joseph and Oliver, but even more so than they understood. In the premortal council, John sat with Joseph as noble and great ones (see Abraham 3:22–23). Assuming John could remember that event, he would have known and appreciated in the eternal scheme the significance of his appearance to these mortal fellow servants. Even if John could not, as yet, remember that great premortal scene, he certainly knew the significance of the restoration of the priesthood to the earth in the last dispensation and understood Joseph's essential role in the marvelous work that was then just beginning. John may have been equally thrilled to be able to call Joseph and Oliver his "fellow servants."

Of the experience, Oliver remembered:

> The Lord, who is rich in mercy, and ever willing to answer the consistent prayer of the humble, after we had called upon Him in a fervent manner, aside from the abodes of men, condescended to manifest to us His will. On a sudden, as from the midst of eternity, the voice of the Redeemer spake peace to us, while the veil was parted and the angel of God came down clothed with glory, and delivered the anxiously looked for message, and the keys of the Gospel of repentance. What joy! what wonder! what amazement! While the world was racked and distracted—while millions were groping as the blind for the wall, and while all men were resting upon uncertainty, as a general mass, our eyes beheld, our ears heard, as in the "blaze of day"; yes, more—above the glitter of the May sunbeam, which then shed its brilliancy over the face of nature! Then his voice, though mild, pierced to the center, and his words, "I am thy fellow-servant," dispelled every fear. We listened, we gazed, we admired! 'Twas the voice of an angel from glory, 'twas a message from the Most High! And as we heard we rejoiced, while His

love enkindled upon our souls, and we were wrapped in the vision of the Almighty! (Joseph Smith—History 1:71, fn).

John announced his mission: acting under the direction of Peter, James, and John, who held the keys of the higher Melchizedek Priesthood, he was there to confer the authority and keys of the lesser Aaronic Priesthood. Laying a hand on each man's head, John declared: "Upon you my fellow servants, in the name of the Messiah I confer the Priesthood of Aaron, which holds the keys of the ministering of angels, and of the gospel of repentance, and of baptism by immersion for the remission of sins; and this shall never be taken again from the earth, until the sons of Levi do offer again an offering unto the Lord in righteousness" (D&C 13).

Following John's instructions, Joseph then baptized Oliver by immersion in the Susquehanna River, and Oliver likewise baptized Joseph (see Joseph Smith—History 1:71).

Before he departed, John told Joseph and Oliver that, while the priesthood he conferred included the authority to baptize, they would later receive further priesthood keys, those keys to include the laying on of hands for the gift of the Holy Ghost (see Joseph Smith—History 1:70).

Having directed John the Baptist to bestow the Aaronic Priesthood, the preparatory priesthood, on Joseph and Oliver, the three presiding Apostles from antiquity—Peter, James, and John—had set the scene for their own appearance to Joseph and Oliver to restore the full authority of the priesthood. The specifics of this scene are not as well-documented as John the Baptist's appearance, but it followed much the same script as had the earlier visit.

Within just weeks after the appearance of John the Baptist, Joseph and Oliver were again in the woods near the Susquehanna River. The two men must have expected this experience because John the Baptist had informed them of "the keys of the Priesthood of Melchizedek, which Priesthood . . . would in due time be conferred on [them]," and John told Joseph and Oliver that Joseph "should be called the first Elder of the Church" and Oliver "the second" (Joseph Smith—History 1:72).

The restoration of the Melchizedek Priesthood occurred as foretold. "Peter, James, and John" appeared to Joseph and Oliver "in the wilderness . . . on the Susquehanna river" (D&C 128:20). The three heavenly ministrants "declar[ed] themselves as possessing the keys of the kingdom, and of the dispensation of the fulness of times" (D&C 128:20), keys that Peter, James, and John had received, themselves, under the hands of Jesus Christ and on the Mount of Transfiguration.

We don't know the exact words used on this occasion, but later revelations recall the event. A few months after the appearance of Peter, James, and John to Joseph and Oliver, the Lord, in another revelation, listed some of the prophets who would accompany him at the Second Coming, those with whom the Lord would "drink of the fruit of the vine . . . on the earth" (D&C 27:5). On that list, the Lord included "Peter, and James, and John, whom I have sent unto you, by whom I have ordained you and confirmed you to be apostles, and especial witnesses of my name, and bear the keys of your ministry and of the same things which I revealed unto them; Unto whom I have committed the keys of my kingdom, and a dispensation of the gospel for the last times; and for the fulness of times, in the which I will gather together in one all things, both which are in heaven, and which are on earth" (D&C 27:12–13).

It is clear, then, that Joseph and Oliver received from Peter, James, and John the "Holy Priesthood, after the Order of the Son of God" (D&C 107:3), which we refer to as the Melchizedek Priesthood, "out of respect or reverence to the name of the Supreme Being, to avoid the too frequent repetition of his name" (D&C 107:4). Along with this came ordination as apostles, the same priesthood office held by Peter, James, and John anciently. The essential office of apostle, held by those who are special witnesses of the name of Christ, had been restored to the earth.

Within a period of not more than a few weeks, Joseph and Oliver received the Aaronic and Melchizedek Priesthoods. Today, men are ordained to this same Aaronic Priesthood and later are ordained to this Melchizedek Priesthood, thus receiving authority, but the keys are another matter. The keys of the kingdom are reserved for those who preside.

Priesthood Keys

Priesthood keys, another feature of the true church of God, are commonly misunderstood, even among members of The Church of Jesus Christ of Latter-day Saints. The distinction between priesthood authority and priesthood keys is essential to an understanding of how the Lord administers His kingdom, both in heaven and on the earth, and to the proper order of administering ordinances.

The heavenly messengers who appeared to Joseph and Oliver bestowed upon their mortal fellow servants not just the authority of the priesthood but also the keys. President Russell M. Nelson defined priesthood keys: "Those keys refer to the right to preside over priesthood authority in the name of the Lord Jesus Christ."[7]

Priesthood keys can be understood by comparing them to other concepts familiar to us. President Nelson, who had a long career as a renowned heart surgeon before accepting the call as an Apostle of the Lord, provided a helpful analogy explaining the purpose and effect of priesthood keys:

> Prior to my call to the Quorum of the Twelve Apostles, I served as a medical doctor and surgeon. I had earned two doctor's degrees. I had been certified by two specialty boards. That long preparation had consumed many years, yet the education itself did not allow me to serve the public. Why? Because I needed legal permission.
>
> That could be granted only by authorities of the state government and directing boards of hospitals in which I desired to work. Once officials holding proper authority granted me a license and permission, then I could care for patients who needed surgical relief from their ailments. After legal administrators had exercised their keys, then I could render the service for which I had been prepared.
>
> In return, I was accountable to those who granted those privileges. I was required to obey legal and ethical expectations and never abuse the power entrusted to me.
>
> Just as the important steps of preparation and permission pertain to medicine (and other professions), they also relate to priesthood service. Those who hold the priesthood—Aaronic and Melchizedek—have authority to render priesthood service. As agents of the Lord, they have the right to perform sacred ordinances of the gospel. Keys authorize the performance of that service.[8]

President Nelson's analogy effectively illustrates two essential concepts related to priesthood keys: legal permission and accountability.

Legal permission to perform ordinances, in the sense that they are authorized by God, can be given only by one who holds priesthood keys. A priesthood holder may exercise the priesthood by performing an ordinance, but for the ordinance to be valid, the ordinance must be authorized by one who holds the applicable keys. For example, although a priest holds the priesthood authority necessary to baptize, he cannot do so unless someone holding the applicable priesthood keys authorizes that baptism. In the case of an eight-year-old child, the bishop holds the keys. The bishop determines the child's preparedness for baptism and authorizes the ordinance. He need not perform the ordinance himself—that can be delegated to a worthy priesthood holder—but he must authorize it before the baptism can be validly performed.

Accountability requires the priesthood holder to answer to the one who holds the priesthood keys, the presiding authority. The priesthood holder must adhere to the direction of the presiding authority. Having performed the ordinance, he is responsible to return and report his exercise of the priesthood to his presiding authority.

Today, we might give the "keys" of the city to a famous person or a hero. But those keys are only honorary and symbolic. The keys that Peter, James, and John received under the hands of Jesus Christ and on the Mount of Transfiguration, on the other hand, were operative and powerful—operative in the sense that they unlocked priesthood authority and powerful because they carried with them the ability to preside in the name of the Lord. And those keys are just as important for the valid performance of priesthood ordinances today as they were in Jesus's day or Joseph's day.

The keys continue to reside on earth because they have been handed down, by the laying on of hands, generation by generation, to the Apostles as they are called to the Quorum of the Twelve Apostles or the First Presidency. President Nelson taught: "All the keys of the kingdom of God on earth are held by members of the First Presidency and members of the Quorum of the Twelve Apostles. The President of the Church—the senior Apostle—presides over the entire Church and is the only person on earth who exercises all the keys in their fulness. He delegates authority by conferring or authorizing the conferral of keys upon other bearers of the priesthood in their specific offices and callings."[9]

Designated priesthood leaders in The Church of Jesus Christ of Latter-day Saints hold priesthood keys. Each one of these men receives these keys from one authorized to bestow them, with the ultimate on-earth authority being the president of the church. Bishops hold keys necessary to preside over wards and administer ordinances such as baptism, confirmation, Aaronic Priesthood ordinations, and the sacrament. Stake presidents hold keys necessary to preside over stakes, including presiding over the bishops in the stake, and administer ordinances such as Melchizedek Priesthood ordinations. Quorum presidents hold keys to preside over their quorums. Mission presidents hold the keys of convert baptism, and temple presidents hold the keys necessary to perform the ordinances of the temple. When a presiding authority is released from his calling, he no longer holds the keys. In this way, the Church and its ordinances are administered in an orderly fashion, with authority passed down from the president of the church. The Lord's Church is a house of order (see D&C 132:8).

Without priesthood keys, the priesthood authority necessary to administer the ordinances cannot be exercised. For example, the deacon who passes the sacrament on Sunday has the priesthood authority to perform that service, but he can only do so as authorized by the bishop. And he is accountable to the bishop for the worthy and faithful performance of that service.

Like John the Baptist and Peter, James, and John, ancient prophets, such as Adam, Noah, Abraham, and Moses held priesthood keys. Each time the world apostatized from the true gospel of Jesus Christ, those keys were lost, and a restoration became necessary. Such a restoration occurred on the Mount of Transfiguration when Peter, James, and John received the keys of the kingdom. Again, after the death of the Apostles of Jesus Christ, the world apostatized, and a new restoration became necessary.

Even though the keys of the Aaronic and Melchizedek Priesthoods were restored in 1829 and the Church was organized in 1830, additional priesthood keys had yet to be restored to the earth. These additional keys were restored at Kirtland, Ohio, on April 3, 1836, at the end of a full week of heavenly manifestations.

One week before the April 3 event, the Saints had dedicated their first temple, ushering in a new era of temple-building and temple-worship, like the temples of Solomon and Herod of old. On that dedicatory occasion, the Saints had experienced an event much like the Pentecost recorded in Acts. On that March day in 1836, "the Savior made His appearance to some, while angels ministered to others, and it was a Pentecost and an endowment indeed, long to be remembered, for the sound shall go forth from this place into all the world, and the occurrences of this day shall be handed down upon the pages of sacred history, to all generations."[10]

About that occasion, Eliza R. Snow remembered: "The ceremonies of that dedication may be rehearsed, but no mortal language can describe the heavenly manifestations of that memorable day. Angels appeared to some, while a sense of divine presence was realized by all present, and each heart was filled with joy inexpressible and full of glory."[11]

One week later, the Saints were again assembled in the temple with Joseph Smith and Oliver Cowdery. The leaders served the sacrament of the Lord's Supper to the members, and then Joseph and Oliver retired to a place behind the pulpit and closed the veil to pray. After solemn and silent prayer, "the veil was taken from [their] minds, and the eyes of [their] understanding were opened" (D&C 110:1). The Lord appeared to them.

First and foremost, the Lord Jesus Christ, "standing upon the breast-work of the pulpit," appeared and accepted the temple (see D&C 110:2, 7). "Under his feet was a paved work of pure gold, in color like amber. His eyes were as a flame of fire; the hair of his head was white like the pure snow; his countenance shone above the brightness of the sun; and his voice was as the sound of the rushing of great waters, even the voice of Jehovah, saying: I am the first and the last; I am he who liveth, I am he who was slain; I am your advocate with the Father" (D&C 110:2–4).

After identifying Himself, the Lord promised to appear to His servants in the temple, on the condition that the temple was not polluted. Many Saints would rejoice as great blessings would be poured out and the Lord's servants would be endowed. It would be just the beginning of the great blessings (see D&C 110:8–10).

When the vision of the Lord closed, three visions followed. Three heavenly messengers conferred keys on Joseph and Oliver, keys that, along with other keys already received, would allow the kingdom to roll forth in the last days.

The first messenger was Moses, who committed unto Joseph and Oliver "the keys of the gathering of Israel from the four parts of the earth, and the leading of the ten tribes from the land of the north" (D&C 110:11). This ancient prophet, the Lawgiver, needs little introduction. Born of the Hebrews in Egypt, saved as an infant by miraculous means, raised among Egyptian royalty, and banished from Egypt, Moses returned to lead his people out of that land. He led them for forty years in the wilderness, to the borders of the promised land, and was translated, taken unto the Lord without tasting death (see Alma 45:19).

Moses's restoration of the keys of the gathering of Israel began the gathering of the Saints in the last days, as foretold by Isaiah: "And he shall set up an ensign for the nations, and shall assemble the outcasts of Israel, and gather together the dispersed of Judah from the four corners of the earth" (Isaiah 11:12).

With the keys of the gathering of Israel restored, the gathering of the Saints began in earnest, both spiritually and temporally. Israel is being gathered spiritually as those who are lost, who do not comprehend the principles of the gospel, accept the true gospel of Jesus Christ, with its saving covenants and ordinances. The temporal gathering proceeds as the heirs of the house of Israel are gathered to the lands of their inheritance.

The second messenger appearing to Joseph and Oliver was Elias, who "committed the dispensation of the gospel of Abraham, saying that in us and our seed all generations after us should be blessed" (D&C 110:12).

The appearance of Elias to restore the keys of the gospel of Abraham raises two questions: who is Elias, and what is the gospel of Abraham? The answer to the first question has not been clearly revealed. However, we can make some educated observations. The answer to the second question is the Abrahamic covenant.

The best answer to the first question may be that Elias was Noah, the one who stands in authority in the priesthood next to Adam. Joseph Fielding Smith, president of the Quorum of the Twelve Apostles at the time, said in a conference talk in 1960: "Elias came and restored the gospel of Abraham. Who was Elias? That question is frequently asked. Well, Elias was Noah, who came and restored his keys."[12] Yet the LDS Bible Dictionary opines that "a man called Elias apparently lived in mortality in the days of Abraham, who committed the dispensation of the gospel of Abraham to Joseph Smith and Oliver Cowdery."[13]

The word *Elias* has several meanings in the scriptures. It may refer (1) to the prophet Elijah or (2), as a title rather than a name, to a person who prepares the way for the Lord (such as John the Baptist) or restores (such as Jesus Christ did during His earthly ministry). On April 3, 1836, it was a restorative function accomplished by Elias.

A query related to this first question is why did Abraham himself not restore the keys of the gospel of Abraham? The answer may be found in Doctrine and Covenants 132:29, which says that "Abraham . . . hath entered into his exaltation and sitteth upon his throne." If he has been exalted, which is the ultimate promise of the Abrahamic covenant, he may have already begun his own godly pursuits and, therefore, may have already moved beyond his ministry on this earth.

The second question—what is the gospel of Abraham?—is the more important question. Regardless of who delivered the keys, it was so important that the keys of the gospel of Abraham were restored that it occurred at the same time that the keys for the gathering of Israel and the sealing of eternal families were restored. The gospel of Abraham restored to Joseph and Oliver is the Abrahamic covenant.[14]

The third messenger was Elijah. He appeared as prophesied in the Old Testament and restored the sealing power. In the closing verses of the Old Testament, Malachi recorded the words of the Lord concerning the great work of the last days. He prophesied: "Behold, I will send you

Elijah the prophet before the coming of the great and dreadful day of the Lord: And he shall turn the heart of the fathers to the children, and the heart of the children to their fathers, lest I come and smite the earth with a curse" (Malachi 4:5–6).

Elijah the Tishbite lived nine hundred years before Jesus Christ was born. He was a powerful prophet whose life is worth studying. But for our purposes the most prominent feature of his life is that the Lord gave him a distinctive power: the sealing power, the power to bind on earth and have it sealed in heaven. Using this sealing power, he produced a drought—"there shall not be dew nor rain these years"—because of the wickedness of King Ahab and his people (see 1 Kings 17:1). After a drought of three and a half years, Elijah again spoke and produced rain in abundance. Elijah was eventually taken up into heaven without tasting death, and he appeared on the Mount of Transfiguration when priesthood keys were bestowed on Peter, James, and John.

Muslims, Jews, and Christians revere Elijah as a great prophet. The Quran recognizes Elijah as a prophet who opposed the worship of false gods. Jewish Passover observances include reserving a vacant seat and opening the door for Elijah's arrival, which is done as a foreshadowing of his arrival to announce the coming of the Messiah. Some Christians believe that John the Baptist was the Elijah of Malachi's prophecy because John announced the coming of the Messiah. Members of The Church of Jesus Christ of Latter-day Saints, however, believe that Elijah's postmortal mission involved the same activity that took place during his appearance on the Mount of Transfiguration. That activity was the bestowal of keys.

The visions of April 3, 1836, were summed up in the last verse of Doctrine and Covenants 110, which reads: "Therefore, the keys of this dispensation are committed into your hands; and by this ye may know that the great and dreadful day of the Lord is near, even at the door" (D&C 110:16).

John the Baptist restored the keys of the Aaronic Priesthood. Peter, James, and John restored the keys of the Melchizedek Priesthood. Moses restored the keys of the gathering of Israel. Elias restored the keys of the Abrahamic covenant. And Elijah restored the keys of the sealing power. Joseph and Oliver, the first and second elder of the Church, held every key necessary to do the work of the Lord on earth in the latter days. Those keys have been passed down from Apostle to Apostle since the days of Joseph Smith and reside in the living Apostles. The senior living Apostle is authorized to exercise all these keys for the benefit of mankind.

What was lost from the earth has been restored. The authority to perform the saving ordinances, with their associated covenants, again resides on the earth. Consequently, the authorized ordinances performed in The Church of Jesus Christ of Latter-day Saints are effective to save.

The president of the Church possesses and is authorized to exercise all priesthood keys relevant to our mortal existence. But the president cannot perform every ordinance. How, then, can millions of members of the Church receive the saving ordinances from someone authorized to exercise the priesthood in performing the ordinance?

The answer is delegation. The president of The Church of Jesus Christ of Latter-day Saints holds all the keys on the earth, and he delegates keys to other priesthood leaders so they can preside in their areas of responsibility. Presidents of quorums, including bishops and stake presidents, as well as mission and temple presidents hold these delegated keys. Counselors and other leaders do not receive keys, but they receive delegated authority to function in their callings.

Thus, for example, when a missionary goes down into the baptismal font and baptizes a convert by immersion for the remission of sins, that baptism is effective because the mission president, either personally or through one of his mission leaders to whom he has delegated authority, authorized that baptism. The mission president holds the keys of convert baptism, keys which he received when he was set apart by the laying on of hands by someone designated by the First Presidency to pass keys on to the mission president.

When a father who holds the priesthood lays his hands on his twelve-year-old son and ordains him to the Aaronic Priesthood, the ordination is effective because the bishop of the ward authorized the ordination. The bishop holds keys necessary to make that authorization, keys which he received by the laying on of hands, usually by his stake president, who also holds keys and was authorized by the First Presidency to pass keys on to the bishop.

When a sealer at the temple addresses members at the altar of the temple and performs the sealing ordinance, that sealing is effective because the sealer has been authorized by the temple president to perform the sealing. The temple president received the keys associated with temple ordinances when he was set apart by someone designated by the First Presidency to pass keys on to the temple president.

Each saving ordinance performed in The Church of Jesus Christ of Latter-day Saints must be authorized by one holding keys. When so authorized, that ordinance is recognized by God. The delegation of keys makes it possible for these ordinances to occur around the world, twenty-four hours each day, even when the president of the Church sleeps in Salt Lake City.

Therefore, covenants, ordinances, priesthood authority, and priesthood keys are inseparably connected. The joint operation of these principles allows us to make effective sacred covenants with God, covenants that will follow us into eternity and allow us to return to our Father's presence.

Each priesthood holder in The Church of Jesus Christ of Latter-day Saints can trace his priesthood authority back, ordination by ordination over the better part now of two centuries, to the ordination of Joseph and Oliver to the Melchizedek Priesthood by Peter, James, and John.

Authority to perform the saving ordinances rests on the priesthood holders. Therefore, if a convert is baptized into The Church of Jesus Christ of Latter-day Saints and someone asks, as did Paul of the disciples in Ephesus, "Unto what then were ye baptized?" (Acts 19:3), the convert can respond, "In the name of the Lord Jesus" (Acts 19:5).

Endnotes

1. Young, in *Journal of Discourses*, 15:127.
2. *Teachings of the Prophet Joseph Smith*, 263.
3. Ibid., 81–82.
4. *Teachings of the Presidents of the Church: Joseph Smith*, 49.
5. Elijah is called "Elias" in Matthew 17:3–4 (LDS Bible Dictionary, s.v. "Elias," 663).
6. Haight, in Conference Report, Oct. 1980, 107.
7. Nelson, "Keys of the Priesthood," 40.
8. Ibid., 40–41.
9. Ibid., 40.
10. Smith, *History of the Church*, 2:432.
11. Snow, quoted in Quentin L. Cook, "Prepare to Meet God," 114.
12. Smith, in Conference Report, Apr. 1960, 72.
13. LDS Bible Dictionary, s.v. "Elias," 663.
14. See chapter 10 for additional discussion of the Abrahamic covenant.

Chapter 9

PRIESTHOOD COVENANTS

---

*And this greater priesthood administereth the gospel and
holdeth the key of the mysteries of the kingdom, even the key
of the knowledge of God. Therefore, in the ordinances
thereof, the power of godliness is manifest.*

—D&C 84:19–20

Priesthood is the eternal power by which exaltation is attainable. It provides for exaltation and everything that leads to exaltation. The Lord shares this grand power with his children on the earth through priesthood covenants. All covenants the Lord makes with us are priesthood covenants because the priesthood is the power of God to exalt us. Therefore, all who come unto Christ are blessed to make priesthood covenants and receive the blessings promised to the great patriarchs—Abraham, Isaac, and Jacob.

Foreordination

Priesthood covenants have their genesis in the premortal life. There, the faithful were prepared and anointed—foreordained—for future opportunities.

The doctrine of foreordination is simple in its definition. According to Elder Neal A. Maxwell, "[God] chose some individuals before they came here to carry out certain assignments, and hence, these individuals have been foreordained to those assignments."[1]

Joseph Smith taught: "Every man who has a calling to minister to the inhabitants of the world was ordained to that very purpose in the Grand Council of heaven before this world was. I suppose I was ordained to this very office in that Grand Council."[2]

To Jeremiah, the Lord said: "Before I formed thee in the belly I knew thee; and before thou camest forth out of the womb I sanctified thee, and I ordained thee a prophet unto the nations" (Jeremiah 1:5).

Concerning latter-day leaders in the Church of Jesus Christ, the Lord said: "Even before they were born, they, with many others, received their first lessons in the world of spirits and were prepared to come forth in the due time of the Lord to labor in his vineyard for the salvation of the souls of men" (D&C 138:56).

Elder Maxwell warned of the danger of misunderstanding or misapplying the doctrine of foreordination: "The combined doctrine of God's foreknowledge and of foreordination is one of the doctrinal roads least traveled by, yet these clearly underline how very long and how perfectly God has loved us and known us with our individual needs and capacities. Isolated from other doctrines or mishandled, though, these truths can stoke the fires of fatalism, impact adversely upon our agency, cause us to focus on status rather than service, and carry us over into predestination."[3]

Foreordination is not predestination. The doctrine of predestination, promoted by some theologians, is that God has decided in advance and decreed all that has and will happen on earth. In particular, God determined before any of us came to this earth who would be saved and who would not be saved. In other words, agency and covenants are unrelated to exaltation. Brigham Young rejected this doctrine: "It is a mistaken idea that God has decreed all things whatsoever that come to pass, for the volition of the creature is as free as air. . . . We . . . are free to choose or refuse the principles of eternal life."[4]

Brigham Young also commented on the difference between foreordination, which we accept, and predestination, which we reject: "God has decreed and foreordained many things that have come to pass, and he will continue to do so; but when he decrees great blessings upon a nation or upon an individual they are decreed upon certain conditions. . . . God rules and reigns, and has made all his children as free as himself, to choose the right or the wrong, and we shall then be judged according to our works."[5]

We can be confident that God's foreknowledge of our future failures does not limit His love for us. Elder Maxwell wrote that God's foreknowledge "does not cause Christ to give up concerning us without providing us with the opportunity to repent and to follow Him. His foreknowledge rests upon His perfect awareness of our weaknesses and capabilities, while His relentlessly redeeming love makes of Him a true and perfect Shepherd. The Father's entire plan of salvation has taken into account beforehand our prospective successes and failures, so that His plan will be fully executed, and His purposes completely fulfilled through Christ."[6]

President Harold B. Lee made it clear that to be foreordained is not to be predestined. In other words, we retain our agency and can fail to fulfill the calling to which we are foreordained. He said:

> Despite that calling which is spoken of in the scriptures as 'foreordination,' we have another inspired declaration: 'Behold, there are many called, but few are chosen. . . .' (D&C 121:34). This suggests that even though we have our free agency here, there are many who were foreordained before the world was, to a greater state than they have prepared themselves for here. Even though they might have been among the noble and great, from among whom the Father declared he would make his chosen leaders, they may fail of that calling here in mortality. Then the Lord poses this question: " . . . and why are they not chosen?" (D&C 121:34). Two answers were given—First, "Because their hearts are set so much upon the things of this world. . . ." And second, they " . . . aspire to the honors of men" (D&C 121:35).[7]

This conditional nature of foreordination is really no different from the conditional nature of our mortal covenants and priesthood ordinations because, even though we may be baptized, ordained, and endowed in this life, we cannot receive the full blessings of those ordinances without faithfulness. We cannot receive "all that [our] Father hath," the ultimate reward of a loving Heavenly Father, unless we are faithful (see D&C 84:33, 38).

An example of not only foreordination but also premortal roles can be found in the Book of Abraham, where the Lord teaches Abraham about the eternal nature of spirits and their premortal existence with God. The Lord tells Abraham that, among the intelligences that God made his spirit children, there were many who excelled and became "noble and great ones" (Abraham 3:22). The role of these noble and great spirits was to participate as a council in creating the earth, led by the greatest among those noble and great ones—Jesus Christ. The role also included the call to be rulers in the Church, in God's kingdom on the earth. The Lord reveals to Abraham that Abraham was one of those who sat in council as a noble and great one. But "sat in council" may be an inadequate description, for the Lord tells Abraham that these noble and great ones participated in creating the earth as a place for spirits to prove their faithfulness to God (see Abraham 3:23–25).

The book of Abraham specifically mentions only two members of the premortal council of noble and great ones: Jesus Christ and Abraham. But that list is expanded greatly in modern scripture. In his Vision of the Redemption of the Dead, President Joseph F. Smith (the nephew of Joseph Smith) was taught that others were "among the noble and great ones who were chosen in the beginning to be rulers in the Church of God" (D&C 138:55). Many of these additional council members are likely suspects, such as many of the prophets (Adam, Abel, Seth, Noah, Shem, Abraham, Isaac, Jacob, Moses, Isaiah, Ezekiel, Daniel, Elias, and Malachi) (see D&C 138:38–46). The list does not include the name of every participant but refers to "many more, even the prophets who dwelt among the Nephites" (D&C 138:49). Though not named by President Smith as members of that council, Enoch, Peter, James, John, Paul and other noble spirits must have been there too.

This council of noble and great ones who participated in creating the earth included not only valiant sons of God but also valiant daughters of God, including "our glorious Mother Eve, with many of her faithful daughters who had lived through the ages and worshiped the true and living God" (D&C 138:39). "Gender is an essential characteristic of individual premortal, mortal, and eternal identity and purpose."[8] And I cannot imagine such an important creative council functioning optimally without the unique and complementary talents and contributions of Mother Eve and her faithful daughters.

Latter-day saints found a place on this great council: Joseph Smith, Hyrum Smith, Brigham Young, John Taylor, and Wilford Woodruff were named. But President Smith also included as noble and great ones "other choice spirits who were reserved to come forth in the fulness of times to take part in laying the foundations of the great latter-day work, including the building of the temples and the performance of ordinances therein for the redemption of the dead" (D&C 138:53–54). This last category—latter-day saints who build temples and perform ordinances for the dead—is huge, both in number and significance. To think that many of us who do temple work for our ancestors participated in the great councils of heaven is truly inspiring and perspective-building.

While we can gain a basic understanding of foreordination in this life, a full comprehension of the subject is inhibited by the veil, by our mortal inability to know and fully comprehend what is outside the mortal experience. Elder Maxwell cautioned against using this lack of full comprehension as a reason to reject foreordination: "When we mortals try to comprehend, rather than accept, foreordination, the result is one in which finite minds futilely try to comprehend omniscience. A full understanding is impossible; we simply have to trust in what the Lord has told us, knowing enough, however, to realize that we are not dealing with *guarantees* from God but extra *opportunities*—and heavier responsibilities. If those responsibilities are in some ways linked to past performance or to past capabilities, it should not surprise us."[9]

We were foreordained or preselected because of our premortal faith and good works (see Alma 13:3). If foreordination were based solely on God's foreknowledge, everyone who was foreordained or preselected would unfailingly achieve that status in this life because God's foreknowledge of our failures as well as our successes is perfect and complete. But our foreordination or preselection came as a result of our premortal faithfulness. Alma taught that those who receive the Melchizedek Priesthood were foreordained not just "according to the foreknowledge of God" but also "on account of their exceeding faith and good works" in the premortal life. Of this, Elder Maxwell said: "Alma speaks about foreordination with great effectiveness and links it to the foreknowledge of God and, perhaps, even to our previous performance (Alma 13:3–5)."[10]

Elder Bruce R. McConkie summarized the doctrine of foreordination. Speaking of the call of President Spencer W. Kimball and his counselors to the First Presidency, he said:

> May I say that there is no chance in the call of these brethren to direct the Lord's work on earth. His hand is in it. He knows the end from the beginning. He ordained and established the plan of salvation and decreed that his everlasting gospel should be revealed to man in a series of dispensations commencing with Adam and continuing to Joseph Smith. And he—the Almighty—chooses the prophets and apostles who minister in his name and present his message to the world in every age and dispensation. He selects and foreordains his ministers; he sends them to earth at the times before appointed; he guides and directs their continuing mortal preparations; and he then calls them to those positions they were foreordained to receive from before the foundations of the earth.[11]

This doctrine raises questions about those who do not receive the Melchizedek Priesthood in the latter days. Were those who (1) did not have the opportunity to receive the Melchizedek Priesthood in this life, but (2) will eventually fully embrace those covenants in the spirit world, when given that opportunity, foreordained to receive the priesthood? I cannot see any other answer than yes. Is God's foreknowledge limited to our mortal lives? Absolutely not. Does the fact that some will not embrace priesthood covenants until first given that opportunity in the spirit world necessarily make them less valiant in the premortal life? I cannot believe that. They are just as eligible for exaltation as those who embraced the priesthood covenants in mortal life. Else why do we perform all of the saving ordinances for them in the temple? And God, who knows the end from the beginning, foreknew even those facts—that some who did not have the opportunity to embrace and magnify priesthood covenants in this life would do so in the spirit world and thus be exalted.

The statement that those who receive and magnify the Melchizedek Priesthood in this mortal life have that opportunity "on account of their exceeding faith and good works" in the premortal life does not logically preclude that there are others who had faith, did good works, and will receive and magnify the Melchizedek Priesthood hereafter. The statement does not exclude others. It is merely a statement that those who are "ordained priests after his holy order" in mortal life were foreordained in the premortal life to that high and holy calling.

The context of Alma's teachings on foreordination helps us understand why Alma did not include in his statement about foreordination those who might receive the priesthood after this life. Alma's sermon was to the Ammonihahites, a people who had rejected the fundamentals of the gospel. Alma taught them that they were in the "snare of the adversary" (Alma 12:6), that our words, works, and thoughts will condemn us if we are not careful (see Alma 12:14), that hell awaits those who persist in sin (see Alma 12:16–18), that this life is a time to prepare to meet God (see Alma 12:24), that nevertheless there is a plan for salvation and they must turn to the Son for remission of sins and redemption (see Alma 12:32–34).

In this context, Alma delved into the plan of salvation, including priesthood and foreordination. Just as men who are ordained to the Melchizedek Priesthood in this life were foreordained with that holy calling in the premortal life, Jesus Christ was chosen and ordained in the premortal life to be our Savior. That was the ultimate point of Alma's sermon.

The "manner" of the calling of priesthood holders is that they were called and prepared in the premortal life because of "their exceeding faith and good works" (Alma 13:3). So also was Jesus Christ chosen because of His exceeding faith and good works—faith and good works that exceeded all others. He is the "great prototype" of foreordination.[12] Therefore, seeing faithful priesthood holders should remind the faithful that there is one great foreordained priest, the Savior Himself, who can save them from their sins. Even though Jesus Christ had not yet been born when Alma gave his sermon, the faithful knew they could look forward to Him for remission of their sins.

In Hebrews we learn that "all those who are ordained unto this priesthood are made like unto the Son of God, abiding a priest continually" (JST, Hebrews 7:3). "Now these ordinances were given after this manner, that thereby the people might look forward on the Son of God, it being a type of his order, or it being his order, and this that they might look forward to him for a remission of their sins, that they might enter into the rest of the Lord" (Alma 13:16).

In a study of covenants, foreordination plays an important role. We lived before this life, and we made choices there that prefigured our choices here. It therefore raises the question of whether foreordination involved covenants. Did we participate as a party with God in the act of foreordination? Yes. Was foreordination involuntary? It could not be. That is not God's way. Even in the premortal life we were agents to act and not to be acted upon. Exceeding faith and good works in the premortal life gave us the opportunity to agree with God to be foreordained or to be preselected for any particular role He had for us in this life.

Jesus Christ is the perfect example of this principle. "And the Lord said: Whom shall I send? And one answered like unto the Son of Man: Here am I, send me. And another answered and said: Here am I, send me. And the Lord said: I will send the first" (Abraham 3: 27). The Savior, with His consent, was thus foreordained to His role.

The premortal covenant between God the Father and the Son is reflected in the Great Intercessory Prayer of Jesus before He suffered in the garden and on the cross. He prayed: "Father, the hour is come; glorify thy Son, that thy Son also may glorify thee. As thou hast given him power over all flesh, that he should give eternal life to as many as thou hast given him. And this is life eternal, that they might know thee the only true God, and Jesus Christ, whom thou hast sent. I have glorified thee on the earth: I have finished the work which thou gavest me to do. And now, O Father, glorify thou me with thine own self with the glory which I had with thee before the world was" (John 17:1–5).

Jesus "verily was foreordained before the foundation of the world" (1 Peter 1:20). He is "the Lamb slain from the foundation of the world" (Revelation 13:8). He said: "I am he who was prepared from the foundation of the world to redeem my people. Behold, I am Jesus Christ. I am the Father and the Son. In me shall all mankind have life, and that eternally, even they who shall believe on my name, and they shall become my sons and my daughters" (Ether 3:14).

In the same manner of foreordination as Jesus Christ was called to be the Savior and Redeemer of all mankind, Melchizedek Priesthood holders were "called and prepared from the foundation of the world according to the foreknowledge of God, on account of their exceeding faith and good works; in the first place being left to choose good or evil; therefore they having chosen good, and exercising exceedingly great faith, are called with a holy calling, yea, with that holy calling which was prepared with, and according to, a preparatory redemption for such" (Alma 13:3).

And this principle and premortal covenant is not limited to men. President Kimball told the women of the Church: "Remember, in the world before we came here, faithful women were given certain assignments while faithful men were foreordained to certain priesthood tasks. While we do not now remember the particulars, this does not alter the glorious reality of what we once agreed to."[13]

Sheri L. Dew related this directly to motherhood: "Just as worthy men were foreordained to hold the priesthood in mortality, righteous women were endowed premortally with the privilege of motherhood."[14]

And President Russell M. Nelson concurred: "In premortal realms, we brethren were foreordained for our priesthood responsibilities. Before the foundation of the world, women were prepared that they may bear children and glorify God."[15]

Not only was Jesus foreordained in the premortal life to be the Christ, but He was also our Savior even then. The Atonement He suffered is infinite, reaching back in time and forward in time. Priesthood ordination has a similar eternal aspect, reaching back in time and forward in time. Elder Orson Pratt described this aspect of ordination reaching back in time with respect to Joseph Smith. He noted the principle that "without [priesthood ordinances] no man can see the face of God, even the Father, and live" (D&C 84:22). However, when God the Father and the Son appeared to Joseph Smith in the Sacred Grove, Joseph was only fourteen years old and had not received the priesthood ordinances. According to Elder Pratt, however, Joseph was foreordained in the premortal life. "He was not without the Priesthood in reality; but was a man chosen, a man ordained, a man appointed from before the foundation of this world . . . ; he could see the face of God the Father and live."[16]

Our foreordination or preselection is manifested not only in priesthood ordination but also in the lineage into which we are born. We are of the seed of Abraham through Israel, disbursed through the many peoples of the earth as leaven in bread. President George Q. Cannon said: "There are men in this Church from almost every race of men, and if representatives from all the races are not now, they will be in. God scattered the seed of Israel through all the nations of the earth, so that in the great gathering of the last days He might be able to get representatives of all the families of men. And we are chosen for this purpose."[17]

Jesus told His disciples that He had already prepared their place in the eternal realms: "Then shall the King say unto them on his right hand, Come, ye blessed of my Father, inherit the kingdom prepared for you from the foundation of the world" (Matthew 25:34). King Benjamin taught his people that they were God's people and that God's reward for His people's righteousness was waiting for them: "The righteous, the saints of the Holy One of Israel, they who have believed in the Holy One of Israel, they who have endured the crosses of the world, and despised the shame of it, they shall inherit the kingdom of God, which was prepared for them from the foundation of the world, and their joy shall be full forever" (2 Nephi 9:18). And Moroni, quoting the Lord, tied these eternal blessings directly to the mortal lineage of Israel: "Come unto me, O ye house of Israel, and it shall be made manifest unto you how great things the Father hath laid up for you, from the foundation of the world" (Ether 4:14).

The doctrine of foreordination extends even to exaltation. "Thus," wrote Elder McConkie, "'the noble and great ones,' who were chosen before they were born (Abra. 3:22–23), who were foreordained to have exaltation, are the ones whom God hath called in this life to be glorified through the gospel in due course."[18]

As in premortal life, so in this life: exceeding faith and good works qualify us to make sacred covenants with God—covenants that will eventually qualify us for exaltation, a reward prepared for us before we even came to this earth, if we continue faithful.

The Oath and Covenant of the Priesthood

Jesus chose and ordained His Twelve Apostles (see John 15:16), and the Apostles passed on priesthood authority by the laying on of hands (see Acts 6:5–6.) This method of transmitting priesthood authority was followed in ancient times. For example, Moses laid hands on Joshua and gave him a charge to serve the children of Israel as Moses had served them (see Numbers 27:18–23). Likewise, we confer priesthood authority today by the laying on of hands by one who has the authority to confer the priesthood. "We believe that a man must be called of God, by prophecy, and by the laying on of hands by those who are in authority, to preach the Gospel and administer in the ordinances thereof" (Articles of Faith 1:5).

All worthy male members of the Church are eligible to receive the priesthood. A young man may receive the Aaronic Priesthood in the year he turns twelve years old, and the young men may be ordained to the offices of teacher and priest in the years they turn fourteen and sixteen years old, respectively. The Aaronic Priesthood is a preparatory priesthood, an appendage to the Melchizedek Priesthood, and is conferred upon a man or young man to prepare him to receive the Melchizedek Priesthood.

Among the most significant revelations of the last dispensation, or of any dispensation, is the oath and covenant of the priesthood, preserved for us in the Doctrine and Covenants. It reveals to us the priesthood agreement between God and man, the agreement by which man may become like God. In nine short verses, it sets forth the Lord's expectations and then pronounces the reward if we are faithful and the concomitant consequence if we are not faithful. It encapsulates the unique Latter-day Saint vision of priesthood authority and its relationship to potential exaltation.

The oath and covenant begins with what the Lord expects in this covenant arrangement, what we must do to receive the blessings later promised. The Lord promises that the Spirit will sanctify us and renew our bodies, remarkable blessings even without considering the glorious blessings promised later in the revelation. "For whoso is faithful unto the obtaining these two priesthoods of which I have spoken, and the magnifying their calling, are sanctified by the Spirit unto the renewing of their bodies" (D&C 84:33).

The two priesthoods are the Aaronic and Melchizedek priesthoods, which can be referred to as separate priesthoods because of their separate offices and duties. But they can also be referred to as one sole priesthood, as is the case later in the revelation, because the Aaronic Priesthood is a part of the Melchizedek Priesthood.

Our commitment is to magnify our calling in the priesthood. President Thomas S. Monson defined this commitment: "It means to build it up in dignity and importance, to make it honorable and commendable in the eyes of all men, to enlarge and strengthen it to let the light of heaven shine through it to the view of other men. And how does one magnify a calling? Simply by performing the service that pertains to it."[19]

After the initial promises and blessings, the revelation turns to the effect of living up to the covenant made—what the priesthood bearer *becomes* as a result of faithfulness in obtaining and magnifying the priesthood.

"They become the sons of Moses and of Aaron and the seed of Abraham, and the church and kingdom, and the elect of God" (D&C 84:34). The "sons of Moses and Aaron" are those who are ordained to the priesthood, not necessarily just the literal seed of Moses and Aaron, who were Levites.[20] They participate in blessings akin to heirship by virtue of their ordination, even if they are not literal heirs in the body. We similarly refer to all modern-day members of The Church of Jesus Christ of Latter-day Saints as the heirs of the pioneers who braved persecution and hardship to preserve for those of us who came along later the blessings of the restored gospel and the culture of faithfulness.

The "seed of Abraham" has to do with the Abrahamic covenant. The phrase refers to the Lord's promise to Abraham that his seed would bear the priesthood and that the whole earth would be blessed by the priesthood ministry of Abraham's seed (see Abraham 2:9–11; Genesis 22:18). It also refers to becoming an heir of eternal life.

The oath and covenant makes this point more explicitly when it provides that those who receive and magnify the priesthood will receive everything that our Heavenly Father has (see D&C 84:38), including "thrones, kingdoms, principalities, and powers, dominions, all heights and depths" (D&C 132:19). They receive eternal life and "continuation of the seeds forever and ever" (D&C 132:19).

Becoming "the church and kingdom, and the elect of God" (D&C 84:34), is the goal of committed priesthood holders. They are the Lord's servants, His agents, who carry the gospel to the earth and offer sacred covenants to others.

This covenant between Melchizedek Priesthood holders and the Lord includes an express oath. The Lord swears an oath that, if the priesthood holder keeps the covenant, "all that my Father hath shall be given unto him" (D&C 84:38). "All those who receive the priesthood, receive this oath and covenant of my Father, which he cannot break, neither can it be moved" (D&C 84:40).

President Joseph Fielding Smith explained why this is an oath: "The covenant on the Lord's part is that if man does as he promises, then all that the Father hath shall be given unto him; and this is such a solemn and important promise that the Lord swears with an oath that it shall come to pass."[21]

On the other hand, the priesthood holder who does not keep the covenant and "altogether turneth therefrom" will not have forgiveness (D&C 84:41). The responsibility of taking upon us this covenant cannot be fully avoided. The Lord declares "wo" to those who refuse to enter into the covenant (D&C 84:42). President Marion G. Romney said: "With such a penalty prescribed for breaking it, one might be prompted to question the advisability of accepting the obligations of the covenant; that is, he might question it until he reads the verse which follows the statement of the penalty. There he learns that those who do not receive the oath and covenant are not *much*, if any, better off than those who receive it and break it. For in that verse the Lord says: 'And wo unto all those who come not unto this priesthood which ye have received' (D&C 84:42)."[22]

The Seed of Abraham

The oath and covenant promises the faithful that they may become the seed of Abraham. That promise is, in its fulness, a promise of exaltation.

There are several facets of the Abrahamic covenant, the covenant God made with Abraham and which is passed along to his descendants. Many of those facets have to do with having mortal posterity, inheriting lands, and taking the priesthood and the gospel to others. But my focus here is on the facet of the Abrahamic covenant promising eternal increase, which is the promise of eternal life.

Brigham Young described this ultimate blessing of eternal increase: "There will be no end to the increase of the faithful. What a pleasing thought! We shall enjoy each other's society in purity, in holiness and in the power of God, and no time will ever come when we may not enjoy this. Such great happiness is beyond the comprehension of mortals."[23] And we receive these blessings because we are "of Abraham" (D&C 132:30–31).

Understanding the greatness of Abraham goes a long way toward understanding why such wondrous blessings were promised to him and his seed. Abraham was a descendant of Noah's son Shem, who was saved on the ark during the flood. Between the time of the flood and Abraham's day, only about four hundred years passed, which is roughly equal to the passing of four hundred years for us since the latter part of the sixteenth century or early part of the seventeenth century. Thus, Abraham was to Shem and Noah as we are today to Christopher Columbus and the early European settlers on the American continents. Nine generations separated Abraham from Shem (see Genesis 11:10–32).

Not all modern scholars are convinced that Abraham was an actual person. Many of them prefer the theory that Abraham was a construct of a later time. They argue that the stories of Abraham and the other patriarchs were created much later to support faith. Contrary to these modern-day theorists, however, Latter-day Saints believe that Abraham was a real person and that the scriptural accounts of him are literal. In other words, we believe in the historicity (the historical authenticity) of the accounts of Abraham in the scriptures.

What made Abraham great? We have some clues in the scriptures. He opposed pervasive wickedness as a young man (see Abraham 1:5). He received the priesthood from Melchizedek (see D&C 84:14). Most well-known was Abraham's willingness to sacrifice his son Isaac to obey the voice of the Lord (see Genesis 22:1–14). But we have all known people who are faithful and many who have sacrificed for the Lord and for others in the name of the Lord. Those actions alone did not make Abraham who he was. The answer lies in premortal life and foreordination. He became a noble and great one before he came to this earth. His faithfulness and sacrifice were a continuation of his pattern of loyalty to God which he established long before his mortal birth. Abraham's response to the test of his faith was evidence of his greatness, of what he had become.

Elder Parley P. Pratt said: "Now, Abraham, by his former superiority of intelligence and nobility, by his former election before the world was, and by conducting himself in this world so as to obtain the renewal of the same according to the flesh, brought upon his posterity, as well as upon himself, that which will influence them more or less to the remotest generations of time, and in eternity."[24]

The Lord promised Abraham that his seed would have eternal life.[25] But all may become Abraham's seed by adoption. The Lord told Abraham: "For as many as receive this Gospel shall be called after thy name, and shall be accounted thy seed, and shall rise up and bless thee, as their father" (Abraham 2:10).

Adoption

Adoption is a concept I feel I understand. As it relates to the Abrahamic covenant, it is similar to the legal concept we are familiar with.

In my parents' family, there are nine children—five of whom are adopted. Before I was born, my parents were married in the temple and had two sons who died at or around childbirth. After the second son died, my parents adopted my older brother. So when I was born naturally to my parents, I had one living older brother. My younger brother was born naturally two years later, and I grew up as the middle brother in a family of three sons. That is how it stood when, as a nineteen–year-old, I left on my two-year mission.

Even before I left the Missionary Training Center in Provo, my parents had adopted another infant son and had him sealed to them. He had severe chromosomal difficulties, however, and lived only eleven months. My parents cared for him for those months, nursing him through many physical challenges.

After this newly adopted son passed away, my parents adopted three more children—a boy and two girls, completing our family of nine children. So I left on my mission with two living brothers and returned two years later with three living brothers and two sisters. Over the years, my older adopted brother and my biological brother passed away, which makes me the oddball biological child of my parents in a family of four living children.

In the case of each of my adopted brothers and sisters, legal processes were invoked to create a parent–child relationship in the eyes of the law. More important, though, is that, also in each case, my parents went to the temple and had my adopted brothers and sisters sealed to them. The last three to be adopted were sealed to my parents in the same sealing room of the Oakland Temple, immediately preceding my marriage to Kim. They came in, dressed in white, and were sealed to my parents by our former stake president, who had been called as a temple sealer.

As a result of the legal proceedings and the temple ordinances, there is no difference between my relationship with our parents and the relationship of my adopted brothers and sisters with our parents, except that our parents' medical history is more relevant to me. When they were legally adopted, they became children of my parents in the eyes of the law. When they were sealed to my parents, they became children of my parents eternally, promised all the same blessings I enjoy as one born in the covenant. Temporally and eternally, we are familial equals.

President Nelson said these concepts also apply to the house of Israel, who are the seed of Abraham: "Some of us are the literal seed of Abraham; others are gathered into his family by adoption. The Lord makes no distinction."[26]

The Apostle Paul also taught this concept, specifying baptism as the point of adoption: "For as many of you as have been baptized into Christ have put on Christ. There is neither Jew nor Greek, there is neither bond nor free, there is neither male nor female: for ye are all one in Christ Jesus. And if ye be Christ's, then are ye Abraham's seed, and heirs according to the promise" (Galatians 3:27–29).

Making and keeping sacred covenants identifies us as the seed of Abraham, whether or not we were born as literal descendants of Abraham. As President Nelson declared: "At baptism we covenant to serve the Lord and keep His commandments. When we partake of the sacrament, we renew that covenant and declare our willingness to take upon ourselves the name of Jesus Christ. Thereby we are adopted as His sons and daughters and are known as brothers and sisters. He is the father of our new life. Ultimately, in the holy temple, we may become joint heirs to the blessings of an eternal family, as once promised to Abraham, Isaac, Jacob, and their posterity. Thus, celestial marriage is the covenant of exaltation."[27]

Rather than being exclusive, the seed of Abraham is inclusive, just as inclusive as we individually desire it to be. "Through the Atonement of Christ, *all* mankind may be saved, by obedience to the laws and ordinances of the Gospel" (Articles of Faith 1:3; italics added). When we make covenants and obtain ordinances, we are numbered with the house of Israel, with Abraham's descendants, even if we are Gentiles, not literally descended from Abraham. Mormon commanded, "Hearken, O ye Gentiles, and hear the words of Jesus Christ. . . . Come unto me, and be baptized in my name, that ye may receive a remission of your sins, and be filled with the Holy Ghost, that ye may be numbered with my people who are of the house of Israel" (3 Nephi 30:1–2).

In His willingness to make covenants, the Lord does not discriminate. He offers the opportunity to all.

In the days long ago when Jesus walked in Palestine, the Jews and the Samaritans despised each other. They both descended from the house of Israel, but the Samaritans had intermarried with the Gentiles and their religion had been contaminated by pagan rituals. The Jews resented the Samaritans because the Samaritans claimed to be the children of Jacob (Israel) and the Jews considered the Samaritans more unclean than other Gentiles, even though they were cousins. So the Jews avoided the Samaritans, even refusing to interact with them.

The Jews lived to the north and the south, and the Samaritans in the middle. When Jews, especially Galileans like Jesus, wanted to travel from Jerusalem in the south to Galilee in the north, they most often traveled an extra day to go around, rather than through, Samaria.

Early in His ministry, Jesus Christ taught in Jerusalem. Then He decided to return to Galilee where He had grown up in the town of Nazareth. Instead of traveling the extra day to go around Samaria, Jesus took His Apostles straight through the middle. At noon on their day of travel through Samaria, Jesus and His Apostles stopped at Jacob's Well, close to the town of Sychar. This was the land that the great patriarch Jacob gave to his son Joseph as an inheritance.

Tired from His morning of travel, Jesus rested at the well while He sent His Apostles into town to purchase food for the travelers. As Jesus waited there, a Samaritan woman came to the well with her water jar to fetch water. Having no means to draw water from the deep well Himself, Jesus asked the woman for a drink. It must have been startling to the woman, as she recognized Jesus as a Jew. While traditions of hospitality in this arid land required that she share her water, she was hesitant to interact with this Jew.

She inquired why a Jew would ask a Samaritan woman for a drink. Jesus answered her in language that we understand today but which she did not understand. He said: "If thou knewest the gift of God, and who it is that saith to thee, Give me to drink; thou wouldest have asked of him, and he would have given thee living water" (John 4:10).

Using the very appropriate metaphor of life-giving water, Jesus was telling this Samaritan woman that what Jesus had to offer her was eternal life. But the woman didn't understand. She noticed that Jesus had no bucket or cord to draw water from the deep well, and she wondered how He could get any kind of water.

Jesus soon changed the subject and, knowing that the unmarried woman was living with a man, asked her to go get her husband. She said she had no husband, and Jesus revealed to her that He knew of her living arrangements. She was impressed and wondered if He was a prophet, and she proclaimed her belief that a Messiah would come. To this, Jesus answered plainly that He was the Messiah.

Eastern orthodox tradition holds that this woman, whom they call Photina, was converted to the gospel and was instrumental in bringing many others to a knowledge of the truth. But regardless of whether she actually repented and followed Jesus, this story illustrates Jesus's willingness to love and teach everyone, not just those who were like Him. It also shows that Jesus's love for the Samaritan woman was not diminished by His knowledge that she was a sinner. He treated her with love and respect and invited her to drink of the water of eternal life.

In the latter-day Church, we strive to be like Jesus. We all belong here. We all need to be here. We need the ordinances; we need the sacrament to renew our covenants. Although we try to be good, we "all have sinned, and come short of the glory of God" (Romans 3:23). "If we say that we have no sin, we deceive ourselves, and the truth is not in us" (1 John 1:8).

To those who may *feel* different, among us you are not "strangers and foreigners, but fellowcitizens with the saints, and of the household of God" (Ephesians 2:19). We are not perfect at making everyone feel loved and accepted, but it is our desire to improve and we ask for your patience and love.

President Dallin H. Oaks said: "As difficult as it is to live in the turmoil surrounding us, our Savior's command to love one another as He loves us is probably our greatest challenge."[28]

To God, there is no favored race or nationality; only the righteous are favored (see 1 Nephi 17:35). President Joseph Fielding Smith said: "Those who are not literal descendants of Abraham and Israel must *become* such, and *when they are baptized and confirmed they are grafted into the tree and are entitled to all the rights and privileges as heirs.*"[29] It is baptism and faithfulness, not race or nationality, that entitles us to the blessings of Israel.

When the Jews tried to claim favored status, John the Baptist told them: "Think not to say within yourselves, We are the children of Abraham, and we only have power to bring seed unto our father Abraham; for I say unto you that God is able of these stones to raise up children into Abraham" (JST, Matthew 3:36). We become favored of God by the covenants we individually make and keep with him. "For they are not all Israel, which are of Israel" (Romans 9:6). "They which are the children of the flesh, these are not the children of God: but the children of the promise are counted for the seed" (Romans 9:8).

We who have made sacred covenants are more alike than we are different. We are members of God's church on earth. We are in the middle of a difficult mortal test to prove whether we will do what God commands (see Abraham 3:25).

There is one way in which we are all alike, and it is the most important defining characteristic that any of us possesses. It is that we are children of God. Every difference pales in comparison to that equality.

The blessings of the great oath and covenant of the priesthood therefore belong to all. It is available for those who desire it and show that desire by making and keeping sacred covenants. President Nelson said:

> The greatest compliment that can be earned here in this life is to be known as a covenant keeper. The rewards for a covenant keeper will be realized both here and hereafter. Scripture declares that "ye should consider on the blessed and happy state of those that keep the commandments of God. For behold, they are blessed in all things, . . . and if they hold out faithful to the end they are received into heaven . . . [and] dwell with God in a state of never-ending happiness."[30]

Nephi explained the favored status of the righteous to his brothers Laman and Lemuel when they complained that Lehi had taken them from their comfortable lives in Jerusalem to bear the hardships of the wilderness. Nephi said that the Jews were ripening for destruction, like other civilizations before them. For that reason, the Lord directed righteous Lehi to take his family and flee (see 1 Nephi 17:43–44). And Jerusalem was soon destroyed (see 2 Nephi 1:4).

In his explanation to his brothers, Nephi used the example of the people who possessed the promised land when the children of Israel, after their forty years of wandering in the wilderness, were led to that land. When the children of Israel arrived, led by the Lord to the promised land, the Lord commanded them to "utterly destroy" the people who were already there: "Thou shalt save alive nothing that breatheth" (Deuteronomy 20:16). Why such treatment?

Nephi explained that they were destroyed because they were wicked: "And after [the children of Israel] had crossed the river Jordan he did make them mighty unto the driving out of the children of the land, yea, unto the scattering them to destruction. And now, do ye suppose that the children of this land, who were in the land of promise, who were driven out by our fathers, do ye suppose that they were righteous? Behold, I say unto you, Nay. Do ye suppose that our fathers would have been more choice than they if they had been righteous? I say unto you, Nay" (1 Nephi 17:32–34).

On another occasion, Nephi told his people that the Lord makes covenants with us not because of our heritage but instead because we repent: "As many of the Gentiles as will repent are the covenant people of the Lord; and as many of the Jews as will not repent shall be cast off; for the Lord covenanteth with none save it be with them that repent and believe in his Son, who is the Holy One of Israel" (2 Nephi 30:2). Commenting on this passage, President Oaks said: "The Book of Mormon promises that all who receive and act upon the Lord's invitation to 'repent and believe in his Son' become 'the covenant people of the Lord' (2 Nephi 30:2). This is a potent reminder that neither riches nor lineage nor any other privileges of birth should cause us to believe that we are 'better one than another' (Alma 5:54; see also Jacob 3:9). Indeed, the Book of Mormon commands, 'Ye shall not esteem one flesh above another, or one man shall not think himself above another' (Mosiah 23:7)."[31]

We are the covenant people because the Lord has made covenants with us, and He makes covenants with us because we have faith and repent. Being righteous and making and keeping sacred covenants with God qualifies us for the blessings of Abraham, Isaac, and Jacob as the seed of Abraham.

Endnotes

1. Maxwell, "Meeting the Challenges of Today," 157.
2. *Teachings of the Prophet Joseph Smith*, 365.
3. Maxwell, "Meeting the Challenges of Today," 155.
4. *Discourses of Brigham Young*, 55.
5. Ibid.
6. Maxwell, *Even as I Am*, 56.
7. Lee, in Conference Report, Oct. 1973, 7.
8. "The Family: A Proclamation to the World" (1995).
9. Maxwell, "Meeting the Challenges of Today,"160, italics in original.
10. Ibid., 156.
11. McConkie, in Conference Report, Apr. 1974, 101.
12. Ibid., 102.
13. *Teachings of the Presidents of the Church: Spencer W. Kimball*, 215–16.
14. Dew, "Are We Not All Mothers?," 96.
15. Nelson, "Roots and Branches," 29
16. Pratt, in *Journal of Discourses*, 22:29–30.
17. Cannon, in *Journal of Discourses*, 22:129.

18. McConkie, *Doctrinal New Testament Commentary*, 3:328.
19. Monson, in Conference Report, Oct. 1999, 66.
20. Smith, *Doctrines of Salvation*, 3:93.
21. Smith, in Conference Report, Apr. 1970, 59.
22. Romney, in Conference Report, Oct. 1980, 64, emphasis in original.
23. Young, in *Journal of Discourses*, 10:5.
24. Pratt, in *Journal of Discourses*, 1:259.
25. Nelson, "Covenants," *Ensign*, 87–88.
26. Ibid., 88.
27. Ibid.
28. Oaks, "Loving Others and Living with Differences," 28.
29. Smith, *Doctrines of Salvation*, 3:246, italics in original.
30. Nelson, "Covenants," *Ensign*, Nov. 2011, 88–89.
31. Oaks, "All Men Everywhere," *Ensign*, May 2006, 79.

PART III

PROGRESSING TOWARD PERFECTION

Chapter 10

THE ATONEMENT
OF JESUS CHRIST

*And he shall go forth, suffering pains and afflictions
and temptations of every kind; and this that the word
might be fulfilled which saith he will take upon him the
pains and the sicknesses of his people. And he will take upon
him death, that he may loose the bands of death which
bind his people; and he will take upon him their infirmities,
that his bowels may be filled with mercy, according to the
flesh, that he may know according to the flesh how to succor
his people according to their infirmities.*

—Alma 7:11–12

The great Jehovah promised in the premortal life that He would atone for our sins. And He perfectly kept His promise by coming to mortality, where He descended below all things and suffered and died for our sins. The Atonement of Jesus Christ activates the plan of salvation by making it possible for us to be exalted even though we live this life imperfectly, which would otherwise disqualify us from dwelling in the presence of our Father. We chose to follow our Father's plan in the premortal life because of our faith that Jesus Christ would suffer for our sins and make it possible for us to return to our Father. And we continue to make and keep covenants in this life for the same reason, because we have faith that we may be saved through the Atonement of Jesus Christ.

The Necessity for Atonement

If making and keeping sacred covenants with God is like getting on and staying on the right train so that we can reach our desired destination of eternal life, then the Atonement of Jesus Christ is the locomotive. Without the Atonement, we could make no progress toward eternal life; there would be no way for us to get any closer to eternal life, no matter how long we stayed on the train of covenants. The Atonement is not only the locomotive, but also the track, because it marked the path to eternal life. It is also the factory where the train and track were created because we would not even be here in mortality and have the possibility of progressing toward eternal life without the Atonement. This life would have had no point, no reason, no object. Without the Atonement of Jesus Christ, our Heavenly Father would not have sent us here. Every aspect of the train analogy except boarding the right train and staying on it, which comprises our agency, is the Atonement of Jesus Christ.

In a book about sacred covenants, the centerpiece is the Atonement of Jesus Christ. It is the same with any discussion about the gospel and the plan of salvation.

With our limited memories, we are tempted to believe that the Atonement of Jesus Christ is merely a happenstance, that we are naturally doomed to death and annihilation, but that we are fortunate that the Savior happened to suffer and die for us. The truth is that the Atonement of Jesus Christ is not happenstance; instead, it is a very favorable term of our contract, our covenant, with our Heavenly Father and our Savior. When we agreed to follow Jesus and submit to the Father's plan for our salvation and happiness, the Lord made the unalterable commitment to provide a Savior.

The Atonement of Jesus Christ is the focal point of the eternities. Everything that occurred before the Atonement pointed forward to it; everything that has occurred and will occur after it hearkens back to it. Without the Atonement, there would have been no purpose in our being spiritually begotten by our Heavenly Parents; there would have been no purpose in creating the earth or coming to mortality. Without the Atonement, there would be no reason to obtain ordinances in this life or to make covenants with our Father. With the Atonement, there is purpose and reason in life.

Our afflictions are consecrated to our gain. Our efforts to be worthy are rewarded. Our covenants with God are meaningful and potentially exalting. Because Jesus atoned for us, we have hope of celestial glory.

Because of the Atonement, all who come to mortality will die but be resurrected with a perfect body. "The spirit and the body shall be reunited again in its perfect form; both limb and joint shall be restored to its proper frame" (Alma 11:43). Because of the Atonement, all have the possibility for exaltation. The decision is entirely up to each person, but exaltation is possible only because our Lord and Savior suffered for us in Gethsemane and suffered again and died for us on the cross at Calvary.

The Savior's Covenant with His Father

Jesus Christ suffered for the sins and infirmities of the world because, as premortal Jehovah, He covenanted with His Father to do so. After Satan presented his plan in opposition to the Father in the council in heaven, Jehovah, in the words of President John Taylor, "addressed the Father, and instead of proposing to carry out any plan of his own, knowing what His Father's will was, said, 'Thy will be done;' I will carry out thy plans and thy designs, and, as man will fall, I will offer myself as an atonement according to thy will, O God. Neither do I wish the honor, but thine be the glory;' and *a covenant was entered into* between Him and His Father, in which He agreed to atone for the sins of the world; and He thus . . . became the Lamb slain from before the foundation of the world."[1]

In the revelation given to Abraham concerning the premortal council, the Lord said:

> And there stood one among them that was like unto God, and he said unto those who were with him: We will go down, for there is space there, and we will take of these materials, and we will make an earth whereon these may dwell; and we will prove them herewith, to see if they will do all things whatsoever the Lord their God shall command them; and they who keep their first estate, shall be added upon; and they who keep not their first estate, shall not have glory in the same kingdom with those who keep their first estate; and they who keep their second estate, shall have glory added upon their heads for ever and ever. (Abraham 3:24–25)

Jehovah could carry out the Atonement precisely because He was "like unto God." He had attained a status both with the Father and with us to merit the trust and faith that He surely *would* make the atoning sacrifice. The Father knew it because He had perfect knowledge of the future event. We, on the other hand, had to have faith that He would carry out the great sacrifice, allowing us to be exalted.

In one magnificent sentence, President Taylor described why we desperately need Jesus Christ: "In the event of man having his free will and being subject to the power of temptation, the weakness of the flesh, the allurements of the world, and the powers of darkness, it was known that he must necessarily fall, and being fallen, it would be impossible for him to redeem himself, and that, according to an eternal law of justice, it would require an infinite, expiatory atonement to redeem man, to save him from the effects and ruin of the Fall, and to place him in a condition where he could again be reinstated in the favor of God, according to the eternal laws of justice and mercy; and find his way back to the presence of the Father."[2]

All of our hopes and dreams of eternal life rely on the covenant that Jehovah, the Son, made with Elohim, the Father. Mormon spoke for all of us when he wrote to his son: "And what is it that ye shall hope for? Behold I say unto you that ye shall have hope through the atonement of Christ and the power of his resurrection, to be raised unto life eternal, and this because of your faith in him according to the promise" (Moroni 7:41).

Here, Mormon refers to the promise that "through the Atonement of Christ, all mankind may be saved, by obedience to the laws and ordinances of the Gospel" (Articles of Faith 1:3). Referring to Mormon's teaching, Elder Neal A. Maxwell said: "Ultimate hope, of course, is tied to Jesus and the great Atonement, with its free gift of the universal Resurrection and the proffer of God's greatest gift, eternal life."[3] And Elder Dieter F. Uchtdorf added: "Hope is a gift of the Spirit. It is a hope that through the Atonement of Jesus Christ and the power of His Resurrection, we shall be raised unto life eternal and this because of our faith in the Savior."[4]

Gethsemane and Calvary

The Lord's mortal life lasted thirty-three years. Born of God to the virgin Mary in Bethlehem, he grew up in Nazareth, where He "increased in wisdom and stature, and in favour with God and man" (Luke 2:52). His public ministry lasted just three years, from His baptism by John in the Jordan River to His Last Supper with His Apostles. He ministered to the people, called priesthood leaders, gave them keys, and taught His everlasting gospel.

His *ministry* complete and His *message* delivered, it was time for Him to complete His *mission*—the mission for which He had been prepared from before the foundation of the world. He was, after all, first and foremost "the Lamb slain from the foundation of the world" (Revelation 13:8). He was the One the Father determined to send (see Abraham 3:27). He covenanted to atone for our sins. What He agreed to do surely would be done, but now was the time.

Jesus went into the Garden of Gethsemane with His eleven faithful Apostles. He left eight of them and took Peter, James, and John with Him until he "began to be sorrowful and very heavy" (Matthew 26:37). He said to them: "My soul is exceeding sorrowful, even unto death: tarry ye here, and watch with me" (Matthew 26:38). The awful pain of the Atonement had begun to descend upon the Son of God.

Leaving Peter, James, and John, who must have been exhausted from the emotional and dangerous proceedings of the past week in Jerusalem, Jesus went by Himself about as far as a rock could be thrown before He fell on His face in the garden and prayed using the familial title "Abba," similar to "Papa" in English: "Abba, Father, all things are possible unto thee; take away this cup from me: nevertheless not what I will, but what thou wilt" (Mark 14:36; Matthew 26:39). Returning to the spot where He had left His three chief Apostles, Jesus found them sleeping. He said: "Peter, What, could ye not watch with me one hour?" (Matthew 26:40). Twice more Jesus returned to His solitary place in the garden and prayed to His Father to let the cup pass from Him. Twice more He recognized that He must do the Father's will and suffer, concluding His prayer with "thy will be done." And twice more He returned to find His chief Apostles sleeping, oblivious to the monumental agony being felt close by (see Matthew 26:42–45).

As Jesus suffered in Gethsemane, His "sweat was as it were great drops of blood" (Luke 22:44). An angel appeared to Him from heaven and strengthened Him (see Luke 22:43). But it was Jesus alone who had to bear the full burden. "He [suffered] temptations, and pain of body, hunger, thirst, and fatigue, even more than man can suffer, except it be unto death; for behold, blood [came] from every pore, so great [was] his anguish for the wickedness and the abominations of his people" (Mosiah 3:7).

Thus the Atonement began in earnest in Gethsemane. President Joseph Fielding Smith explained:

> I think it is understood by many that the great suffering of Jesus
> Christ came through the driving of nails in His hands and in His feet,

and in being suspended upon a cross, until death mercifully released Him. That is not the case. As excruciating, as severe as was that punishment, coming from the driving of nails through His hands and through His feet, and being suspended, until relieved by death, yet still greater was the suffering which He endured in carrying the burden of the sins of the world—my sins, and your sins, and the sins of every living creature. This suffering came before He ever got to the cross, and it caused the blood to come forth from the pores of his body, so great was that anguish of His soul, the torment of His spirit that He was called upon to undergo.[5]

Rising from His suffering in the garden, Jesus returned to His Apostles and left the garden. The leaders of the Jews and the Roman guards took Him. Peter wanted to defend Him, boldly wielding a sword and striking the high priest's servant. But Jesus would not allow it. He reproved Peter and immediately healed the injury.

Through the night, Jesus was illegally and unjustly tried, falsely accused. But He would not defend himself; He could not defend himself, because He was greater than they all. They could not have had power over Him without His willing submission.

Sentenced to die by the leaders of the Jews, with the approval of Pilate, the Roman governor, Jesus was taken to Calvary and crucified between two thieves. Roman soldiers drove nails through His hands and feet and lifted Him up on the cross. Along with the excruciating physical suffering of crucifixion, the full pain and anguish He felt in Gethsemane returned.

On the cross, Jesus cried to His Father, this time using the more formal "Eloi," meaning "my Lord," "why hast thou forsaken me?" (Mark 15:34). Never in His life had Jesus done anything to distance Himself from His Father. He was perfect, and He reaped the benefit of that perfection, enjoying a closeness with God the Father. But now, on the cross, that closeness was gone. He had to feel *every* pain caused by our unrighteousness, and perhaps for Him the most excruciating pain was the withdrawal of the Father. It is a condition so grave that we call it spiritual death. And it is a condition Jesus felt—such terrible spiritual pain to go along with the momentous physical and mental pain He endured.

Finally, Jesus Christ, the great Jehovah, must have known that the ultimate price had been paid, the debts were extinguished, and His mission was accomplished. He said, "It is finished, thy will is done" (JST, Matthew 27:54). No one could take His life from Him because He is the Son of God. But, having suffered all the pain, abandonment, and every other conceivable negative feeling relating to mortality and imperfection, He knew that He must now voluntarily and willingly lay down His life. So He succumbed, and His spirit left His body.

Elder Jeffrey R. Holland wrote:

> The Atonement of Jesus Christ is the foreordained but voluntary act of the Only Begotten Son of God. He offered his life, including his innocent body, blood, and spiritual anguish as a redeeming ransom (1) for the effect of the Fall of Adam upon all mankind and (2) for the personal sins of all who repent, from Adam to the end of the world. Latter-day Saints believe this is the central fact, the crucial foundation, the chief doctrine, and the greatest expression of divine love in the plan of salvation. The Prophet Joseph Smith declared that all 'things which pertain to our religion are only appendages' to the atonement of Christ.[6]

The effect of the Atonement of Jesus Christ is both retroactive and prospective. It is retroactive not only because it pertained to humans who preceded Jesus Christ in mortality but also to our premortal life. In a revelation given to Joseph Smith, the Lord said that we were born innocent twice: (1) when we were spiritually born and (2) when we were physically born: "Every spirit of man was innocent in the beginning; and God having redeemed man from the fall, men became again, in their infant state, innocent before God" (D&C 93:38). Because we had agency and sinned in the premortal life, we could not have been born innocent into this life unless there was a redemption from our premortal sins—a preparatory redemption. This preparatory redemption was discussed by Alma. He said that, in the premortal life, we were empowered to choose between good and evil, which required a preparatory redemption so that we could be born into this life innocent and pure (see Alma 13:3).

We know that the choices we made in the premortal life, though generally good, were not as good as the choices that Jesus Christ made, resulting in His godhood. Yet we are born innocent into this world. Brigham Young said on several occasions that we were born pure and clean into this life: "The spirits that live in these tabernacles were pure as the heavens, when they entered them."[7]

Elder Holland drew together the Atonement of Jesus Christ and the covenants we make with God by noting that, because we rely on the Atonement for salvation, we are indebted to the Savior, and what He requires is a life of discipleship. He said:

As a consequence of the Atonement, we need not be in subjection to the devil, but we must be willing, as Jacob taught, to "become subject unto [Christ]." What that subjection means does not involve anything slavish or restrictive nor does it require any payment of money or worldly gifts. What that subjection means, what these people choosing redemption "owe" to Christ, their new master, is a life of discipleship, beginning with faith, repentance, and baptism and leading on to all the ordinances and covenants of the gospel and a life of loving kindness. Clearly all of humankind is still in debt even after the full effect of the Atonement has transpired. But fortunately he to whom we are indebted is Christ the Merciful rather than Lucifer the Miserable. We still have obligations, but they are of a much higher and happier sort. We are in debt, but we are not in bondage.[8]

With His Atonement, Jesus Christ fulfilled the solemn covenants He made with the Father and with us in the premortal life. President Taylor wrote: "The plan, the arrangement, the agreement, the covenant was made, entered into and accepted before the foundation of the world; it was prefigured by sacrifices, and was carried out and consummated on the cross."[9]

Our faith in Jesus Christ—the faith we showed by accepting the Lord's plan and believing that Jehovah would provide a way for us to be redeemed from our sins—was not in vain. His is the perfect example of a covenant made and kept. In the same way, we must make and keep covenants, which will allow us to enjoy the full blessings of the Atonement of Jesus Christ.

Now Their King He Shall Be Known

Joseph Smith said that "Jesus [is] the Mediator of the new covenant."[10] President Joseph Fielding Smith added that "the new and everlasting covenant is the sum total of all gospel covenants and obligations."[11] It is "new" in the sense that it was restored to Joseph Smith in the latter days, and it is "everlasting" because it existed before our lives here and will exist forever.[12]

Our Father sent His Son to die that we might live. "For God so loved the world that he gave his only begotten Son, that whosoever believeth in him should not perish, but have everlasting life" (John 3:16). And doing so was not a gratuity but fulfillment of the covenant the Father made with us before we came to earth.

This covenant relationship permeates our religious experience. As members of The Church of Jesus Christ of Latter-day Saints, we do not use the crucifix in making covenants or in performing ordinances, despite our deep belief in and reliance on the Atonement of Jesus Christ and our acknowledgment that the crucifix can be a powerful symbol. An explanation of this peculiarity in our worship highlights how we feel about the Savior and how we relate to Him, how we covenant with Him.

Before sunset on the Friday of His crucifixion, the Lord's mortal body was taken down from the cross and hastily laid in the tomb owned by Joseph of Arimathea. The third day after the crucifixion, Sunday, some of the women, Jesus's friends, came to the tomb to prepare His body properly for burial. They discovered that the stone covering the entry to the tomb had been rolled away. Inside the tomb, an angel told them: "He is not here, but is risen" (Luke 24:6).

Mary Magdalene wept at the tomb, not yet understanding the resurrection. She saw Jesus, but thought it was the gardener and asked, "Sir, if thou have borne him hence, tell me where thou hast laid him, and I will take him away." Jesus said to her, "Mary." And she recognized Him. Jesus told her, "Touch me not; for I am not yet ascended to my Father" (John 20:15–17).

Later the same day, Jesus appeared to ten of the Apostles, excluding Judas, who had betrayed Jesus and then taken his own life, and Thomas, who was simply absent. The appearance was miraculous because the Apostles were in a closed room when Jesus came and stood in their midst. But He showed them that He had a body of flesh and bone, with the prints in His hands and the wound in His side. Thomas doubted the other Apostles' story. But eight days later, Jesus again appeared to the Apostles, this time with Thomas present, and Thomas added his witness to the testimony of the other Apostles, saying, "My Lord and my God" (John 20: 28).

After forty days of ministering to His disciples in Palestine, Jesus went with the Apostles to the Mount of Olives. As the Apostles watched, Jesus ascended into heaven. Two angels appeared and said, "Ye men of Galilee, why stand ye gazing up into heaven? this same Jesus, which is taken up from you into heaven, shall so come in like manner as ye have seen him go into heaven" (Acts 1:11).

Later, Jesus appeared to the inhabitants of the American continent, and ministered to them for several days. On that occasion, Jesus said:

> Behold, I am Jesus Christ the Son of God. I created the heavens and the earth, and all things that in them are. . . . And as many as have received me, to them have I given to become the sons of God; and even so will I to as many as shall believe on my name, . . . Behold, I have come unto

the world to bring redemption unto the world, to save the world from sin. Therefore, whoso repenteth and cometh unto me as a little child, him will I receive, for of such is the kingdom of God. Behold, for such I have laid down my life, and have taken it up again; therefore repent, and come unto me ye ends of the earth, and be saved. (3 Nephi 9:15, 17, 21–22)

Jesus was not dead; He was very much alive, even immortal.

For many years, however, the heavens were closed because of the wickedness of man. Within a short time after the crucifixion and resurrection of Jesus Christ, priesthood authority was lost from the earth, and, without the guidance of living prophets and apostles, the Christian world was plunged into spiritual darkness. As Isaiah foresaw, they "transgressed the laws," "changed the ordinance," and broke "the everlasting covenant" (Isaiah 24:5).

Finally, in 1820, the heavens were opened once more. Young Joseph Smith went into a grove to pray concerning which church he should join. He described what happened: "I saw a pillar of light exactly over my head, above the brightness of the sun, which descended gradually until it fell upon me. . . . When the light rested upon me I saw two Personages, whose brightness and glory defy all description, standing above me in the air. One of them spake unto me, calling me by name and said, pointing to the other— This is My Beloved Son. Hear Him!" (Joseph Smith—History 1:16–17).

Sixteen years later, after (1) the translation of the Book of Mormon, (2) the restoration of the Church of Jesus Christ as it existed at the time of Christ, and (3) the construction of the first temple in this dispensation, the Savior came to His temple on April 3, 1836, in connection with the restoration of priesthood keys (see D&C 110:4). These postmortal appearances of Jesus Christ establish that He lives. We do not focus on the crucifix in our worship of Jesus Christ because He is not there on the cross; neither is He in the tomb. He is risen. He reigns in the heavens. Elder Quentin L. Cook said that "while we rejoice in the supernal significance of Gethsemane and Calvary, our focus has always been on the resurrected Lord."[13]

The resurrection of Jesus Christ was just as important to us as His suffering and death. Without His resurrection, we could not be resurrected. "For since by man came death, by man came also the resurrection of the dead. For as in Adam all die, even so in Christ shall all be made alive" (1 Corinthians 15:21–22). I think most of us are familiar with that scripture from First Corinthians, but perhaps not with the next four verses: "But every man in his own order: Christ the firstfruits; afterward they that are Christ's at his coming. Then cometh the end, when he shall have delivered up the kingdom to God, even the Father; when he shall have put down all rule and all authority and power. For he must reign, till he hath put all enemies under his feet. The last enemy that shall be destroyed is death" (1 Corinthians 15:23–26).

As Alma the Younger prophesied: "Yea, every knee shall bow, and every tongue confess before him. Yea, even at the last day, when all men shall stand to be judged of him, then shall they confess that he is God; then shall they confess, who live without God in the world, that the judgment of an everlasting punishment is just upon them; and they shall quake, and tremble, and shrink beneath the glance of his all-searching eye" (Mosiah 27:31).

The testimony of Jesus Christ and the truth of His restored gospel is obtained by the witness of the Holy Ghost. Yet there are also outward evidences that this church is the true Church of Jesus Christ. One of those evidences is the similarity of The Church of Jesus Christ of Latter-day Saints to the primitive Christian Church, soon after the death and resurrection of Jesus Christ. The focus of those early saints was also on the resurrected Christ rather than the crucifix.

Frederic Farrar, an English Bible scholar, studied the question of why the primitive Saints, those living just after the time of Jesus Christ, did not preserve a record of where all the events of the life of Christ took place. Farrar's explanation highlights the similarities between how we worship and how the primitive saints worshipped.

Farrar wrote:

> That the sites where events took place which have swayed the whole temporal and eternal destinies of the human race could have been forgotten, might well seem passing strange; but the earliest generations of believers, in the days of primitive Christianity, attached no importance to localities or relics. The Lord Christ was to them far less the human Jesus, who, for one brief lifetime, had moved among men, than He was the Risen, the Eternal, the Glorified Christ, their Lord and their God. They habitually contemplated Him, not as on the Cross, but as on the Throne; not as the humiliated sufferer, but as the King exalted far above all heavens. They never regarded Him as *taken away* from them, but on the contrary as *nearer to them* than He had been while on earth even to the disciple whom He loved, and who bowed his head upon His breast. So far from being *absent from them*, He was, as He had expressly taught, ever *with them* and *within them*. To minds pervaded by such thoughts, the scenes of His *earthly* pilgrimage were comparatively as nothing.[14]

As did the primitive Saints, we worship Him as a living, redeeming, glorified God, not as a perpetual sufferer.

Elder Parley P. Pratt, one of the early latter-day Apostles, penned the words of one of our sacrament hymns:

> Jesus, once of humble birth,
> Now in glory comes to earth.
> Once he suffered grief and pain;
> Now he comes on earth to reign.
> Once a meek and lowly Lamb,
> Now the Lord, the great I Am.
> Once upon the cross he bowed;
> Now his chariot is the cloud.
> Once he groaned in blood and tears;
> Now in glory he appears.
> Once rejected by his own,
> Now their King he shall be known.
> Once forsaken, left alone,
> Now exalted to a throne.
> Once all things he meekly bore,
> But he now will bear no more.[15]

Never again will He sleep in an animal's manger while others luxuriate at the inns.

Never again will He flee to Egypt to escape the murderous intent of a wicked king.

Never again will He be taken before a tribunal of sinners to be judged for offending them.

Never again will He be spit upon and fitted with a crown of thorns.

Never again will He submit to cruel lashing and painful assaults.

Never again will He be laden with His own cross and paraded to His death.

Never again will He be nailed to a cross and suffer death.

Never again will He be burdened with our every sin, every grief, and every pain, and descend below all things.

It is finished.

Now their King He shall be known.

Forever, our King, our Savior and Redeemer, He shall be known— Christ, the Mediator of the New Covenant.

Endnotes

1. Taylor, *Mediation and Atonement of Our Lord and Savior Jesus Christ*, 97; italics added.
2. Ibid., 96.
3. Maxwell, "Plow in Hope," 60.
4. Uchtdorf, "The Infinite Power of Hope," 21.
5. Smith, in Conference Report, Apr. 1944, 50.
6. *Encyclopedia of Mormonism*, s.v. "Atonement of Jesus Christ," 1:82–83.
7. *Discourses of Brigham Young*, 51.
8. Holland, *Christ and the New Covenant*, 231.
9. Taylor, *Mediation and Atonement of Our Lord and Savior Jesus Christ*, 171.
10. *Teachings of the Prophet Joseph Smith*, 12.
11. Smith, *Doctrines of Salvation*, 1:156, emphasis omitted.
12. *Encyclopedia of Mormonism*, s.v. "New and Everlasting Covenant," 3:1008.
13. Cook, "We Follow Jesus Christ," 84.
14. Farrar, *The Life of Lives: Further Studies in the Life of Christ*, 276–277; italics in original.
15. Pratt, "Jesus, Once of Humble Birth," in *Hymns of The Church of Jesus Christ of Latter-day Saints*, no. 196.

Chapter 11

REPENTANCE, MERCY,
AND RESTORATION

---

*Whosoever repenteth, and hardeneth not his heart, he shall
have claim on mercy through mine Only Begotten Son, unto
a remission of his sin.*

—Alma 12:34

Making covenants with God, by itself, does not exalt us. It merely
puts us on the path toward exaltation. By making a covenant, we
board the train to eternal life. But inevitably we sin. We stray from
the path. We get on the wrong train. Blessedly, the Atonement of Jesus Christ
accounts for our imperfection and allows us to get back on the path, to board
the right train again. The process by which we make that adjustment, by which
we accept the offer of the Savior's atoning sacrifice, is repentance. Like making
the covenant in the first place, accepting the redeeming power of the Atonement of Jesus Christ is another exercise of free will. By continually exercising
our free will consistent with God's will, we become like Him. We become His.

Justice and Mercy

Mercy is what we hope to receive when we repent. It can be understood only in the context of justice. The eternal principles of justice and
mercy, working together, can facilitate our journey to eternal life. But neither of them, alone, can help us.

To be just is to be right with the law. God is just; He is perfectly right with the law. His perfect justice is so basic to His being that He would not be God if He were not just.

Justice requires punishment for sin. "Justice claimeth the creature and executeth the law, and the law inflicteth the punishment; if not so, the works of justice would be destroyed, and God would cease to be God" (Alma 42:22). Justice also requires that a blessing must be bestowed for obedience to God's laws. It is perfectly so and perfectly predictable.

The eternal justice of God is not to be confused with the justice meted out by human governments, as with criminal proceedings. Criminal law certainly makes an attempt at justice, but the law and the institution are both imperfect, making the attempt to do justice fall short of perfection. For example, what is the perfect punishment for a crime? Legislators and voters tangle with that question unceasingly. At times, it is politically correct to make terms of punishment more severe; at other times the expediency of politics dictates less severe punishment. And each case is treated differently—whether to investigate a crime, whether to prosecute a crime, whether to engage in plea bargaining with the accused, how to prosecute the crime, and what punishment to impose. It is entirely possible that two similar individuals who commit a crime together will receive very different outcomes, ranging from no conviction to many years in prison or even death. To the unbiased onlooker, any human criminal justice system can seem arbitrary and unpredictable even if the actors in the criminal justice system try their best to achieve justice.

On the other hand, God's justice is neither arbitrary nor unpredictable. His is the perfect rule of law. "There is a law, irrevocably decreed in heaven before the foundations of this world, upon which all blessings are predicated. And when we obtain any blessing from God, it is by obedience to that law upon which it is predicated" (D&C 130:20–21).

We should want it no other way because justice is what lends predictability to our lives. How miserable life would be if we could not predict the consequences of our actions. Arbitrary consequences would completely disrupt any plans we might have for the future. In our everyday lives, we rise in the morning, seek nourishment for our bodies, try to treat others with charity, do the necessary work with hope of sufficient recompense to support ourselves, and lie down again at night to rest. What chaos would ensue if gravity did not attract, if eating did not nourish, if being sociable produced no friendly relationships, if work did not pay, and if resting did not refresh?

We predictably obtain blessings by obeying God's laws. That predictability is the basis of our faith. We express our faith in God by being obedient to His laws because we predict that obedience will invoke blessings and will draw us closer to God.

Justice and predictability go hand in hand. Predictability in the law of the land, even if the predictably is not as dependable as with God's laws, enables us to order our lives. If there is no justice, the law is unstable. If the law is unstable, changing at the whim of the tyrant, or even at the too-frequent shift in the will of the people, we lose the capacity to act with a predictable end in mind. Through the ages, courts have recognized the need to maintain predictability and, with some exceptions, have insisted on deciding similar cases the same way sometimes for no better reason than to ensure that individuals will be able to act knowing what the outcome will be. Deciding similar cases the same way over time is called *stare decisis*, meaning that the principles of law on which a court rested a previous decision must be followed again if the facts are substantially the same. The California Supreme Court, in a case in which one of the parties argued for an approach to the law different from the approach that had been taken before, declined to adopt a new and different approach, saying: "This is so parties can 'regulate their conduct and enter into relationships with reasonable assurance of the governing rules of law.'"[1]

Elder D. Todd Christofferson explained that this need for predictability is a necessary prerequisite to agency: "Choice . . . requires law, or predictable outcomes. We must be able by a particular action or choice to cause a particular outcome or result—and by the opposite choice create the opposite outcome. If actions don't have fixed consequences, then one has no control over outcomes and choice is meaningless."[2] He continued: "We need the justice of God—a system of fixed and immutable laws that He Himself abides by and employs—so that we can have and exercise agency. This justice is the foundation of our freedom to act and is our only path to ultimate happiness."[3]

We are not perfect at prediction. We may not fully understand the laws of nature or the complicated business and personal relationships involved in our decisions. And the fact that others will exercise their agency in unpredictable ways may render our best predictions unrealized. But with God, we can depend on ultimate predictability—that is, our obedience to His laws will eventually result in blessings, while disobedience will eventually result in pain and suffering. God "is the same yesterday, today, and forever; and the way is prepared for all men from the foundation of the world, if it so be that they repent and come unto him" (1 Nephi 10:18). "Jesus Christ [is] the same yesterday, and to day, and for ever" (Hebrews 13:8). "For do we not read that God is the same yesterday, today, and forever, and in him there is no variableness neither shadow of changing?" (Mormon 9:9). "He cannot walk in crooked paths; neither doth he vary from that which he hath said; neither hath he a shadow of turning from the right to the left, or from that which is right to that which is wrong; therefore, his course is one eternal round" (Alma 7:20). It takes faith, but the faithful soul can fully depend on the favorable consequences, the blessings, of obeying God's law.

God's justice allows us to have hope. Alma counseled his people to be humble and prayerful and to be led by the Spirit, that they might have faith on the Lord and "a hope that ye shall receive eternal life" (Alma 13:29).

Because God cannot vary from His promises and because He is perfectly just, we will receive the promised blessings if we obey. For the same reasons, punishment will be inflicted if we choose the path of sin. Those two aspects of justice are inseparable. Without the possibility of punishment, there can be no possibility of reward. Without one, the other is not operative.

But, while God is just, He is also merciful. That is important because we are not perfect and ultimately deserve punishment. We "all have sinned, and come short of the glory of God" (Romans 3:23). Likewise, if we say we can avoid justice, the truth is not in us and punishment lies in our future, if not in our present. Because we have sinned and are not perfect, we cannot qualify for God's kingdom, the celestial kingdom, on our own merit. "No unclean thing can dwell with God; wherefore, ye must be cast off forever" (1 Nephi 10:21).

This is where mercy enters to satisfy the demands of justice. The punishment for our sins must be inflicted, but in God's merciful plan there is a perfect proxy to receive that punishment. The sacrifice of God's beloved Son potentially satisfies the demands of justice. But there is a condition: because God will not force us to accept the Son's suffering, we must exercise our agency and accept that suffering for our sins. The way we accept that suffering is by repenting.

"Whoso repenteth and is baptized in my name shall be filled; and if he endureth to the end, behold, him will I hold guiltless before my Father at that day when I shall stand to judge the world" (3 Nephi 27:16). "No unclean thing can enter into his kingdom; therefore nothing entereth into his rest save it be those who have washed their garments in my blood, because of their faith, and the repentance of all their sins, and their faithfulness unto the end" (3 Nephi 27:19). In other words, the only way to be clean and qualify for exaltation is to be washed clean by the Atonement of Jesus Christ. There is no other way.

Elder Christofferson commented on this need for something that would take from us the taint of (and eternal punishment for) sin, something that would allow us to enter into the celestial kingdom despite our imperfection in this life. He said: "We really cannot look to the law or to justice to preserve and perfect us when we have broken the law. So being just, but also being motivated by love, our Heavenly Father created mercy. He did this by offering as propitiation for our sin His Only Begotten Son, a Being who could, with His Atonement, satisfy justice, putting us right with the law so that it is once again supporting and preserving us, not condemning us."[4]

"Redemption cometh in and through the Holy Messiah; for he is full of grace and truth. Behold, he offereth himself a sacrifice for sin, to answer the ends of the law, unto all those who have a broken heart and a contrite spirit; and unto none else can the ends of the law be answered" (2 Nephi 2:6–7).

The topic of justice and mercy reminds me of an incident I witnessed years ago as a young lawyer in Nevada. I was working for the Nevada Supreme Court, and I attended a session of the Nevada Board of Pardons. Nevada has an unusual system for determining whether a person should be pardoned after that person has been convicted of a crime. Instead of giving the pardoning power to the chief executive, as do most states, like the United States which gives the pardoning power to the president, Nevada gives that power to a board consisting of the governor, the state attorney general, and all five of the justices of the Nevada Supreme Court. Particularly for the justices of the supreme court, the duty to sit as members of the Board of Pardons is unusual and uncomfortable because the justices are so committed to and comfortable with enforcing the rule of law, seeing that justice is done. The Board of Pardons is all about whether to grant mercy, whether to pardon a convicted person of crimes or whether to commute the sentence of a convicted person. Commuting a sentence usually means that the conviction still stands, but the prisoner no longer is required to serve prison time.

On the occasion I witnessed, the Board of Pardons was assembled in the chambers of the Nevada Supreme Court. One by one, convicted felons presented their cases to the board, usually through an attorney appointed to advocate on their behalf. For the most part, the Board of Pardons was not granting much clemency that day. Finally, a prisoner was wheeled into the courtroom in a wheelchair. He was young, perhaps in his thirties, but he was obviously unwell. His attorney stood and explained to the board that he had been convicted of murder and was serving a life sentence, but that he had AIDS and was not expected to live much longer. The plea to the board was for a commutation of his sentence so that he could leave prison and die in his mother's home.

Once the attorney completed his presentation, it was the Board of Pardon's responsibility to vote publicly whether to grant or deny clemency. Beginning with the state attorney general, his vote was to grant. Next to vote was the most junior justice of the Nevada Supreme Court. "Grant," he said. After that, each of the remaining four justices, ending with the chief justice, voted to grant a commutation of the prisoner's sentence so that he could go home and die.

At this point in the solemn and hushed proceedings, I was surprised that a woman who had been sitting behind me rose and, sobbing, began thanking the Board of Pardons for allowing her to take her son home and let him die in her arms. It was a heart-wrenching, emotional scene. Everyone in the courtroom was affected. But there was something that everyone in that courtroom knew, except for the prisoner's mother. It was that the governor would be the last to vote, and he held a veto. No matter whether all of the other members of the board voted to grant clemency, the governor's vote to deny clemency would end the matter in denial. Not only that, but everyone in the courtroom, except for the prisoner's mother, knew that this governor had never before granted clemency under those circumstances—to release a convicted murderer from prison. All eyes, including my own, were on the governor. I saw him squirm and struggle in his chair, with a look of resentment that the mother had put him in this uncomfortable situation. Finally, in a low, subdued voice, the governor voted, "Grant."

I include this story not to show how the Savior exercises His mercy but instead to contrast His bestowal of mercy. Our Savior offers mercy freely and willingly. With everything He has suffered and everything He stands for, He offers to grant clemency, to take upon Himself our sins and to suffer their effects, which suffering He has already felt. But we must accept that offer. We must accept the Savior's offer of clemency by repenting, simple as that. We need not worry that He will be unwilling to grant mercy; He is willing, ready, and capable. But He will not force us to repent. He will not force us to heaven. It is for us to decide.

Abinadi described how the Savior grants clemency at the judgment when we have repented. He said that the Savior "stand[s] betwixt [the repentant sinners] and justice; having . . . taken upon himself their iniquity and their transgressions, having redeemed them, and satisfied the demands of justice" (Mosiah 15:9).

Because of the Savior's offer to stand between us and justice, we must choose. Alma the Younger explained the choice to his son Corianton: "O my son, whosoever *will* come *may* come and partake of the waters of life freely; and whosoever *will not* come the same is *not compelled* to come; but in the last day it shall be restored unto him according to his deeds. If he has desired to do evil, and has not repented in his days, behold, evil shall be done unto him, according to the restoration of God" (Alma 42:27–28; italics added).

Even if we desire exaltation, justice will not allow it unless mercy somehow intercedes. We invoke God's mercy by repenting.

Repentance

Because repentance is our way of accepting the Atonement of Jesus Christ, which is His offer of mercy, so that we, though imperfect in this life, can eventually qualify for eternal life, it is crucial for us to know how to repent and to find the will to repent.

King Benjamin warned of the consequences of not repenting in this life: "Therefore if that man repenteth not, and remaineth and dieth an enemy to God, the demands of divine justice do awaken his immortal soul to a lively sense of his own guilt, which doth cause him to shrink from the presence of the Lord, and doth fill his breast with guilt, and pain, and anguish, which is like an unquenchable fire, whose flame ascendeth up forever and ever. And now I say unto you, that mercy hath no claim on that man; therefore his final doom is to endure a never-ending torment" (Mosiah 2:38–39).

"Repentance," we are told in the Church's *True to the Faith* reference work, "is much more than just acknowledging wrongdoings. It is a change of mind and heart that gives you a fresh view about God, about yourself, and about the world. It includes turning away from sin and turning to God for forgiveness. It is motivated by love for God and the sincere desire to obey His commandments."[5]

Repentance isn't so much the erasure of sins (although it has that effect) as it is the changing of the heart. What is a carnal and sinful heart must become a converted heart, a Christ-like heart. As we exercise our agency to receive ordinances, we also exercise our agency to repent and come unto Jesus Christ. There is no compulsion.

The unrepentant sinner naturally degenerates to a state of wickedness. "For the natural man is an enemy to God, and has been from the Fall of Adam" (Mosiah 3:29). "To be carnally minded is death" (Romans 8:6). And "the natural man receiveth not the things of the Spirit of God: for they are foolishness unto him: neither can he know them, because they are spiritually discerned" (1 Corinthians 2:14). "But remember that he that persists in his own carnal nature, and goes on in the ways of sin and rebellion against God, remaineth in his fallen state and the devil hath all power over him. Therefore he is as though there was no redemption made, being an enemy to God; and also is the devil an enemy to God" (Mosiah 16:5). "Mercy hath no claim on that man; therefore his final doom is to endure a never-ending torment" (Mosiah 2:39).

Repentance, on the other hand, turns the heart to God and activates God's mercy. "Whosoever repenteth, and hardeneth not his heart, he shall have claim on mercy through mine Only Begotten Son, unto a remission of his sins" (Alma 12:34). "Mercy claimeth the penitent" (Alma 42:23).

In the last chapter of the Book of Mormon, Moroni admonished us to repent and explained the blessings of doing so:

> Yea, come unto Christ, and be perfected in him, and deny your-selves of all ungodliness; and if ye shall deny yourselves of all ungodli-ness, and love God with all your might, mind and strength, then is his grace sufficient for you, that by his grace ye may be perfect in Christ; and if by the grace of God ye are perfect in Christ, ye can in nowise deny the power of God. And again, if ye by the grace of God are perfect in Christ, and deny not his power, then are ye sanctified in Christ by the grace of God, through the shedding of the blood of Christ, which is in the covenant of the Father unto the remission of your sins, that ye become holy, without spot. (Moroni 10:32)

Repentance is no temporary fix. It must be lasting and complete. We must remember that these are eternal covenants, without end. They are not like merit badges with finite requirements that we check off and then wear on a sash. We do not earn eternal life by accumulating accomplish-ments like trophies on a shelf; we gain eternal life by becoming like God.

The Lord said: "I, the Lord, require the hearts of the children of men" (D&C 64:22). The Lord not only requires our hearts but will also judge us by our hearts (see D&C 137:9). It is not enough to follow the Lord half-heartedly. He requires our whole-hearted effort.

Alma the Younger's story is a fitting model for the process of repentance. He and the four princes (the sons of Mosiah) rebelled against their fathers. They were "numbered among the unbelievers" and drew many away from the church established by Alma's father (Mosiah 27:8). Alma "became a great hinderment to the prosperity of the church of God" (Mosiah 27:9). To Alma's everlasting benefit, God sent an angel to confront Alma and the princes. The angel's words were like thunder, causing the earth to shake, and Alma and the princes fell to the earth (see Mosiah 27:10–11).

You may wonder that this does not sound like repentance. It sounds more like the wrath of God, which it is. But it can be the start of repentance. A crisis may occur. Alma's crisis was literally earth-shaking. Ours need not be as earth-shaking, but it must have the same effect: we must become humble.

Alma was compelled to be humble, as he was confronted by an angel who showed him the power of God. We may be compelled to be humble too, but it is even better if we humble ourselves without being compelled. Later, Alma taught, contrary to his own experience, "Blessed are they who humble themselves without being compelled to be humble" (Alma 32:16).

Alma's response to being humbled was to repent. After the angel warned Alma not to seek to destroy the Church anymore, Alma was dumb and paralyzed. Though he could not speak or move, his mind was active. He wished to be banished rather than face God to be judged. He lay in that condition for three days. But he remembered his father's prophecies about the coming of the Son of God to atone for the sins of the world. Grasping that lifeline, he cried out: "O Jesus, thou Son of God, have mercy on me, who am in the gall of bitterness, and am encircled about by the everlasting chains of death" (Alma 36:18).

Repentance is not easy. It is a change of heart, which can be very hard. It is a turning to Christ after we have failed to give Him His due. Alma "wad[ed] through much tribulation, repenting nigh unto death" (Mosiah 27:28). In this extremity, in this moment of peril, Alma reached out to God, and "the Lord in mercy [saw] fit to snatch [Alma] out of an everlasting burning." And he was "born of God" (Mosiah 27:28).

After much tribulation came relief in Christ, whose yoke is easy: "My soul hath been redeemed from the gall of bitterness and bonds of iniquity. I was in the darkest abyss; but now I behold the marvelous light of God.

My soul was racked with eternal torment; but I am snatched, and my soul is pained no more" (Mosiah 27:29).

Restoration

Justice and agency require restoration and judgment. Because our Heavenly Father is perfectly just and He has given us the right to choose our destiny (by our covenants and actions), we cannot expect that, after we are resurrected, He will turn us into righteous, worthy individuals if we do not repent in this life. In the resurrection, we will continue to be what we have become through our desires and actions in mortality.

Why won't a God, who loves us perfectly and has all power, use that love and power to save us in the celestial kingdom, regardless of what we have done or become? Simply because that would destroy justice and God would cease to be God. He has all power to act within the limits of His own law, but He will not act contrary to that law.

Our bodies will eventually rise in the resurrection, but the essence of who we are will not change. If we are mortals striving on the covenant path to become celestial beings, we will be restored to that state. If we are caught up in the telestial pursuit of crimes and base passions, we will be restored to that telestial path.

This is especially sweet for those who keep on the covenant path in this life because, when they die and go to the spirit world, they will find that they are on the same covenant path. Though they are not perfect when they die, they will still be on the path to perfection in the next life. Worthiness is our journey on the path to eternal life; perfection is the destination.

Bruce R. McConkie described this restoration:

> What we are doing as members of the Church is charting a course leading to eternal life. There was only one perfect being, the Lord Jesus. If men had to be perfect and live all of the law strictly, wholly, and completely, there would be only one saved person in eternity. The Prophet taught that there are many things to be done, even beyond the grave, in working out our salvation.
>
> And so what we do in this life is chart a course leading to eternal life. That course begins here and now and continues in the realms ahead. We must determine in our hearts and in our souls, with all the power and ability we have, that from this time forward we will press on in righteousness; by so doing we can go where God and Christ are.

If we make that firm determination and are in the course of our duty when this life is over, we will continue in that course in eternity. That same spirit that possesses our bodies at the time we depart from this mortal life will have power to possess our bodies in the eternal world. If we go out of this life loving the Lord, desiring righteousness, and seeking to acquire the attributes of godliness, we will have that same spirit in the eternal world, and we will then continue to advance and progress until an ultimate, destined day when we will possess, receive, and inherit all things.[6]

The concept of having the same spirit in the eternal world—of being restored to what we were before—troubled Alma's son Corianton. He had succumbed to the temptations of the world, and Alma, concerned for his son's eternal welfare, warned him to be careful about returning to those sins: "The plan of restoration is requisite with the justice of God; for it is requisite that all things should be restored to their proper order. Behold, it is requisite and just, according to the power and resurrection of Christ, that the soul of man should be restored to its body, and that every part of the body should be restored to itself" (Alma 41:2). Alma warned Corianton not to risk eternal punishment by supposing that God would restore Corianton to righteousness even though he was wicked: "And now behold, my son, do not risk one more offense against your God. . . . Do not suppose, because it has been spoken concerning restoration, that ye shall be restored from sin to happiness. Behold, I say unto you, wickedness never was happiness" (Alma 41:9–10).

Restoration not only means that righteousness will be restored to righteousness, but it also means that the intelligence we obtain in this life will still be ours in the next life. All that we have learned, including our knowledge of good and evil and the wisdom we have gained from enduring mortal experiences and afflictions, will still be part of us. "Whatever principle of intelligence we attain unto in this life, it will rise with us in the resurrection. And if a person gains more knowledge and intelligence in this life through his diligence and obedience than another, he will have so much the advantage in the world to come" (D&C 130:18–19).

Wishfully thinking that we can live a telestial life here and repent later, to be saved in the celestial kingdom is a flawed strategy: "Ye cannot say, when ye are brought to that awful crisis, that I will repent, that I will return to my God. Nay, ye cannot say this; for that same spirit which doth possess your bodies at the time that ye go out of this life, that same spirit will have power to possess your body in that eternal world" (Alma 34:34).

Now is the time to repent because we don't know when this mortal probation will end. We don't know how much longer we have. The Lord told His disciples that He would come like a thief in the night, unexpected: "The coming of the Lord is as a thief in the night. And it is like unto a man who is an householder, who, if he watcheth not his goods, the thief cometh in an hour of which he is not aware, and taketh his goods, and divideth them among his fellows" (JST, Luke 12:44–45). "And he said unto them, Verily I say unto you, be ye therefore ready also; for the Son of man cometh at an hour when ye think not" (JST, Luke 12:47).

There are two ways for the Lord to come to us: (1) His second coming or (2) our death. Because we don't know when either of these will occur, we must constantly prepare for both. Alma taught that death results in a return to God: "Now, concerning the state of the soul between death and the resurrection. Behold, it has been made known unto me by an angel, that the spirits of all men, as soon as they are departed from this mortal body, yea, the spirits of all men, whether they be good or evil, are taken home to that God who gave them life" (Alma 40:11).

Jesus also taught, using the parable of the rich man, that He will judge us according to the desire of our hearts:

> The ground of a certain rich man brought forth plentifully:
> And he thought within himself, saying, What shall I do, because I have no room where to bestow my fruits?
> And he said, This will I do: I will pull down my barns, and build greater; and there will I bestow all my fruits and my goods.
> And I will say to my soul, Soul, thou hast much goods laid up for many years; take thine ease, eat, drink, and be merry.
> But God said unto him, Thou fool, this night thy soul shall be required of thee: then whose shall those things be, which thou hast provided?
> So is he that layeth up treasure for himself, and is not rich toward God. (Luke 12:16–21)

Notice in this parable that the rich man had not actually executed his plan of building bigger barns, filling them, then retiring to eat, drink, and be merry. Instead, he died the very night that he made the plan. The judgment that came against him was based on his intent, the desires of his heart.

The moral of these parables, keeping in mind the law of restoration, is that we must keep on the covenant path at all times. Our hearts must be turned to the Lord, and our desires must be to serve Him. We must be covenant keepers and endure faithfully to the end, as President Russell M. Nelson has taught, to have never-ending happiness.[7] Getting to that state of never-ending happiness requires us to rely on the merits of Jesus Christ. After all we can do, it is His grace that will save us (see 2 Nephi 25:23).

The allegory of the raindrop teaches that it is only through the combination of our struggling to rise, exercising our agency to be the best we can be, along with the Atonement of Jesus Christ, that we can rise to celestial heights. The raindrop started out happy in the sky as a bit of water vapor, living in the clouds, basking in the sun's light, but wanting more experience. She eventually became water through condensation and finally fell to earth, alighting in the mountain top. She percolated down through the ground and into a stream, and it was an exciting ride. She had experiences she could never have known in the clouds. But the raindrop missed the sun and wanted to return to the sky. She was cold and remembered the warmth of the sun. Despite her desire to ascend, gravity always pulled her down. She ran downhill in the stream and into a river. There were times when she was in a very still patch, where she could rise, but only to the surface of the water. Other times, when the water ran fast, she just hung on for the ride, and quite a ride it was, through rapids and over waterfalls. But always the progress was down. Gravity always had its way, even though the rain drop wanted to return to the sky. Finally, she flowed with the river into the ocean and sank into the depths. She struggled again, always remembering her goal to return to the sky. After much effort, she managed to get to the surface of the ocean, but, at that point, she realized that, as water, she could not return to the sky. She did her best to stay at the surface, hoping someday to have the help she needed to ascend. One day, the sun came out. And because the rain drop was doing everything she could to stay on the surface of the water, the sun shone on her. She evaporated and returned to the sky, where she could once again enjoy the warmth of the sun.

Lehi taught, "There is no flesh that can dwell in the presence of God, save it be through the merits, and mercy, and grace of the Holy Messiah" (2 Nephi 2:8). So we must reconcile ourselves with God, which can be done only through the Atonement of Jesus Christ.

Resurrection is a restoration of a different sort. Instead of being restored to what we are in this life, we will become immortal. But even the resurrection is a restoration depending on what we have become in this life. In that case, we call it the judgment, but it is really no more than a restoration and a recognition of what we have become. President Nelson related this restoration to covenants and ordinances: "One day we will meet our Maker and stand before Him at Judgment. We will be judged according to our ordinances, covenants, deeds, and the desires of our hearts."[8] Nephi said that the essence of the final judgment is that we will have the reward of what we have become in this life: "If their works have been filthiness they must needs be filthy; and if they be filthy it must needs be that they cannot dwell in the kingdom of God" (1 Nephi 15:33). Likewise, Moroni said: "He that is filthy shall be filthy still; and he that is righteous shall be righteous still" (Mormon 9:14).

"The Final Judgment," said President Dallin H. Oaks, "is not just an evaluation of a sum total of good and evil acts—what we have *done.* It is an acknowledgment of the final effect of our acts and thoughts—what we have *become.* It is not enough for anyone just to go through the motions. The commandments, ordinances, and covenants of the gospel are not a list of deposits required to be made in some heavenly account. The gospel of Jesus Christ is a plan that shows us how to become what our Heavenly Father desires us to become."[9]

This restoration (resurrection and judgment) will not come to all at once. It will begin with the most righteous (some of them have already been resurrected) and end with the most wicked, who will not be resurrected until the end of the millennium, the thousand years when Christ reigns personally on the earth. The most righteous "are Christ's, the first fruits, they who shall descend with him first, and they who are on the earth and in their graves, who are first caught up to meet him" (D&C 88:98). The most wicked will be resurrected last and "shall remain filthy still" (D&C 88:102).

The reward for keeping on the covenant path is to become like Christ and to become Christ's. It is to do all we can do that by His grace we may be saved. But, inevitably, it is hard to stay on the covenant path because we are weak.

Weakness

Sometimes, in our constant self-evaluation, we are tempted to equate weakness with sin. Because we are weak, we assume that we are sinners. While it is true that we are sinners (see Romans 3:23), our sins do not consist of our weaknesses. Instead, our sins consist of succumbing to our weaknesses.

Weakness is difficulty in the face of trial, an absence of strength. Weaknesses can come in many forms, anywhere from weakness making us prone to partake of something desirable but forbidden to weakness when action is required. An example of the former is the alcoholic's tendency to crave alcohol, and an example of the latter is a procrastinator's tendency to put off good works. Until the alcoholic actually partakes of alcohol and the procrastinator forgoes the opportunity to perform the good work, the tendency, the propensity, is not sinful.

The Lord's example gives us reason to take heart that our weaknesses are not sins and will not be counted against us. In Gethsemane, the Lord experienced difficulty in the face of trial—weakness, if you will. In the depths of misery, He cried out: "Father, if thou be willing, remove this cup from me: nevertheless not my will, but thine, be done" (Luke 22:42). So grievous was the suffering that an angel attended him, to strengthen Him (see Luke 22:43).

Since we recognize Jesus as being sinless in mortality, a constant in the theology of The Church of Jesus Christ of Latter-day Saints (see Hebrews 4:15), this weakness in Gethsemane could not have been sin. Yet, weakness it was, else why would He need strengthening? Thus, it is of some comfort to us that we can acknowledge our weaknesses without bemoaning them as sins.

Mortal weakness is good for our souls. That can be hard to fathom, especially in the midst of trials. The Lord said: "I give unto men weakness that they may be humble; and my grace is sufficient for all men that humble themselves before me; for if they humble themselves before me, and have faith in me, then will I make weak things become strong unto them" (Ether 12:27). The Lord will never tempt us or force us to sin (see James 1:13), but He gives us weakness to humble us and allow us to progress.

We should be careful not to misunderstand the statement that God "give[s] unto men weakness" (Ether 12:27). The nature of mortality is to have weaknesses, but, just like many of our strengths, many of those weaknesses are ones we developed in the eternity before we came here. We may have been faithful enough in the premortal life to merit foreordination for some important mortal work, but we may also have developed a weakness that follows us into mortality. Examples may be difficulty accepting counsel, heightened sensitivity to peer pressure, or other personality traits that came with us into this life. On the other hand, there are mortal weaknesses that we probably did not have, at least in full-fledged form, in the premortal life. The propensity to bite our fingernails may be one of this latter group of weaknesses.

The process of turning weakness into strength was on display in Gethsemane. The Lord was weak but perfectly humble. He recommitted to doing His Father's will. And the Father sent an angel to strengthen Him, enabling Him to accomplish the infinite Atonement, which required more strength than any simple mortal is capable of exerting. If we are to return to our Heavenly Father, our lives must be echoes of that great redeeming event—initial weakness, humility, faith, and ultimate strength.

Endnotes

1. *Hernandez v. Restoration Hardware* (2018) 4 Cal. 5th 260, 273.
2. Christofferson, "A Message at Christmas."
3. Ibid.
4. Ibid.
5. *True to the Faith*, s.v. "Repentance," 132.
6. McConkie, "The Seven Deadly Heresies," 177–78.
7. Nelson, "Covenants," 89.
8. Nelson, "Personal Preparation for Temple Blessings," 34.
9. Oaks, in Conference Report, Oct. 2000, 41; italics in original.

Chapter 12

THE SACRAMENT

Jesus took bread, and brake it, and blessed it, and gave to his disciples, and said, Take, eat; this is in remembrance of my body which I give a ransom for you.

—JST, Matthew 26:22

Each Sunday we have the opportunity to renew our covenants by partaking of the sacrament. The sacrament is the perfect confluence of covenant principles. Our sins violate the covenants we have made, but we can renew those covenants, as if we had not violated them, if we repent of our sins and partake of the sacrament. During the sacrament, we remember our reliance on Jesus Christ's sacrifice by eating the blessed bread and drinking the blessed water. In doing so, we renew our covenants with God.

The Last Supper and the Burial of Jesus

In Jerusalem for the Passover, Jesus desired to eat a Passover feast with His Apostles. On that occasion in an upper room, He took bread and broke it and blessed it, and He gave it to His Apostles, saying, "This is my body which is given for you: this do in remembrance of me" (Luke 22:19). Likewise, He gave them a cup of wine, representing "the new testament in my blood, which is shed for you" (Luke 22:20). Referring to the sacramental wine, Jesus told His Apostles: "I will not drink henceforth of this fruit of the vine, until that day when I drink it new with you in my Father's kingdom" (Matthew 26:29).

Brigham Young explained the Savior's statement about drinking the fruit of the vine again in His Father's kingdom: "[Jesus] came here to redeem fallen man, he being the heir of the family that receive bodies on this earth, that they, through obedience to his requirements and commandments and the ordinances of his house; may be sanctified and prepared to return to the presence of the Father and there sit down with Jesus, where he will administer to them again in fulfillment of his saying to them, 'I will not drink, henceforth of this fruit of the vine, until the day when I drink it anew, with you, in my Father's kingdom.'"[1]

After this last gathering with His Apostles, Jesus went to Gethsemane and on to the cross, providing the infinite Atonement essential to His Father's plan to redeem us and exalt us. The sacrifice accomplished, Jesus declared, "It is finished," and He died.

What happened after He died reminds us of how significant the sacrament is. And the experience of the faithful women and a wealthy ruler right after Jesus died provided a pattern for us in approaching the sacrament.

We don't know much about Joseph of Arimathea. He was a wealthy ruler of the Jews, a member of the Sanhedrin. At a time when most of the rulers of the Jews were against Jesus or even conspired to kill Him, Joseph was faithful and did not participate in the condemnation leading to the crucifixion of Jesus. Joseph apparently heard and believed in the words of Jesus. So when Jesus was crucified on that Friday, leaving little time before the Sabbath to prepare His body and entomb Him, Joseph was emboldened. He used his standing and authority to go to Pilate, and he "begged the body of Jesus Christ" (Matthew 27:58). He asked Pilate if he could take control of the body. This is not what the rest of the rulers of the Jews wanted. They wanted to have control because Jesus said that after three days He would rise again.

But Pilate granted the request of Joseph of Arimathea, who had purchased a tomb that had never been used. Joseph and just a few other faithful followers took the body of Jesus down from the cross, and they took it to Joseph's tomb, where very hasty provision was made for His burial. Mary Magdalene, Mary the mother of the James and John, and other women did not abandon Jesus, even in death and even though many of the Apostles fled. The women put His body in the tomb and they covered Him with a cloth. The Jews had a quite lengthy and involved burial procedure involving anointing the body and wrapping it. Only some of the preparation could be done before nightfall, when the Sabbath would begin, and they would need to roll the stone across the opening of the tomb. So they prepared Him as best they could and covered His body with a cloth.

When we arrive at sacrament meeting on Sunday, we enter a room that has been prepared with a remembrance of the sacrifice of Jesus Christ. We enter the chapel, and we see a cloth covering the sacrament table. The chapel becomes an ordinance room as we prepare ourselves to partake of the emblems of the death of Jesus Christ.

After the priests have pulled back the covering on the table and have broken the bread in remembrance of the breaking of the body of Jesus Christ for our benefit, the bread is blessed and passed to us. Likewise, the water is blessed and passed to us.

O that, when we take the sacrament, we might always have the care that those women had for Jesus Christ—that when we partake of the bread we might remember Him like the women remembered Him, that we might remain faithful to Him in the same way that Joseph of Arimathea remained faithful to Him while others fled.

The deacons pass the emblems to us, and as we partake of the sacrament, we renew our commitment to Him, our loyalty to Him. Every Sunday we have that opportunity. When we miss it, we should feel deeply the absence of the opportunity to see that sacrament table, to remember the body of Jesus Christ in the tomb, and to renew our covenants with Him. When we partake of the sacrament, we should remember that Peter and John ran to the garden, entered the tomb, and found the cloth that had covered Jesus's body folded and put to the side. We should remember that Mary Magdalene wept at the tomb, thinking someone had taken Jesus's body, but then exulted when she found that He was risen. We should remember that all of the covenants we make and keep are effective because the tomb was empty on that first Easter morning. The sacrament is an opportunity to remember and recommit.

The Sacrament of the Lord's Supper

On April 6, 1830, the sacred emblems were once again administered to the faithful followers of the Lord. On that day, Joseph Smith formally organized the latter-day Church of Jesus Christ and, as directed by revelation, broke the bread and blessed the bread and wine, inviting those who had been baptized to partake.

Joseph recounted: "We were commanded to bless bread and break it with them, and to take wine, bless it, and drink it with them."[2]

The sacrament is not a saving ordinance in the sense we normally use that term. A saving ordinance is one that we must receive, either personally or by proxy, to qualify for exaltation. But the sacrament is a saving ordinance in a broader sense because partaking of the sacrament renews our covenants with God and draws us closer to Him. Drawing closer to Him, in its ultimate sense, is to be exalted.

Brigham Young said the sacrament "is as necessary to our salvation as any other of the ordinances and commandments that have been instituted in order that the people may be sanctified, that Jesus may bless them and give unto them his spirit, and guide them and direct them that they may secure unto themselves life eternal."[3]

The Lord said: "It is expedient that the church meet together often to partake of bread and wine in the remembrance of the Lord Jesus" (D&C 20:75).

Paul's instructions to the Corinthians about receiving the sacrament reflect the profound importance of the ordinance and the necessity of doing it worthily:

> For I have received of the Lord that which also I delivered unto you, That the Lord Jesus the same night in which he was betrayed took bread. And when he had given thanks, he brake it, and said, Take, eat: this is my body, which is broken for you: this do in remembrance of me. After the same manner also he took the cup, when he had supped, saying, This cup is the new testament in my blood: this do ye, as oft as ye drink it, in remembrance of me. For as often as ye eat this bread, and drink this cup, ye do shew the Lord's death till he come. Wherefore whosoever shall eat this bread, and drink this cup of the Lord, unworthily, shall be guilty of the body and blood of the Lord. But let a man examine himself, and so let him eat of that bread, and drink of that cup. For he that eateth and drinketh unworthily, eateth and drinketh damnation to himself, not discerning the Lord's body. (1 Corinthians 11:23–29)

Renewing Our Covenants

Speaking as a special witness of Jesus Christ to the world in a presentation prepared by the First Presidency and Quorum of the Twelve Apostles, then-Elder Dallin H. Oaks said:

> The sacrament of the Lord's Supper is a renewal of the covenants and blessings of baptism. We are commanded to repent of our sins and

to come to the Lord with a broken heart and a contrite spirit and partake of the sacrament. In partaking of the bread, we witness that we are willing to take upon us the name of Jesus Christ and always remember Him and keep His commandments. When we comply with this covenant, the Lord renews the cleansing effect of our baptism. We are made clean and can always have His Spirit to be with us. The administration of the sacrament and the renewal of covenants and cleansing that take place in the partaking of the sacrament are the most important acts in the Sabbath worship of Latter-day Saints. We do this in remembrance of the blood of the Only Begotten Son, Jesus Christ. He is at the center of our faith. He is our Savior and our Redeemer.[4]

We bring to the sacrament ordinance our offering of a broken heart and a contrite spirit (see D&C 59:8). In return, the Lord promises that we will have His spirit to be with us. "The ordinance of the sacrament," said Elder David A. Bednar, "is a holy and repeated invitation to repent sincerely and to be renewed spiritually. The act of partaking of the sacrament, in and of itself, does not remit sins. But as we prepare conscientiously and participate in this holy ordinance with a broken heart and a contrite spirit, then the promise is that we may *always* have the Spirit of the Lord to be with us. And by the sanctifying power of the Holy Ghost as our constant companion, we can *always* retain a remission of our sins."[5]

The sacrament connects us to the past, present, and future. In partaking of the emblems of His death, the bread and water, in remembrance of His body and blood, we remember the atoning sacrifice of Jesus Christ, recalling the single most significant event in eternity. We renew our covenants, as if to receive them anew. And we look with longing and determined preparation to that day when we will again partake of those emblems with the Savior in His Father's kingdom.

When the Savior administered the sacrament to His Apostles at the Last Supper, He told them, "I will not drink henceforth of this fruit of the vine until that day when I shall come and drink it new with you in my Father's kingdom" (JST, Matthew 26:26). To Joseph Smith, the Lord said: "I will drink of the fruit of the vine with you on the earth" (D&C 27:5).

President John Taylor also spoke of that future day, saying that, when he receives the sacrament, he reflects on our relationships with God and with each other and on "our hopes concerning the future; the second appearing of our Lord Jesus Christ, when, we are given to understand, he will gird himself and wait upon us, and we shall eat bread and drink wine with him in his Father's kingdom."[6]

Alma said that "all is as one day with God, and time only is measured unto men" (Alma 40:8). In a way, at least metaphorically, we can step outside our boundaries and limitations of time as we receive the sacrament each Sunday and draw together the past, present, and future. We can join God to embrace eternity, if just for a moment.

That They May Have His Spirit to be With Them

The Atonement of Jesus Christ is the greatest gift from God to man, and the Holy Ghost is the delivery system for the blessings of the Atonement while we are in mortality. Therefore, the promise in the sacrament prayer that we may have His Spirit to be with us is a promise that we will receive the full blessings of the Atonement of Jesus Christ.

Elder Bruce R. McConkie summarized the blessings of the Atonement of Jesus Christ brought to us by the Holy Ghost:

> The Holy Ghost is God's minister; he is appointed to teach and testify, to bear witness of the Father and the Son, and to reveal all needful things to men. As the Testator, he bequeaths salvation, through an eternal testament, to the heirs of God. The Holy Ghost is the Revelator. Almost always the first great revelation received by any person is a testimony of the truth and divinity of the Lord's work on earth. "And by the power of the Holy Ghost ye may know the truth of all things." (Moroni 10:5.) He is the Comforter. Those who enjoy his companionship find their whole souls are filled with comfort and joy. And the very reason men are commanded to repent and be baptized is so they "may be sanctified by the reception of the Holy Ghost, that [they] may stand spotless before [the Lord] at the last day." (3 Nephi 27:20)[7]

To speak of the Holy Ghost as a "delivery system" may be too base, as He is a god in His own right. But the term is descriptive. He is the witness, the comforter, the sanctifier, delivering the blessings of the Atonement to those who will accept those blessings.

When Jesus journeyed through Samaria and stopped at Jacob's Well, where he spoke to the woman and asked for a drink, the woman had drawn fresh water from far below. Jesus then said: "If thou knewest the gift of God, and who it is that saith to thee, Give me to drink; thou wouldest have asked of him, and he would have given thee living water" (John 4:10). Surprised that a man with no bucket or line to draw water from the deep well offered water to her, the woman said: "Sir, thou hast nothing to draw with, and the well is deep: from whence then hast thou that living water?" (John 4:11).

The woman was justifiably perplexed. This Jewish man offered her water, but he had no bucket or line. He had no way to retrieve the water to give to her.

What followed this Samaritan woman's question was a concise sermon on the Savior's Atonement, that Jesus is the source of life. But I want to focus on the practical implication of the woman's understandable confusion, noting that this Man who offered water had nothing to draw the water with.

Water is a source of life. Without it, we cannot live. And a well is a source of fresh, drinkable water. But that water can do us no good if it remains in an aquifer far below us. There must be some sort of system to deliver the water to us: a well, for example, with a system to move the water to the surface, either manually or through some sort of automation. Water in the aquifer cannot save a person dying of thirst unless the water is delivered to that person. The same is true of the living water offered by Jesus Christ. The Atonement cannot save us if we do not have access to the blessings of the Atonement.

That system for providing the blessings of the Atonement of Jesus Christ is through the Holy Ghost. Through the Holy Ghost, we receive a testimony of the Atonement. From the Holy Ghost, we have peace and comfort. By the Holy Ghost, we are sanctified. And through the Holy Ghost, we are sealed up unto eternal life. As we worthily partake of the sacrament, we receive the promise that we will have the Holy Ghost to be with us. It is a promise of surpassing beauty and eternal value.

Endnotes

1. Young, in *Journal of Discourses*, 19:91.
2. *Doctrine and Covenants Student Manual*, 34.
3. Young, in *Journal of Discourses*, 19:92.
4. Oaks, "Special Witnesses of Christ," 13.
5. Bednar, "Always Retain a Remission of Your Sins," 61–62; italics in original.
6. Taylor, in *Journal of Discourses*, 15:266.
7. McConkie, *A New Witness for the Articles of Faith*, 70.

Chapter 13

TEMPLE COVENANTS

---

*And there you shall be endowed
with power from on high.*

—D&C 38:32

On the covenant path, our ultimate destination is eternal life in the celestial kingdom, but our mortal destination is the temple. In the temple, we make further sacred covenants that bind us to our Savior. We are endowed with power, we are sealed to our families, and we obtain the strength and resolve to continue on the covenant path.

Gathering to the Temple

In his message to the members of the Church from the temple after he was ordained and set apart as the seventeenth president of the Church in 2018, President Nelson continued the inspired emphasis on following the covenant path to the temple: "The end for which each of us strives is to be endowed with power in a house of the Lord, sealed as families, faithful to covenants made in a temple that qualify us for the greatest gift of God—that of eternal life. The ordinances of the temple and the covenants you make there are key to strengthening your life, your marriage and family, and your ability to resist the attacks of the adversary. Your worship in the temple and your service there for your ancestors will bless you with increased personal revelation and peace and will fortify your commitment to stay on the covenant path."[1]

The scriptures are full of references to the temple, but many of them are metaphorical. Important gospel precepts are taught in the scriptures using metaphors. Jesus Christ is referred to in the scriptures as the Lamb of God and the Bread of Life. He is the unblemished sacrificial lamb who died for our sins. His Atonement sustains us spiritually, just as bread sustains us physically.

A common metaphor used in the scriptures is the harvest—sometimes the harvest of olives or grapes, but most often the harvest of wheat. For example, a section of the Doctrine and Covenants familiar to all missionaries tells us: "The field is white already to harvest; and lo, he that thrusteth in his sickle with his might, the same layeth up in store that he perisheth not, but bringeth salvation to his soul" (D&C 4:4).

In this verse, the field of wheat is the world of potential members of the Lord's church. The whiteness of the field indicates that the time for missionary work is here. And the harvest is the missionary work. Missionaries thrust in their sickles with their might when they labor diligently to bring souls unto Christ. These missionaries are not just the full-time missionaries, but all members of the Church.

John the Baptist used the harvest metaphor in his teaching: "I indeed baptize you with water; but one mightier than I cometh, the latchet of whose shoes I am not worthy to unloose: he shall baptize you with the Holy Ghost and with fire: Whose fan is in his hand, and he will throughly purge his floor, and will gather the wheat into his garner; but the chaff he will burn with fire unquenchable" (Luke 3:16–17).

Here, the gathering of the wheat into the garner is the gathering of the members of the Church to the temples where they are instructed and protected. The chaff represents those who reject the truth.

Elsewhere in scriptural uses of the harvest metaphor, sheaves are the cut wheat stalks that are gathered together in bundles. They represent newly baptized members. Although they have been baptized, they are still vulnerable to the storms that could destroy them because they have not been gathered to the garners.

The garners are the storage for the wheat, the silos where it is taken after it is harvested. Until the wheat is in the garner, it lies in the field, vulnerable to disease, fungus, and pests. If a storm comes while the wheat is cut but still in the field, the crop can be lost.

My family visited northeastern Oregon in the summer one year while the wheat was being harvested. Using huge machinery, the workers harvested the wheat, spewing it into large bins to be transported directly to the silos or garners. But in the old days, the harvest involved much more manual labor—cutting the stalks, gathering the wheat into sheaves, and transporting the sheaves to the garner. Until the sheaves could be transported to the garners, they stood vulnerable in the fields.

The great missionary Ammon, one of the sons of Mosiah, used this imagery of the wheat harvest in teaching about the harvest of souls, bringing souls unto Christ and protecting them from the evil influences and the storms of wickedness in the last days. Ammon was particularly successful both in baptizing thousands of Lamanites and retaining them as faithful saints.

When I was young, I was impressed by the way Ammon served King Lamoni and saved the king's sheep. As evildoers tried to scatter and steal the sheep, Ammon bravely stepped in to protect the sheep. Seemingly outnumbered, he fended off the attackers, cutting off their arms as they raised them to strike him.

When I served as a full-time missionary, I marveled at the thousands that were converted through Ammon's instrumentality. Starting with King Lamoni's conversion, the conversions spread through King Lamoni's people and to many other Lamanites. These humble people not only made baptismal covenants, but they also covenanted not to return to their warlike ways, burying their weapons.

As a priesthood leader, I gained a new appreciation for Ammon's story. None of the Lamanite converts fell away and abandoned the covenants they had made. In his abridgement of the records of Alma, Mormon made this observation: "As sure as the Lord liveth, so sure as many as believed, or as many as were brought to the knowledge of the truth, through the preaching of Ammon and his brethren, according to the spirit of revelation and of prophecy, and the power of God working miracles in them—yea, I say unto you, as the Lord liveth, as many of the Lamanites as believed in their preaching, and were converted unto the Lord, never did fall away" (Alma 23:6).

After this impressive missionary and retention success, Ammon spoke to his brothers, congratulating them for their faithfulness and the great effect it had on the Lamanites. In his address, Ammon invoked the harvest doctrine. He said:

> Behold, the field was ripe, and blessed are ye, for ye did thrust in the sickle, and did reap with your might; yea, all the day long did ye labor; and behold the number of your sheaves! And they shall be gathered into the garners, that they are not wasted.

> Yea, they shall not be beaten down by the storm at the last day;
> yea, neither shall they be harrowed up by the whirlwinds; but when the
> storm cometh they shall be gathered together in their place, that the
> storm cannot penetrate to them; yea, neither shall they be driven with
> fierce winds whithersoever the enemy listeth to carry them.
>
> But behold, they are in the hands of the Lord of the harvest, and
> they are his; and he will raise them up at the last day. (Alma 26:5–7)

Referring to the harvest doctrine, Elder Neal A. Maxwell said: "Clearly, when we baptize, our eyes should gaze beyond the baptismal font to the holy temple. The great garner into which the sheaves should be gathered is the holy temple."[2] To Elder Maxwell's statement, Elder David A. Bednar added: "This instruction clarifies and emphasizes the importance of sacred temple ordinances and covenants—that the sheaves may not be wasted."[3] Elder Bednar continued: "We should not be surprised by Satan's efforts to thwart or discredit temple worship and work. The devil despises the purity in and the power of the Lord's house. And the protection available to each of us in and through temple ordinances and covenants stands as a great obstacle to the evil designs of Lucifer."[4]

Another way that we gather to the temple, other than being physically present there, is to live a life worthy of entering the temple. The questions that are asked in a temple recommend interview provide the standard of worthiness: Do you have a testimony of God, the Atonement of Jesus Christ, and the gospel? Do you sustain the church leaders? Do you live the laws of chastity and tithing and the Word of Wisdom? Do you strive to live all of the commandments? Do you keep the covenants you have made?

Living by this standard of worthiness, when combined with service to others, dedicated scripture study, and sincere prayer, will provide a shield against the darts of the adversary, against the influences of evil, against the storms of worldliness. As Ammon said, those who gather to the temple "are in the hands of the Lord of the harvest, and they are his; and he will raise them up at the last day" (Alma 26:7).

In a latter-day revelation, the Lord declared: "The time of harvest is come, and my word must needs be fulfilled. Therefore, I must gather together my people, according to the parable of the wheat and the tares, that the wheat may be secured in the garners to possess eternal life, and be crowned with celestial glory, when I shall come in the kingdom of my Father to reward every man according as his work shall be; While the tares shall be bound in bundles, and their bands made strong, that they may be burned with unquenchable fire" (D&C 101:64–66).

In the last days (our time) the Saints must gather to the temple to find protection from the storm. Obviously, we do not all move into the temple. Instead, our gathering to the temple involves physical and spiritual aspects.

In the temple, saving ordinances are provided to both the living and the dead. You and I may go there to receive our endowment—literally, a gift from God consisting of instruction and covenants. We are taught how to return to our Heavenly Father. This instruction and these covenants are sacred. We baptize, confirm, and ordain to the priesthood on behalf of the dead. They then have the opportunity to accept the gospel and these ordinances in the spirit world. We can become saviors (with a lowercase "s") on Mount Zion because we help provide the saving ordinances that can be performed only in this life (see Obadiah 1:21).

This proxy or vicarious work is an important part of our worship in the temple. It is not a concept foreign to Christianity that we perform this work. In teaching about the resurrection, the Apostle Paul asked: "Else what shall they do which are baptized for the dead, if the dead rise not at all? why are they then baptized for the dead?" (1 Corinthians 15:29).

In fact, every good Christian believes in the principle allowing the use of a proxy when the person needing something cannot provide it. The Atonement of Jesus Christ is the ultimate vicarious work. Jesus suffered for our sins, in our place, and died for us, so that we can return to our Heavenly Father clean, even though we have sinned. Jesus was our proxy in punishment.

Latter-day Saints are a chosen people, appointed in the premortal world to be in partnership with the Lord for the salvation of the living and the dead. We learn by revelation through Joseph Smith that "these . . . principles in relation to the dead and the living . . . cannot be lightly passed over, as pertaining to our salvation. For their salvation is necessary and essential to our salvation. . . . For we without them cannot be made perfect; neither can they without us be made perfect" (D&C 128:15, 18). Joseph said: "The greatest responsibility in this world that God has laid upon us is to seek after our dead."[5]

During New Testament times, Saints performed baptisms for the dead. But this saving doctrine was lost in the apostasy for hundreds of years. Without the doctrine, Christian churches really had no option other than to conclude that those who died without the opportunity to hear the gospel of Jesus Christ and to be baptized could not be saved. President George Q. Cannon said:

> The belief upon this point is illustrated by the reply of a certain Bishop to the inquiry of the king of the Franks, when the king was about to submit to baptism at the hands of the Bishop. The king was a heathen, but had concluded to accept the form of religion then called Christianity. The thought occurred to him that if baptism were necessary for his salvation, what had become of his dead ancestors who had died heathens. This thought framed itself into an inquiry which he addressed to the Bishop. The prelate, less politic than many of his sect, bluntly told him they had gone to hell. "Then, by Thor, I will go there with them," said the king, and thereupon refused to accept baptism or to become a Christian.[6]

Temple ordinances are necessary to salvation. "The dead who repent will be redeemed, through obedience to the ordinances of the house of God. And after they have paid the penalty of their transgressions, and are washed clean, shall receive a reward according to their works, for they are heirs of salvation" (D&C 138:58–59). Brigham Young said:

> When we take up the religion that has been revealed—the Gospel in its fullness, we find that it is simply a code of laws, ordinances, gifts and graces which are the power of God unto salvation. The laws and ordinances which the Lord has revealed in these latter days, are calculated to save all the sons and daughters of Adam and Eve who have not sinned against the Holy Ghost, for all will be saved in a kingdom of glory, though it may not be in the celestial kingdom, for there are many mansions. These ordinances reach after every one of the children of our Father in heaven, and not only them, but after all the earth, the fullness of the earth, all things that dwell upon it, to bring them back into the presence of God, or into some kingdom or place prepared for them, that they may be exalted to a higher state of intelligence than they now dwell in.[7]

So we gather to the temple to receive and provide saving ordinances, along with eternally significant instruction. Every worthy member, beginning in the year the member turns twelve, can go to the temple. Those who have not yet been endowed can perform baptisms for the dead. Those who have been endowed may also receive endowments and sealings for the dead.

The Endowment

In temples, worthy members of The Church of Jesus Christ of Latter-day Saints are endowed with power.

President Brigham Young said: "Your endowment is, to receive all those ordinances in the house of the Lord, which are necessary for you, after you have departed this life, to enable you to walk back to the presence of the Father, passing the angels who stand as sentinels, being enabled to give them the key words, the signs and tokens, pertaining to the holy Priesthood, and gain your eternal exaltation in spite of earth and hell."[8]

In the temple, Latter-day Saints are washed and anointed. They are instructed on the plan of salvation, the Creation, and the Atonement of Jesus Christ. And they make covenants. The covenants, according to Elder James E. Talmage, include the "covenant and promise to observe the law of strict virtue and chastity, to be charitable, benevolent, tolerant and pure; to devote both talent and material means to the spread of truth and the uplifting of the [human] race; to maintain devotion to the cause of truth; and to seek in every way to contribute to the great preparation that the earth may be made ready to receive . . . Jesus Christ."[9]

The endowment provides the covenants and the knowledge essential for exaltation. For that reason, it is an ordinance of exaltation—a saving ordinance—along with baptism, confirmation, and priesthood ordination for the men. President Nelson said: "In the temple we receive our ultimate blessings, as the seed of Abraham, Isaac, and Jacob."[10]

The endowment is not the beginning of our relationship with God but instead is a continuation of that relationship. The ordinances of exaltation leading up to the endowment—baptism, confirmation, and ordination to the priesthood—are a preparation for the endowment, steps to the exalting ordinances of the temple.

"The receiving of the endowment," said President Harold B. Lee, "requires the assuming of obligations by covenants which in reality are but an embodiment or an unfolding of the covenants each person should have assumed at baptism."[11] And Elder Robert D. Hales added: "Temples are the greatest university of learning known to man, giving us knowledge and wisdom about the Creation of the world. Washings and anointings tell us who we are. Endowment instructions give guidance as to how we should conduct our lives here in mortality."[12]

In this fallen world, the temple provides glimpses of who we really are. Joseph Smith said: "You have got to learn to be Gods yourselves, and to be kings and priests to God, the same as all Gods have done before you, namely, by going from one small degree to another, and from a small capacity to a great one; from grace to grace, from exaltation to exaltation, until you attain to the resurrection of the dead, and are able to dwell in everlasting burnings, and to sit in glory, as do those who sit enthroned in everlasting power."[13]

In this statement, Joseph Smith speaks of going "from exaltation to exaltation." This may seem illogical. If exaltation is the end goal, how can one go from one exaltation to another? Joseph also provided an answer to this question. Speaking of his own future progress through eternity, he taught: "When I get my kingdom, I shall present it to my Father, so that he may obtain kingdom upon kingdom, and it will exalt him in glory. He will then take a higher exaltation, and I will take his place, and thereby become exalted myself."[14]

This concept also helps us to understand better the statement of God's mission as recorded in Moses, that His *work and glory* is to bring to pass our immortality and eternal life (see Moses 1:39). When we are exalted, it also further exalts Him.

The Sealing

The temple endowment prepares us for temple sealings, where eternal families are created.

A few years ago, my oldest daughter went to the temple and put on a simple white temple dress that her mother made for her before her mission. Mindy knelt at an altar with the young man she had chosen to marry, and her grandfather, who was called and set apart as a sealer, performed an ordinance, marrying them for this life and sealing that marriage for eternity. It was very simple and meaningful.

After the sealing, Mindy put on a beautiful wedding dress with beads and lace, and the wedding party went out of the temple into the bright sunshine for pictures, pictures, and more pictures. The families went to a restaurant for lunch generously provided by the groom's family. And finally, everyone gathered at the meetinghouse for a celebration with music, a reception line, food, dancing, and smiles. People scurried about, completing their assignments.

The proceedings after the temple ceremony were very complex and momentous, but nothing that happened the rest of the day surpassed the eternal significance of what happened so simply in the sealing room of the temple that morning. The power of the priesthood, manifested in the sealing power, stood eternally above the later events, even though the later events were beautiful and inspiring and required so much planning and work.

Mindy's sealing was possible only because the authority to perform such sealings was restored to the earth as part of the restoration of the gospel in these last days. With the same authority, children are sealed to parents, and the generations are welded together in a "whole and complete and perfect union" (D&C 128:18).

On September 21, 1823, three and a half years after Joseph Smith's First Vision, an angel appeared to Joseph at night. This angel was Moroni, the last Nephite prophet, the one who had hidden the golden plates in the ground centuries earlier and who held the keys of the Book of Mormon. Moroni instructed Joseph through the night. A point that Moroni emphasized was the coming of Elijah. He quoted Malachi's statement, although with slightly different wording than is found in our modern Bibles: "Behold, I will reveal unto you the Priesthood, by the hand of Elijah the prophet, before the coming of the great and dreadful day of the Lord. . . . And he shall plant in the hearts of the children the promises made to the fathers, and the hearts of the children shall turn to their fathers. If it were not so, the whole earth would be utterly wasted at his coming" (Joseph Smith—History 1:38–39).

On April 3, 1836, Elijah appeared to Joseph Smith and Oliver Cowdery, the first and second elders of the Church. Joseph described the event:

> Elijah the prophet, who was taken to heaven without tasting death, stood before us, and said: Behold, the time has fully come, which was spoken of by the mouth of Malachi—testifying that he [Elijah] should be sent, before the great and dreadful day of the Lord come—To turn the hearts of the fathers to the children, and the children to the fathers, lest the whole earth be smitten with a curse—Therefore, the keys of this dispensation are committed into your hands; and by this ye may know that the great and dreadful day of the Lord is near, even at the doors. (D&C 110:13–16)

The priesthood that existed on the earth at the time of Christ was lost through an apostasy, a falling away. Therefore, for sealings to take place today, it was necessary for this sealing power to be restored. Because the keys were lost after the death of the Apostles, it was necessary to have them restored to the earth anew so that they could be used in sacred ordinances for the living and the dead.

The date on which Elijah returned to restore the sealing power was during the Jewish Passover celebration. About the appearance of Elijah, President Joseph Fielding Smith said: "It was, I am informed, on the third day of April, 1836, that the Jews, in their homes at the Paschal feast, opened their doors for Elijah to enter. On that very day Elijah did enter—not in the home of the Jews to partake of the Passover with them, but he appeared in the House of the Lord."[15]

The keys of the sealing power are held by each of the living Apostles—fifteen of them, including the First Presidency. But the President of the Church is the only person on the earth authorized to exercise the keys. He does so by authorizing the ordinances performed in the temple.

Receiving these temple ordinances, culminating in the sealing, is essential to our salvation, but not sufficient. We must also endure to the end.

"And verily, verily, I say unto you, that whatsoever you seal on earth shall be sealed in heaven; and whatsoever you bind on earth, in my name and by my word, saith the Lord, it shall be eternally bound in the heavens; and whosesoever sins you remit on earth shall be remitted eternally in the heavens; and whosesoever sins you retain on earth shall be retained in heaven" (D&C 132:46).

Sealing by the Holy Spirit of Promise is the ratification, the seal of approval given by the Holy Ghost when a person who has received an ordinance lives worthily. That ratification is necessary for the ordinance to have binding effect in heaven. Therefore, if we are baptized, ordained to the priesthood, endowed in the temple, and sealed to our family but then live unworthily, those ordinances will not be effective in heaven.

Concerning the application of this principle to temple marriage, Elder Bruce R. McConkie said: "If both parties are 'just and true,' if they are worthy, a ratifying seal is placed on their temple marriage; if they are unworthy, they are not justified by the Spirit and the ratification of the Holy Ghost is withheld. Subsequent worthiness will put the seal in force, and unrighteousness will break any seal."[16]

Those who are married in the temple for time and eternity must live righteously to have that sealing ratified by the Holy Spirit of Promise. Specifically, each spouse must live the covenants made in that sealing ceremony. The effectiveness of that sealing is assured by enduring to the end in observing the covenants made. On the other hand, the failure to endure to the end breaks the covenant and sealing. The Holy Spirit of Promise withdraws its ratification, and the sealing has no eternal effect.

In a revelation the Lord gave to Joseph Smith, He said:

> And again, verily I say unto you, if a man marry a wife by my word, which is my law, and by the new and everlasting covenant, and it is sealed unto them by the Holy Spirit of promise, by him who is anointed, unto whom I have appointed this power and the keys of this priesthood; and it shall be said unto them—Ye shall come forth in the first resurrection; and if it be after the first resurrection, in the next resurrection; and shall inherit thrones, kingdoms, principalities, and powers, dominions, all heights and depths. (D&C 132:19)

The path to eternal life that we entered by the gate of baptism leads to the temple. In the temple, we make covenants and receive ordinances and instruction that help us to continue on the path toward eternal life and protect us in the process.

Endnotes

1. Nelson, "As We Go Forward Together," 7.
2. Maxwell, quoted in David A. Bednar, "Honorably Hold a Name and Standing," 97.
3. Bednar, "Honorably Hold a Name and Standing," 97.
4. Bednar, "Honorably Hold a Name and Standing," 99–100.
5. *Teachings of the Presidents of the Church: Joseph Smith*, 475.
6. Cannon, *The Life of Joseph Smith, the Prophet*, 510–11.
7. Young, in *Journal of Discourses*, 15:122.
8. *Discourses of Brigham Young*, 416.
9. Talmage, *The House of the Lord: A Study of Holy Sanctuaries Ancient and Modern*, 100.
10. Nelson, "The Gathering of Scattered Israel," 80.
11. Lee, *Teachings of Presidents of The Church: Harold B. Lee*, 106.
12. Hales, "Temple Blessings."
13. *Teachings of the Prophet Joseph Smith*, 346–47.
14. *Teachings of the Prophet Joseph Smith*, 347–48.
15. Smith, in Conference Report, Apr. 1936, 75.
16. McConkie, *Mormon Doctrine*, 362.

Chapter 14

COVENANTING AS EQUALS WITH GOD

Men should be anxiously engaged in a good cause, and do many things of their own free will, and bring to pass much righteousness. For the power is in them, wherein they are agents unto themselves.

—Doctrine and Covenants 58:27–28

We are free to agree to be exalted or to settle for less. God will not force us. Instead, He stands ready to honor His part of the agreement. In this eternally significant covenant setting, we covenant with a Being who, in His omniscience, knows whether we will ultimately be exalted. He knows that someday in our future we may be gods like Him, or not. But the choice is ours.

When Kim and I bought our train tickets to travel from Florence to Milan, Italy, we entered into an agreement with the state railroad to transport us to Milan. There was no compulsion; we were not compelled to buy the tickets. But we wanted to reach our destination, so it was necessary to enter into the agreement to be transported there. We and the state railroad were willing parties to the contract. When we discovered we were mistakenly on the train to Venice, there was no compulsion to find the correct train to Milan. We could have been thrown off the train to Venice because we had no right to be on that train, but no one compelled us to board the correct train to Milan when we found it in Bologna. It was our desire to reach the proper destination that prompted us to get off the Venice-bound train in Bologna and board the Milan-bound train. In the matter of whether to buy a ticket and whether to board the Milan-bound train, we were equals with the state railroad in whether to enter into that contract.

Likewise, we are equals with God in deciding whether we want to make and keep the covenants that will get us to the celestial kingdom. He will not compel us to make the covenants, and He will not compel us to keep the covenants. Those matters are entirely of our own choosing. "Whosoever will come may come and partake of the waters of life freely; and whosoever will not come the same is not compelled to come" (Alma 42:27). In the matter of covenant-making and covenant-keeping, we are agents unto ourselves, just like God is an agent unto Himself.

Kim and I have made the covenants necessary in this life to eventually be exalted. We have bought the tickets. We were both baptized and confirmed. I received the Melchizedek Priesthood. We were both endowed in the temple, and we were sealed in the temple. I also believe we are on the right train to exaltation, even if we certainly have a journey left ahead of us before we reach our destination. We do our best to keep the covenants we have made, and we strive to obey the commandments and serve those around us, repenting daily. It is not a passive activity as the train analogy might imply. We are not perfect. However, we believe that through the Atonement of Jesus Christ we may be saved.

The wonder and grandeur of covenant-making and covenant-keeping is the power to become gods. Knowing God is essential to our progress toward becoming like Him. Jesus said: "And this is life eternal, that they might know thee the only true God, and Jesus Christ, whom thou hast sent" (John 17:3). Joseph Smith said that we must comprehend the character of God to comprehend ourselves.[1] And, comprehending our own true character, we comprehend the magnitude of the covenants we make with God.

Joseph Smith taught:

> God himself was once as we are now, and is an exalted man, and sits enthroned in yonder heavens! That is the great secret. If the veil were rent today, and the great God who holds this world in its orbit, and who upholds all worlds and all things by his power, was to make himself visible,—I say, if you were to see him today, you would see him

like a man in form—like yourselves in all the person, image, and very form as a man; for Adam was created in the very fashion, image and likeness of God, and received instruction from, and walked, talked and conversed with him, as one man talks and communes with another.[2]

When we think of the opposite of God, we may think of Satan, as in good versus evil. But there is another way to consider what is the opposite of God—that is, *we* are the opposite of God, as in child versus Father. Opposites really are two almost-identical things with one essential difference. That holds true in how we compare to God. We are like God with one pending and crucial difference that we are not yet exalted as He is.

The essential characteristics of God the Father may be summed up as follows: (1) He is an eternal being; (2) He is of a godly species; (3) He is an agent unto Himself; (4) He has an immortal, perfect body of flesh and bones; and (5) He is exalted. The only way we are essentially unlike our Father is that we are not exalted. But that takes some explaining.

1. God the Father is an eternal being.

Every week when we partake of the sacrament, we pray to "God, the Eternal Father" (D&C 20:77). God said: "Man of Holiness is my name; Man of Counsel is my name; and Endless and Eternal is my name, also" (Moses 7:35). He is "infinite and eternal, from everlasting to everlasting" (D&C 20:17). He is self-existent.

We are also eternal beings. Our intelligence is the essential part of our being, and it has always existed. This eternal nature was revealed through Joseph Smith: "[The Bible] does not say in the Hebrew that God created the spirit of man. It says 'God made man out of the earth and put into him Adam's spirit, and so became a living body.' The mind or the intelligence which man possesses is co-equal with God himself."[3] We are coequal with God.

Joseph Smith added: "Intelligence is eternal and exists upon a self-existent principle. It is a spirit from age to age, and there is no creation about it."[4]

Latter-day Saint philosopher Truman Madsen put in simple terms the majesty of our eternal nature:

> There is no beginning to our "beginning."
> Mind has no birthday and memory has no first.
> Age is relative only to stages, not existence. No one is older, or younger, than anyone else.

We have always been alone, separate from, and always together, coexistent with, other intelligences.

Creation is never totally original; it is always a combination of prior realities. . . .

Whatever may be said of the spirit and body, death does not destroy self, but only delimits it. . . .

Through all transformations of eternity, no self can change completely into another thing. Identity remains.

In an ultimate sense, no existent self ever loses his mind nor his consciousness.

In sum, nothing is something we never were and never can be.[5]

2. God the Father is of a godly species.

Although God the Father was once mortal, He has progressed beyond that condition and is now exalted, meaning He is a god. By a natural process, God the Father became a god.

We are also of a godly species. President Lorenzo Snow echoed Joseph Smith's teaching: "As man now is, God once was: As God now is, man may be."[6]

In mortality we trace our lineage back through the generations to Adam—generation after generation of progenitors. However, our spiritual lineage is simple: we are first generation descendants of a Heavenly Father and a Heavenly Mother. We are literal children of Gods, and as literal children of Gods we are of the same species.

The Apostle Paul said: "The Spirit itself beareth witness with our spirit, that we are the children of God: And if children, then heirs; heirs of God, and joint-heirs with Christ; if so be that we suffer with him, that we may be also glorified together" (Romans 8:16–17).

While God the Father has already attained godhood, we have not. But the potential is within us to become like Him. We can accept or refuse, but the potential is there.

This is not just an abstract principle but has found fulfillment already in some who have preceded us on earth—namely, Abraham, Isaac, and Jacob. They "did none other things than that which they were commanded; and because they did none other things than that which they were commanded, they have entered into their exaltation, according to the promises, and sit upon thrones, and are not angels but are gods" (D&C 132:37).

Neither the Lord nor the Lord's Church has abandoned this exalting doctrine that we are of a godly species on a path to godhood.

Elder Dieter F. Uchtdorf said: "We are eternal beings, without beginning and without end. We have always existed. We are the literal spirit children of divine, immortal, and omnipotent Heavenly Parents! We come from the heavenly courts of the Lord our God. We are of the royal house of Elohim, the Most High God."[7]

3. God the Father is an agent unto Himself.

God is free to choose. One might ask, if God is free to choose, why are we not in danger of His failing to keep the covenants we so desperately rely on for our journey down the path to eternal life? That is where our faith comes in—our faith that God will always keep covenants, not because He *cannot* break them so much as that He perfectly *will not* break them. Truman Madsen wrote that "this is a 'cannot' that reduces to an eternal 'will not.' It is impossible because He has so chosen, not because external forces prevent it."[8]

In the oath and covenant of the Melchizedek Priesthood, the Lord declares that "all those who receive the priesthood, receive this oath and covenant of my Father, which he cannot break, neither can it be moved" (D&C 84:40).

We are also agents unto ourselves.

Joseph Smith received, in revelation, this great truth: "Verily I say, men should be anxiously engaged in a good cause, and do many things of their own free will, and bring to pass much righteousness; For the power is in them, wherein they are agents unto themselves. And inasmuch as men do good they shall in nowise lose their reward" (D&C 58:27–28).

This gift of agency is of divine origin and is essential to our divine nature. Brother Madsen wrote: "Made in imitation of the Divine, man's free agency is the boldest, most powerful, most sweeping, and most exciting commitment possible."[9]

The ultimate exercise of our agency is to choose to be exalted. The power is in us, thanks to the divine nature we inherit from our Father in combination with the Atonement of His Son Jesus Christ.

4. God the Father has an immortal, perfect body of flesh and bone.

Joseph Smith, who saw God the Father on more than one occasion (see, for example, D&C 76: 20–24; Joseph Smith—History 1:17), declared: "The Father has a body of flesh and bones as tangible as man's" (D&C 130:22). "And God said, Let us make man in our image" (Genesis 1:26), literally.

God is immortal, meaning that He has power over death and that His spirit and body will never be separated. "The Father hath life in himself" (John 5:26). James Talmage said that God the Father "already passed through the experiences of mortal life, including death and resurrection, and was therefore a Being possessed of a perfect, immortalized body of flesh and bones."[10]

We will *inevitably* have immortal, perfect bodies of flesh and bone, and in the economy of God all that is inevitable is accomplished.

We have bodies of flesh and bone; that is apparent. Our spirits reside in these bodies during this mortal stage of our eternal existence; however, someday we will each die, meaning that our spirits will leave our bodies. But that condition, in which our spirits and bodies are separated, will be temporary. Eventually, spirit and body will reunite in the resurrection, and each resurrected body will be immortal, never again to be separated.

Resurrection will come to all who have lived in mortality on this earth: "Now, this restoration shall come to all, both old and young, both bond and free, both male and female, both the wicked and the righteous" (Alma 11:44).

Amulek tutored Zeezrom on the literal and permanent nature of resurrection: "This mortal body is raised to an immortal body, that is from death, even from the first death unto life, that they can die no more; their spirits uniting with their bodies, never to be divided; thus the whole becoming spiritual and immortal, that they can no more see corruption" (Alma 11:45).

Resurrection is universal because of the Atonement. Because Jesus Christ suffered and died for us and was resurrected, all will likewise be resurrected, receiving an immortal, perfect body of flesh and bones. The Atonement reaches back to the beginning and forward to the last person who will be born on this earth to provide that gift of resurrection. Therefore, we will inevitably be like our Heavenly Father in that we will have a perfect, immortal body of flesh and bones.

Even though we have not yet been resurrected, as we have not yet died, there is no essential difference between us and God the Father in whether, in the end, we will have a perfect, immortal body of flesh and bones. It will happen because Jesus Christ, our perfect Savior, unalterably provided for it as part of His Atonement and resurrection.

This condition of inevitability can be compared to the teachings of prophets concerning the Atonement of Jesus Christ before the Savior was born on this earth. Abinadi said: "And now if Christ had not come into the world, speaking of things to come as though they had already come, there could have been no redemption" (Mosiah 16:6). As the Atonement was inevitable before it was accomplished because a perfect being had covenanted to accomplish it, so our immortality is inevitable because the causal event, the Atonement, has already taken place. Indeed, it could just as easily be said that immortality was inevitable even before the Atonement and resurrection of Jesus Christ because a perfect being covenanted to provide it.

Brother Madsen wrote: "Immortality is in no sense conditional. It is inevitable and universal."[11]

So it is both logical and reasonable to conclude that, as far as God is concerned, we are of the class of beings (His children) who will inevitably be resurrected beings with a perfect, immortal body of flesh and bones, even though for us, in our limited sense of time and sequence, we don't see it yet. "Time only is measured unto men" (Alma 40:8).

5. God the Father is exalted.

God "sits enthroned in yonder heavens."[12] Exaltation is eternal life, both in quality (the kind of life God lives) and in quantity (it will last forever).

"What is eternal life?" asked President Joseph Fielding Smith. He answered, "It is to have 'a continuation of seeds forever and ever.' No one receives eternal life except those who receive the exaltation."[13]

We have the possibility of being exalted, but that is not inevitable. Joseph Smith taught about the process of eventual exaltation: "You have got to learn how to be Gods yourselves, and to be kings and priests to God, the same as all Gods have done before you, namely, by going from one small degree to another, and from a small capacity to a great one; from grace to grace, from exaltation to exaltation, until you attain to the resurrection of the dead, and are able to dwell in everlasting burnings, and to sit in glory, as do those who sit enthroned in everlasting power."[14]

Joseph Smith added that the process is "to inherit the same power, the same glory and the same exaltation, until you arrive at the station of a God, and ascend the throne of eternal power, the same as those who have gone before."[15]

Exaltation is our destiny if we choose it because the possibility has been provided to all who come to this earth. Our Heavenly Father, a higher intelligence, in His infinite love and wisdom, has provided a way for us, who are lower intelligences, to be like Him.

Does our potential for exaltation diminish God by making us equal to Him? No. As we gain our exaltation, the Father obtains a higher exaltation. His power is to provide the opportunity and ability for us to become gods. If we were to say He had no such power, we would say He is not omnipotent and diminish Him.

I have described our exaltation as not being inevitable; however, there is one class of individuals for whom exaltation is inevitable: those who have had their calling and election made sure. Peter encouraged the Saints to "give diligence to make your calling and election sure: for if ye do these things, ye shall never fall" (2 Peter 1:10). By doing so, he taught, they would receive "a more sure word of prophecy" (2 Peter 1:19).

Referring to these teachings of Peter, Joseph Smith explained that "the more sure word of prophecy means a man's knowing that he is sealed up unto eternal life, by revelation and the spirit of prophecy, through the power of the Holy Priesthood" (D&C 131:5). Joseph added: "When the Lord has thoroughly proved [a person], and finds that the [person] is determined to serve Him at all hazards, then the [person] will find his [or her] calling and election made sure."[16]

But the fact that it is even possible to have our calling and election made sure in this life further proves that we are more like God the Father than unlike Him. Indeed, we are much like Him. We are eternal beings, as is He. We are of the same species as our Father. We are agents unto ourselves, as He is. Immortality is inevitable. And we have the potential, even the promise, of exaltation, to live that life that He lives and have eternal increase, if we desire it sufficiently to make it happen.

While, in our minds, the last difference between us and God has not been eliminated, all things are present before God. Past, present, and future are present. His vision is not limited, obscured, or dimmed by time. We don't see the glory within ourselves, but our Father does. We may perceive in ourselves a promising potential, but He fully knows and appropriately treats us as gods in embryo.

Elder Neal A. Maxwell said: "The Lord Himself said that He 'knoweth all things, for all things are present' before Him (D&C 38:2). We read, too, that 'all things are present with me, for I know them all' (Moses 1:6). Therefore, God's omniscience is not *solely* a function of prolonged and discerning familiarity with us—but of the stunning reality that the past and present and future are part of an 'eternal now' with God!"[17]

Thus, the similarities between God and us are substantial and striking. The differences are few and potentially absent altogether.

The essential differences between God and those who have not received saving ordinances are (1) receiving the saving ordinances in which we make sacred covenants with God, (2) faithfulness, which we often refer to as enduring to the end, and (3) time, during which we continue to become like Him.

The essential difference between God and those who have received saving ordinances are (1) faithfulness and (2) time.

And the only essential difference between God and those who have had their callings and elections made sure is time.

When we apply these principles and doctrines concerning how similar we are to God and how the past, present, and future are before Him in one eternal now, we can understand that to God we are as He is, just not yet.

By making and keeping sacred covenants, we may become all that He is.

Endnotes

1. *Teachings of the Prophet Joseph Smith*, 343.
2. Ibid., 345; italics omitted.
3. Ibid., 353.
4. Ibid., 354.
5. Madsen, *Eternal Man*, 26.
6. Snow, *Biography and Family Record of Lorenzo Snow*, 46.
7. Uchtdorf, "How Great the Plan of Our God!," 21.
8. Madsen, *Eternal Man*, 70, n. 19.
9. Ibid., 70.
10. Talmage, *Jesus the Christ*, 39.
11. Madsen, *Eternal Man*, 26.
12. *Teachings of the Prophet Joseph Smith*, 345.
13. Smith, *Doctrines of Salvation*, 2:9, emphasis omitted.
14. *Teachings of the Prophet Joseph Smith*, 346–47.
15. Ibid., 347.
16. Ibid., 150.
17. Maxwell, *All These Things Shall Give Thee Experience*, 8.

Works Cited

Bednar, David A. "Always Retain a Remission of Your Sins," *Ensign*, May 2016, 61–62.

—. "Honorably Hold a Name and Standing," *Ensign*, May 2009, 99–100.

—. "If Ye Had Known Me," *Ensign*, Nov. 2016, 104.

Callister, Tad R. *The Infinite Atonement*. Salt Lake City: Deseret Book, 2000.

Cannon, George Q. "Discourse by President George Q. Cannon," *The Latter-day Saints' Millennial Star* 15, no. 42 (Oct. 16, 1893), 670.

—.*The Life of Joseph Smith, the Prophet*. Salt Lake City: Juvenile Instructor Office, 1888.

Christofferson, D. Todd. "The Divine Gift of Repentance," *Ensign*, Nov. 2011, 39.

—. "A Message at Christmas," BYU Devotional, Dec. 12, 2017.

—. "The Power of Covenants," *Ensign*, May 2009, 22.

Classic Speeches: 22 Selections from Brigham Young University Devotional and Fireside Speeches. Provo: Brigham Young University, 1994.

Conference Reports of The Church of Jesus Christ of Latter-day Saints. Salt Lake City: The Church of Jesus Christ of Latter-day Saints, 1898 to present.

Cook, Quentin L. "We Follow Jesus Christ," *Ensign*, May 2010, 84.

Dew, Sheri L. "Are We Not All Mothers?," *Ensign*, Nov. 2001, 96.

Dickens, Charles. *A Christmas Carol*. Toronto: Bantam Books, 1986.

Discourses of Brigham Young. Selected and arranged by John A. Widtsoe. Salt Lake City: Deseret Book, 1954.

Doctrine and Covenants Student Manual. Salt Lake City: The Church of Jesus Christ of Latter-day Saints, 1981.

Encyclopedia of Mormonism, s.v. "New and Everlasting Covenant," 3:1008.

Eyring, Henry B. "The Book of Mormon as a Personal Guide," *Ensign*, Sep. 2010, 4.

—. "Gathering the Family of God," *Ensign*, May 2017, 20.

—. "The Holy Ghost as Your Companion," *Ensign*, Nov. 2015, 105.

"The Family: A Proclamation to the World," *Liahona*, October 2004, 49; *Ensign*, November 1995, 102.

Farrar, F.W. *The Life of Lives: Further Studies in the Life of Christ*. London: Cassell and Co., 1900.

First Presidency, "The Origin of Man," *The Improvement Era*, Nov. 1909, 81.

—. "Pre-existent States," *The Improvement Era*, Mar. 1912, 417.

Flood v. Kuhn (1972) 407 U.S. 258.

Hales, Robert D. "Seeking to Know God, Our Heavenly Father, and His Son, Jesus Christ," *Ensign*, Nov. 2009, 30.

—. "Temple Blessings," BYU Devotional, Nov. 15, 2005.

Hernandez v. Restoration Hardware (2018) 4 Cal. 5th 260, 273, quoting 9 Witkin, Cal. Procedure (5th ed. 2008) Appeal, § 481, at p. 541.

Hinckley, Gordon B. "We Look to Christ," *Ensign*, May 2002, 90.

Holland, Jeffrey R. *Christ and the New Covenant*. Salt Lake City: Deseret Book, 1997.

Hymns of The Church of Jesus Christ of Latter-day Saints. Salt Lake City: The Church of Jesus Christ of Latter-day Saints, 1985.

Journal of Discourses. 26 vols. London: Latter-day Saints' Book Depot, 1855–1856.

Judd, Frank F., Jr., Eric D. Huntsman, and Shon D. Hopkin, eds. *The Ministry of Peter, the Chief Apostle*. Provo: Religious Studies Center; Salt Lake City: Deseret Book, 2014.

Kimball, Spencer W. "Absolute Truth," BYU Devotional, Sep. 6, 1977.

—. *The Miracle of Forgiveness*. Salt Lake City: Bookcraft, 1969.

The Life and Teachings of Jesus Christ and His Apostles. 2nd ed., rev. Salt Lake City: The Church of Jesus Christ of Latter-day Saints, 1978.

Ludlow, Daniel H., ed. *Encyclopedia of Mormonism*. 4 vols. New York: Macmillan Publishing Co., 1992.

Madsen, Truman G. *Eternal Man*. Salt Lake City: Deseret Book, 1970.

Matthews, Robert J. *A Burning Light: The Life and Ministry of John the Baptist*. Provo: Brigham Young University Press, 1972.

Maxwell, Neal A. *All These Things Shall Give Thee Experience*. Salt Lake City: Deseret Book, 1980.

—. Quoted in David A. Bednar, "Honorably Hold a Name and

—. "Plow in Hope," *Ensign*, May 2001, 60.

—. *Even as I Am*. Salt Lake City: Deseret Book, 1982.

McConkie, Bruce R. *A New Witness for the Articles of Faith*. Salt Lake City: Deseret Book, 1985.

—. "The Salvation of Little Children," *Ensign*, Apr. 1977, 4, quoted in *Doctrine and Covenants Student Manual*, 221.

—. *Doctrinal New Testament Commentary*. 3 vols. Salt Lake City: Bookcraft, 1973.

—. *Mormon Doctrine*. Salt Lake City: Bookcraft, 1966.

Monson, Thomas S. "Dare to Stand Alone," *Ensign*, Nov. 2011, 60, quoting David Brooks, "If It Feels Right . . . ," *New York Times*, Sep. 12, 2011, nytimes.com.

—. "The Race of Life," *Ensign*, May 2012, 91.

Nelson, Russell M. *Accomplishing the Impossible*. Salt Lake City: Deseret Book, 2015.

—. "As We Go Forward Together," *Ensign*, Apr. 2018, 7.

—. "Covenants," *Ensign*, Nov. 2011, 88.

—. "The Gathering of Scattered Israel," *Ensign*, Nov. 2006, 80.

—. "Keys of the Priesthood," *Ensign*, Oct. 2005, 40.

—. "Personal Preparation for Temple Blessings," *Ensign*, May 2001, 34.

—. "Roots and Branches," *Ensign*, May 2004, 29

—. "Salvation and Exaltation," *Ensign*, May 2008, 10.

Oaks, Dallin H. "Loving Others and Living with Differences," *Ensign*, Nov. 2014, 28.

—."Special Witnesses of Christ," *Ensign*, Apr. 2001, 13.

Packer, Boyd K. "The Reason for Our Hope," *Ensign*, Nov. 2014, 6.

Perry, L. Tom. "The Gospel of Jesus Christ," *Ensign*, May 2008, 46.

—. "The Power of Deliverance," *Ensign*, May 2012, 95.

Roberts, B.H. *Joseph Smith: The Prophet-Teacher, a Discourse*. Salt Lake City: Deseret News, 1908.

Smith, Joseph. *History of the Church of Jesus Christ of Latter-day Saints*. Edited by B.H. Roberts. 7 vols. Salt Lake City: Deseret Book, 1932–1951.

Smith, Joseph Fielding. *Doctrines of Salvation*. 3 vols. Salt Lake City: Bookcraft, 1954.

Snow, Eliza R. *Biography and Family Record of Lorenzo Snow*. Salt Lake City: Deseret News Co., 1884.

Snow, Lorenzo. "Discourse Delivered by Apostle Lorenzo Snow in the Tabernacle at Brigham City, March 6, 1887," *The Latter-day Saints' Millennial Star* 49, no. 16 (Apr. 18, 1887), 244.

Snow, Lorenzo. Quoted in Quentin L. Cook, "Prepare to Meet God," *Ensign*, May 2018, 114.

Talmage, James E. *The House of the Lord: A Study of Holy Sanctuaries Ancient and Modern*. Salt Lake City: The Church of Jesus Christ of Latter-day Saints, 1912.

—. *Jesus the Christ*. Salt Lake City: Deseret Book, 1975.

Taylor, John. *Mediation and Atonement of Our Lord and Savior Jesus Christ*. Salt Lake City: Deseret News Publishing Co., 1892.

Teachings of the Presidents of the Church: Harold B. Lee. Salt Lake City: The Church of Jesus Christ of Latter-day Saints, 2000.

Teachings of the Presidents of the Church: Joseph Smith. Salt Lake City: The Church of Jesus Christ of Latter-day Saints, 2007.

Teachings of the Presidents of the Church: Spencer W. Kimball. Salt Lake City: The Church of Jesus Christ of Latter-day Saints, 2006.

Teachings of the Prophet Joseph Smith. Selected and arranged by Joseph Fielding Smith. Salt Lake City: Deseret Book, 1976.

True to the Faith. Salt Lake City: The Church of Jesus Christ of Latter-day Saints, 2004.

Uchtdorf, Dieter F. "How Great the Plan of Our God!," *Ensign*, Nov. 2016, 21.

—. "The Infinite Power of Hope," *Ensign*, Nov. 2008, 21.

Van der Hoeven, Johan. *Karl Marx: The Roots of His Thought*. Toronto: Wedge Publishing Foundation, 1976.

Washington, George, *George Washington's Rules of Civility and Decent Behavior in Company and Conversation*. Chestertown, MD: Literary House Press of Washington College, 2007.

Whitney, Orson F. *Life of Heber C. Kimball, an Apostle*. Salt Lake City: The Kimball Family, 1888.

Widtsoe, John A. *A Rational Theology as Taught by the Church of Jesus Christ of Latter-day Saints*. 4th ed., rev. Salt Lake City: Deseret Book, 1937.

—. "The Worth of Souls," *The Latter-day Saints' Millennial Star* 96, no. 9 (Mar. 1, 1934), 131–132.

Index

INDEX

Woodruff, Wilford 136
worthiness 77, 80, 90, 93, 101, 108–
    110, 113, 125, 127, 140, 142,
    157, 178, 188, 191, 194, 196,
    198–199, 202

Young, Brigham 14, 18–19, 22, 24,
    44, 56, 64, 77, 107, 117, 134,
    136, 144, 161, 186, 188, 198, 199
Zacharias 79
Zeezrom 71, 210

About the Author

Jeffery A. Hogge has been an appellate court attorney for more than thirty years, assisting judges in California and Nevada to craft judicial opinions deciding a wide range of legal issues. He is the author of *Norton Parker Chipman: A Biography of the Andersonville War Crimes Prosecutor*, as well as articles and essays for legal and religious publications. Born and raised in California, he graduated from Brigham Young University with a BA in linguistics and returned to California for his law degree. He is a lifelong member of The Church of Jesus Christ of Latter-day Saints, served a mission in Italy, and has served in many ward, stake, and mission leadership callings, most recently as stake president. He and his wife, Kim, have six children and live in Elk Grove, California. For more information, see jeffhogge.com.

Scan to visit

jeffhogge.com